MODERN TEACHING OF POPULATION EDUCATION

MODERN TEACHING OF POPULATION EDUCATION

[Strictly According to the UGC Syllabus for B.Ed. Course]

By

UDAI VEER

ANMOL PUBLICATIONS PVT. LTD.

NEW DELHI - 110 002 (INDIA)

ANMOL PUBLICATIONS PVT. LTD.
4374/4B, Ansari Road, Daryaganj
New Delhi - 110 002
Ph.: 23261597, 23278000
Visit us at: www.anmolpublications.com

Modern Teaching of Population Education

First Published, 2004

ISBN 81-261-1877-6

PRINTED IN INDIA

Published by J.L. Kumar for Anmol Publications Pvt. Ltd., New Delhi - 110 002 and Printed at Mehra Offset Press, Delhi.

Contents

Preface

Education is a vast discipline and Teachers' Training is a vital part of it. The responsibilities of the educationists and educators are focused on the task of providing better training to the future teachers for their better learning and proper development. Needless to say that this responsibility can only be exercised, if the trainers are equipped with the required knowledge of the subject concerned. That's why it becomes essential for making adequate provisions for each course to the student-teachers or teacher trainees. The present series is designed for providing a solid workable base for all course-papers. It has been prepared strictly according to the syllabus of the B.Ed class, prescribed by the UGC for different universities.

No doubt, there are so many other books on the subject, available in the market, written by worthy authors. However, every writer has his or her own style and way of presentation. The present work also has its own features and characteristics.

In preparation of this series of texts, the editor had to refer to the works of other authors and information sources. The editor feels a deep sense of gratitude for incorporating their ideas in the text. Hopefully, this series would serve as a 'ready to refer' tool for all teachers, teacher-students and others.

— **Editor**

Population Statistics
At a Glance

I

States and Union Territories by Population Size

Rank 2001	State/ Union Territory	Population 2001	Per cent to total Population of India 2001	1991	Rank 1991
1	2	3	4	5	6
1.	Uttar Pradesh	16,60,52,859	16.17	15.60	1
2.	Maharashtra	9,67,52,247	9.42	9.33	2
3.	Bihar	8,28,78,796	8.07	7.62	5
4.	West Bengal	8,02,21,171	7.81	8.04	3
5.	Andhra Pradesh	7,57,27,541	7.37	7.86	4
6.	Tamil Nadu	6,21,10,839	6.05	6.59	6
7.	Madhya Pradesh	6,03,85,118	5.88	5.74	7
8.	Rajasthan	5,64,73,122	5.50	5.20	9
9.	Karnataka	5,27,33,958	5.14	5.31	8
10.	Gujarat	5,05,96,992	4.93	4.88	10
11.	Orissa	3,67,06,920	3.57	3.74	11
12.	Kerala	3,18,38,619	3.10	3.44	12
13.	Jharkhand	2,69,09,428	2.62	2.58	14
14.	Assam	2,66,38,407	2.59	2.64	13
15.	Punjab	2,42,89,296	2.37	2.40	15
16.	Haryana	2,10,82,989	2.05	1.95	17
17.	Chhattisgarh	2,07,95,956	2.03	2.08	16
18.	Delhi	1,37,82,976	1.34	1.11	18
19.	Jammu and Kashmir	1,00,69,917	0.98	0.92	19
20.	Uttaranchal	84,79,562	0.83	0.84	20
21.	Himachal Pradesh	60,77,248	0.59	0.61	21
22.	Tripura	31,91,168	0.31	0.33	22
23.	Manipur	23,88,634	0.23	0.23	23
24.	Meghalaya	23,06,069	0.22	0.21	24
25.	Nagaland	19,88,636	0.19	0.14	25
26.	Goa	13,43,998	0.13	0.14	26
27.	Arunachal Pradesh	10,91,117	0.11	0.10	27
28.	Pondicherry	9,73,829	0.09	0.10	28
29.	Chandigarh	9,00,914	0.09	0.08	30
30.	Mizoram	8,91,058	0.09	0.08	29
31.	Sikkim	5,40,493	0.05	0.05	31
32.	Andaman and Nicobar Islands	3,56,265	0.03	0.03	32
33.	Dadra and Nagar Haveli	2,20,451	0.02	0.02	33
34.	Daman and Diu	1,58,059	0.02	0.01	34
35.	Lakshadweep	60,595	0.01	0.01	35

Source : Provisional Population Totals, Paper-1 of 2001, Series-1, Census of India, 2001.

II

Ranking of States/UTs by Literacy Rate Among Persons, Males and Females, 2001

Rank	Persons: State/ Union Territory	Persons: Literacy rate	Males: State/ Union Territory	Males: Literacy rate	Females: State Union Territory	Females: Literacy rate
1	2	3	4	5	6	7
1.	Kerala	90.92	Kerala	94.20	Kerala	87.86
2.	Mizoram	88.49	Lakshadweep	93.15	Mizoram	86.13
3.	Lakshadweep	87.52	Mizoram	[illegible]	Lakshadweep	81.56
4.	Goa	82.32	Pondicherry	88.89	Chandigarh	76.65
5.	Delhi	81.82	Goa	88.88	Goa	75.51
6.	Chandigarh	81.76	Daman and Diu	88.40	Andaman and Nicobar Islands	75.29
7.	Pondicherry	81.49	Delhi	87.37	Delhi	75.00
8.	Andaman and Nicobar Islands	81.18	Maharashtra	86.27	Pondicherry	74.13
9.	Daman and Diu	81.09	Andaman and Nicobar Islands	86.07	Daman and Diu	70.37
10.	Maharashtra	77.27	Himachal Pradesh	86.02	Himachal Pradesh	68.08
11.	Himachal Pradesh	77.13	Chandigarh	85.65	Maharashtra	67.51
12.	Tripura	73.66	Uttaranchal	84.01	Tripura	65.41
13.	Tamil Nadu	73.47	Tamil Nadu	82.33	Tamil Nadu	64.55
14.	Uttaranchal	72.28	Tripura	81.47	Punjab	63.55
15.	Gujarat	69.97	Gujarat	80.50	Nagaland	61.92
16.	Punjab	69.95	Haryana	79.25	Sikkim	61.46
17.	Sikkim	69.68	Manipur	77.87	Meghalaya	60.41

Cond.

III

1	2	3	4	5	6	7
18.	West Bengal	69.22	Chhattisgarh	77.86	Uttaranchal	60.26
19.	Manipur	68.87	West Bengal	77.58	West Bengal	60.22
20.	Haryana	68.59	Madhya Pradesh	76.80	Manipur	59.70
21.	Nagaland	67.11	Sikkim	76.73	Gujarat	58.60
22.	Karnataka	67.04	Rajasthan	76.46	Karnataka	57.45
	India	65.38	Karnataka	76.29	Haryana	56.31
23.	Chhattisgarh	65.18	Orissa	75.95	Assam	56.03
24.	Assam	64.28	**India**	75.85	**India**	54.16
25.	Madhya Pradesh	64.11	Punjab	75.63	Chhattisgarh	52.40
26.	Orissa	63.61	Dadra and Nagar Haveli	73.32	Andhra Pradesh	51.17
27.	Meghalaya	63.31	Assam	71.93	Orissa	50.97
28.	Andhra Pradesh	61.11	Nagaland	71.77	Madhya Pradesh	50.28
29.	Rajasthan	61.03	Andhra Pradesh	70.85	Rajasthan	44.34
30.	Dadra and Nagar Haveli	60.03	Uttar Pradesh	70.23	Arunachal Pradesh	44.24
31.	Uttar Pradesh	57.36	Jharkhand	67.94	Dadra and Nagar Haveli	42.99
32.	Arunachal Pradesh	54.74	Meghalaya	66.14	Uttar Pradesh	42.98
33.	Jammu and Kashmir	54.46	Jammu and Kashmir	65.75	Jammu and Kashmir	41.82
34.	Jharkhand	54.13	Arunachal Pradesh	64.07	Jharkhand	39.38
35.	Bihar	47.53	Bihar	60.32	Bihar	33.57

Source : Provisional Population Totals, Paper—1 of 2001, Series-1, Census of India, 2001.

IV

States and Union Territories by Density 1991 and 2001

Rank in 2001	*State/ Union Territory*	*Density* 2001	1991	*Rank in 1991*
1.	Delhi	9,294	6,352	1
2.	Chandigarh	7,903	5,632	2
3.	Pondicherry	2,029	1,683	3
4.	Lakshadweep	1,894	1,616	4
5.	Daman and Diu	1,411	907	5
6.	West Bengal	904	767	6
7.	Bihar	880	685	8
8.	Kerala	819	749	7
9.	Uttar Pradesh	689	548	9
10.	Punjab	482	403	11
11.	Tamil Nadu	478	429	10
12.	Haryana	477	372	12
13.	Dadra and Nagar Haveli*	449	282	15
14.	Goa	363	316	13
15.	Assam	340	286	14
16.	Jharkhand	338	274	16
17.	Maharashtra	314	257	18
18.	Tripura	304	263	17
19.	Andhra Pradesh	275	242	19
20.	Karnataka	275	235	20
21.	Gujarat	258	211	21
22.	Orissa	236	203	22
23.	Madhya Pradesh	196	158	23
24.	Rajasthan	165	129	26
25.	Uttaranchal	159	133	24
26.	Chhattisgarh	154	130	25
27.	Nagaland	120	73	31
28.	Himachal Pradesh	109	93	27
29.	Manipur	107	82	28
30.	Meghalaya	103	79	29
31.	Jammu and Kashmir	99	74	30
32.	Sikkim	76	57	32
33.	Andaman and Nicobar Islands*	43	34	33
34.	Mizoram	42	33	34
35.	Arunachal Pradesh	13	10	35

Source: Provisional Population Totals, Paper—1 of 2001, Series-1, Census of India, 2001.

V

Population 1901-2001

Census years	Population	Decadal Growth		Change in Decadal growth		Average annual exponential growth rate (per cent)	Progressive growth rate over 1901 (per cent)
		Absolute	Per cent	Absolute	Per cent		
1	2	3	4	5	6	7	8
1901	23,83,96,327	—	—	—	—	—	—
1911	25,20,93,390	1,36,97,063	5.75	—	—	0.56	5.75
1921	25,13,21,213	-7,72,177	-0.31	-1,44,69,240	-6.05	-0.03	5.42
1931	27,89,77,238	2,76,56,025	11.00	2,84,28,202	11.31	1.04	17.02
1941	31,86,60,580	3,96,83,342	14.22	1,20,27,317	3.22	1.33	33.67
1951	36,10,88,090	4,24,27,510	13.31	27,44,168	-0.91	1.25	51.47
1961	43,92,34,771	7,81,46,681	21.64	3,57,19,171	8.33	1.96	84.25
1971	54,81,59,652	10,89,24,881	24.80	3,07,78,200	3.16	2.20	129.94
1981	68,33,29,097	13,51,69,445	24.66	2,62,44,564	-0.14	2.22	186.64
1991	84,33,87,888	16,30,58,791	23.86	2,78,89,346	-0.80	2.14	255.03
2001	1,02,70,15,247	18,06,27,359	21.34	1,75,68,568	-2.52	1.93	330.80

Source : Provisional Population Totals, Paper - 1 of 2001, Series - 1, Census of India, 2001.

VI

Distribution of Villages According to Population : 1991

Sl. No.	States/UTs	Less than 1,000	1,000 to 1,999	2,000 to 4,999	5,000 to 9,999	10,000 and over	Total
1	2	3	4	5	6	7	8
	INDIA	**3,90,093**	**1,14,395**	**62,915**	**10,597**	**2,779**	**5,80,781**
1.	Andhra Pradesh	11,856	6,433	6,510	1,474	313	26,586
2.	Arunachal Pradesh	3,538	82	25	3	1	3,649
3.	Assam	17,784	4,988	1,793	111	9	24,685
4.	Bihar	45,164	12,768	7,647	1,604	330	67,513
5.	Goa	156	78	94	31	1	360
6.	Gujarat	8,528	5,432	3,418	575	75	18,028
7.	Haryana	2,627	2,021	1,703	364	44	6,759
8.	Himachal Pradesh	16,361	495	136	5	—	16,997
9.	Karnataka	17,113	5,861	3,422	570	100	27,066
10.	Kerala	7	16	102	252	1,007	1,384
11.	Madhya Pradesh	56,568	11,426	3,264	261	7	71,526
12.	Maharashtra	24,111	10,632	4,715	762	192	40,412
13.	Manipur	1,834	192	135	16	3	2,182
14.	Meghalaya	5,316	129	38	1	—	5,484
15.	Mizoram	616	61	19	2	—	698
16.	Nagaland	929	170	108	8	1	1,216
17.	Orissa	39,309	5,761	1,812	103	4	46,989
18.	Punjab	7,447	3,130	1,628	209	14	12,428
19.	Rajasthan	27,123	7,060	3,255	420	31	37,889
20.	Sikkim	336	79	29	3	—	447
21.	Tamil Nadu	4,915	4,625	4,764	1,247	271	15,822
22.	Tripura	195	203	348	94	15	855
23.	Uttar Pradesh	74,866	24,523	11,949	1,336	129	1,12,803
24.	West Bengal	22,701	8,065	5,819	1,117	208	37,910
25.	A. and N. Islands	445	44	15	—	—	504
26.	Chandigarh	7	6	8	3	1	25
27.	D. and N. Haveli	27	17	25	1	1	71
28.	Daman and Diu	9	6	6	2	1	24
29.	Delhi	29	44	86	19	21	199
30.	Lakshadweep	2	—	4	1	—	7
31.	Pondicherry	174	48	38	3	—	263

VII

Population of Million Plus Cities

Sl. No.	City	Population in '000s 1991	1981	1951	Growth ratio 1991	1981	Sex ratio 1991	1981	Literacy rate 1991	1981
1.	Kolkata	11,022	9,194	4,670	2.36	1.97	830	781	77	65
2.	Greater Mumbai	12,596	8,243	2,967	4.25	2.78	828	772	82	68
3.	Delhi	8,419	5,729	1,437	5.86	3.99	830	808	76	63
4.	Chennai	5,422	4,289	1,542	3.52	2.78	933	930	81	67
5.	Bangalore	4,130	2,922	786	5.25	3.72	902	896	79	64
6.	Hyderabad	4,344	2,546	1,131	3.84	2.25	920	919	71	58
7.	Ahmedabad	3,312	2,548	877	3.78	2.91	889	869	80	63
8.	Kanpur	2,030	1,639	705	2.88	2.32	822	804	72	55
9.	Pune	2,494	1,686	609	4.09	2.77	903	880	81	67
10.	Nagpur	1,664	1,302	485	3.43	2.68	915	910	82	66
11.	Lucknow	1,669	1,008	497	3.36	2.03	871	832	71	58
12.	Jaipur	1,518	1,015	304	4.99	3.34	868	861	70	54
13.	Surat	1,519	924	237	6.41	3.90	828	840	76	60
14.	Kochi	1,141	825	212	5.38	3.89	997	989	94	79
15.	Vadodara	1,127	782	211	5.34	3.71	899	888	82	68
16.	Indore	1,109	829	311	3.57	2.67	900	885	77	61
17.	Coimbatore	1,101	920	287	3.84	3.21	930	924	80	67
18.	Patna	1,100	919	326	3.37	2.82	829	815	77	58
19.	Madurai	1,086	907	371	2.93	2.44	954	952	82	68
20.	Bhopal	1,063	671	102	10.42	6.58	894	870	72	57
21.	Visakhapatnam	1,057	604	108	9.79	5.59	937	933	72	56
22.	Ludhiana	1,043	607	154	6.77	3.94	795	815	72	62
23.	Varanasi	1,031	797	370	2.79	2.15	861	842	64	47

Source : Paper 2. 1992, Final Population Total.

VIII

Rural and Urban Population : 1901- 1991

Census Year	Population (Million)		Percentage of total population	
	Rural	Urban	Rural	Urban
1901	213	26	89.2	10.8
1911	226	26	89.7	10.3
1921	223	28	88.8	11.2
1931	246	33	88.0	12.0
1941	275	44	86.1	13.9
1951	299	62	82.7	17.3
1961	360	79	82.0	18.0
1971	439	109	80.1	19.9
1981	524	159	76.7	23.3
1991	629	218	74.3	25.7

Source: Census of India 1991, Series 1, India, Paper 2 of 1992. Final Population Totals.

Growth of Urbanisation by Class of Towns

	Class of town	Population in '000s					
		1901	1951	1961	1971	1981	1991
I	1,00,000 and above	5,570	23,483	34,736	52,808	82,227	1,22,291
II	50,000 - 99,999	2,948	7,548	9,530	14,712	22,037	28,764
III	20,000 - 49,999	4,346	11,115	15,728	19,865	26,719	35,273
IV	10,000 - 19,999	5,847	9,331	11,241	13,929	17,588	21,079
V	5,000 - 9,999	5,332	8,463	6,304	6,089	6,788	7,397
VI	Less than 5,000	1,650	2,047	805	853	1,062	967
	All classes	25,693	61,987	78,343	1,08,256	1,56,420	2,15,772
	Urban population as percentage to total Population	10.84	17.29	19.97	19.91	23.34	25.72

Source : Part II-A(ii) - A-Series - Towns and Urban Agglomerations 1991 with their Populations 1901-1991.

IX

Sex Ratio : 1901-2001

Census Year	Sex ratio (females per 1,000 males)
1901	972
1911	964
1921	955
1931	950
1941	945
1951	946
1961	941
1971	930
1981	934
1991	927
2001	933

Source : Provisional Population Totals, Paper—1 of 2001, Series-1, Census of India, 2001.

Literact Rate : 1951-2001

Census Year	Persons	Males	Females
1951	18.33	27.16	8.86
1961	28.30	40.40	15.35
1971	34.45	45.96	21.97
1981	43.57	56.38	29.76
1991	52.21	64.13	39.29
2001	65.38	75.85	54.16

Source : Provisional Population Totals, Paper—1 of 2001, Series-1, Census of India, 2001.

X

Population by Religion

	1961		1971		1981		1991	
Religious group	*Number (million)*	*Per cent to total*	*Number (million)*	*Per cent to total*	*Number (million)*	*Per cent to total*	*Number (million)*	*Per cent to total*
Hindus	366.5	83.5	453.4	82.7	549.7	82.6	672.6	82.41
Muslims	46.9	10.7	61.4	11.2	75.6	11.4	95.2	11.67
Christians	10.7	2.4	14.3	2.6	16.2	2.4	18.9	2.32
Sikhs	7.8	1.8	10.4	1.9	13.1	2.0	16.3	1.99
Buddhists	3.2	0.7	3.9	0.7	4.7	0.7	6.3	0.77
Jains	2.0	0.5	2.6	0.5	3.2	0.5	3.4	0.41
Other	1.6	0.4	2.2	0.4	2.8	0.4	3.5	0.43
Total	439.2	100.0	548.2	100.0	665.3	100.0	816.2	100.00

Source : (i) Census of India, Series 1, India, Part II c (i); (ii) Census of India 1981, Series 1, Paper 3 of 1984 (Religion); (iii) Census of India, Series 1, Paper I of 1995 (Religion).

1

Origin and Development

History

One of the most rapidly growing educational innovations in the world. Population education has a relatively short history. Formerly only a handful of countries had any type of consolidated effort to include population education in the school curriculum. Now nearly one hundred countries were at varying stages in the development of population education, family life education, family health education, sex education, or other related programmes. Following is a brief account of the historical development of Population Education:

Alva Myrdal 1941: 'Alva Myrdal in 1941' made the first attempt to voice the need for population education. In her book Nation and Family she tried to convince the Govt. and people of United States of America that a conscious population policy was essential to realise the social policy. She emphasised the role of education in the development of a new population policy. Which she called family education. However, for about two decades no significant progress was made with regard to the inclusion of population content in curricula.

UNESCO 1948 : The United Nations, Particularly UNESCO, took a keen interest and initiative in the direction of efforts made at the individual level for introducing population content in the curriculum. In his Annual Report for 1948 Sir Julian Huxley, the first Director General of UNESCO, emphasised that over-population could drastically affect the future civilisation and its rate of advance. Huxley was particularly concerned about the undernourishment of much of the world's population and with the problem of erosion and depletion of natural resources writing that "Population must be balanced against resources, or civilisation will perish," Huxley suggested that UNESCO's task must include educating the people of the world to realise the gravity of the problems involved.

Articles 1962 : The Match 1962 issue of Teacher's College Record, Columbia University, tied an article by Warren S. Whomson entitled The Population Explosion' and mother article 'Population-Gap in the Curriculum' by Philip M. Hauser. Both there articles drew attention to the need to include population content in the school curriculum.

Project 1964 : A project to prepare instructional materials related to population education was undertaken at Teacher College, Columbia University, under the leadership of Professor Solm Wayland in the year 1964. Designed as prototype materials for the preservice training of secondary school teachers two documents were resulted, entitled, (i) Teaching Population Dynamics, and (ii) Critical Stages of Reproduction.

Conference 1968 : In 1968 a general conference of UNESCO declared that the purpose of UNESCO's activities in the field of population should be to promote a better understanding of the serious responsibility which population growth imposes on individuals, nations and the whole international community.

Policies 1970-72 : During this period UNESCO authorised the Director General to assist Member States, on request in the elaboration of population and family planning policies. In 1972 UNESCO recommended that the Director General promote a clearer insight among the public, into the wine, causes and consequences of demographic trends by means of education and information. At its seventeenth session the General Conference of UNESCO adopted resolution authorising the Director General to pursue and undertake activities designed inter alia for the promotion of population education.

Workshop 1970 : Sponsored by the UNESCO Regional Office for Education in Asia and held in Bangkok in September-October 1970 the workshop on Family and Population Education was a landmark in the history of population education. Experts and educators from 13 Member States in Asia addressed themselves to the task of preparing a statement of objectives for population education. They suggested strategies for organising programmes, outlining content for incorporation into school curricula in the social sciences and natural sciences, and preparing a set of draft sample instructional materials in mathematics, science and social studies. In course of time several of the participants of the workshop played key roles in developing population education programmes in their own countries.

World Plan of Action : The World Plan of Action, stated that governments should consider making provision in both the formal and non-formal educational programmes for informing their people on the consequences of existing or alternative futility behaviour for the well-beings of the family, for the educational and psychological development of children and for the general welfare of society, so that an informed and responsible attitude to marriage and reproduction will be promoted. Population education was instituted in nine countries in response to the recommendation.

The programme of population education picked up quite fast in the seventies. After the 1970 Regional Workshop, with the financial support of the United Nations Food for Population Activities (UNFPA) and the technical assistance of UNESCO five countries in Asia launched national programmes in population education.

Seminar on Education

The National Seminar on Population Education was organized by the Ministry of Education and Youth Services in collaboration with the Ministry of Health and Family Planning, on 2nd and 3rd of August, 1969 at Mumbai, with. Dhairwandry Rama Rao, President, International Planned Parenthood Federation, Mumbai as the chairperson. The Department of Social Sciences and Humanities of the NCERT provided the academic services to this Seminar. It was attended by the representatives of

Ministry of Education and Youth Services, Ministry of Health and Family Planning State Representatives, USAID, Ford Foundation, Pathfinder Fund and NCERT and twenty-two other specialists in allied fields.

Objectives and Motives

1. To review the work already done so far in population education by the different agencies, official and non-official, in the country.
2. To clarify the concept and objectives of population education; and
3. To develop a practical and realistic plan of action for the introduction of population education in the curricula at different stages of education.

Suggestions

Challenge-The country is faced with a new challenge which arises out of the enormous increase in population, the needs of which are not being met adequately by the economic development.

Education-Steps should be educate the student at various levels to meet these challenges. Population education should be an integral plan of education at all levels.

Objectives of Education-The objectives of Population education should be (i) to enable the students to understand that family size is controllable, (ii) that population limitation can facilitate the development of a higher quality of life in the nation, and (iii) that a small section contribute materially to the quality of living for the individual family.

Information-Students at all levels have a right to accurate information about the effect of changes in family size and in national population on the individual, the family, and the nation so that this body of knowledge is utilized to control family size and national population with beneficial impact on the economic development of the nation and the welfare of the individual families.

Curriculum-Population education should be introduced into the curriculum of schools and colleges by including it in so far as it my be possible, in the areas of study now common in the educational curriculum such as social studies, sciences, health education, mathematics, languages, etc. It may be possible to achieve all the objectives in view by including population education suitably in the curricula of appropriate subjects already comprised in the curriculum.

Correlation -Careful attention must be given to offering ideas and information which we appropriate to the age levels and the cultural orientation of children, adolescents and adults in schools and colleges and outside the educational system.

Gradual development -Population education is a new area of curriculum to most schools and colleges. Steps will therefore, have to be taken to introduce it gradually so that the curriculum is developed, teachers trained it pilot projects conducted and evaluated.

Population Education Cell- A separate "Population Education Cell" should be established in the NCERT in order to develop suitable curricula of population education at the school stage. This cell should work in close collaboration with the Central Health Education Bureau, Central Family Planning Institute and other agencies interested in the programme, both official and voluntary.

Implementation-Immediate steps must be taken :

(a) To clearly define the content of population education at different steps and evolve suitable methods for teaching and examination, and

(b) To prepare books, supplementary reading materials, audiovisual aids, teachers guides, etc. needed for the successful implementation of the programme.

Education out of schools-Special steps may be taken to draw a suitable programme in population education for the youth who are not entitled in the schools and use the facilities as well as the personal available in all education institutions for this purpose.

Training-(a) Immediate steps should be taken to organise courses; on population education in teachers' colleges at the primary as well as the secondary levels.

(b) Suitable steps should be taken to organize in-service training for the teachers who were already working.

(c) There should be specialists on population education among the teacher educators at the post-graduate level.

Research-Efforts should be made to promote research on population education in the teachers' college as well as in the liberal arts colleges and other institutions of higher education. In the universities efforts have to be made to develop inter-disciplinary research in population problems.

Courses, Guidance and Extension-(a) At the college level, steps should be taken by the universities to design a course in demography at the undergraduate level so that those who were interested in population problem could be specialized at the post-graduate level in demography.

(b) College level guidance bureau should be strengthened by qualified staff who would help the students to solve personal problem in connection with family relations, marriage counselling, etc.

(c) Extension lectures should be organized on population problems in each college and university every year in order to ensure a widespread awareness of the problems among the youths and the teachers.

Steps by U.G.C-To achieve the purpose in the two resolutions stated above, the Resolution Nos. 12 and 13, University Grants Commission may be requested to take the necessary steps to enable the affiliated colleges and the universities to take up new task-courses of study, research and extension lectures.

Parent-Teacher Co-operation-Teachers organisations and parent-teacher associations should discuss the problem and help in the implementation of population education programmes.

Step for Govt. Experiments-The seminar welcomes the willingness of the States to try this programme on an experimental basis provided the details of the curricula, materials and necessary guidance were made available. The Seminar, therefore, recommends that the following steps my be taken :

(i) ***Statement***-The Government of India, Ministries of Education and Health in consultation with the State

Governments should draw up an statement showing the broad objectives of the programme, it broad content as it would be introduced at different stages, and the manner in which the pilot projects for the programme would be developed, administered and financially supported.

(ii) ***Programme***-On the basis of this statement, the NCERT and the Central Health Education Bureau, Central Family Planning institute collaborating with the State Education Departments and other organizations interested in the programme -official and voluntary-should go into the details of the programme and produce (a) detailed curricula, (b) hand-books for teachers dealing with among other things, methods of reaching and examination, and (c) other materials which should be available in English, Hindi and other Indian languages, in good time.

(iii) ***Introduction on a pilot bases***-The programme should then be introduced on a pilot basis in different categories of institutions of the various categories and levels.

Support to Projects-The Seminar notes with satisfaction that some universities and other organizations have already started pilot projects and recommends that they should be supported.

Evaluation and Improvement- Adequate arrangements should also be made to watch the progress of these pilot projects to evaluate them and improve the materials and techniques in the light of the experience gained.

Standing Committee-The Government of India should take immediate steps to act up a standing committee which could watch the progress in the implementation of these recommendations by various organisations at different levels.

National Population Education Project

National Population Education Project (School Education) was launched in April 1980 with a view to institutionalise population education in the school education system. This project a being implemented by NCM on behalf of the Ministry of Human

Resource Development. The Ministry of Health and Family Welfare is the nodal agency for this project. This project is being implemented in all States and UTs. It is also being implemented in the Higher and Adult Education Sector. The objective of inculcating the message of mail family unions; and other population related issues in the mind of school and college students and the clientele of adult and non-formal education is being achieved through National Population Education Project. The National Population Education Programme is now being implemented through three projects of School and Non-Formal Education, Higher Education and Adult Education. Three cycles of the project that have been completed so have laid stress on— (i) integrate population education in the syllabi and textbooks; (ii) develop prototype curricular, instructional and training materials for all stages of school education; (iii) conduct teacher training programmes in population education throughout the country; and (iv) incorporation of sustainable development, agencies and other related concerns in the population education elements in textbooks of the NCERT.

The fourth cycle of the project is about to commence shortly with the aim of introducing adolescence education, process of growing up, HIV/AIDS education, drug abuse in school and teacher education.

QUESTIONS

1. Trace the history of Population Education.
2. Account for the history of Population Education in India.

2

The Concept and Perspective

India seeks to establish an egalitarian society through constitutional means. Education has a dynamic role to play by including right values, beliefs and attitudes in children, who are the future citizens. They should be made aware of the trends in population growth, the gap between the available resources and increasing numbers, the negative effects of population growth on social and natural environment and the blessings of a small family.

Population Education is not a sophisticated name for family planning. It is not sex education, either. It expects the students to be sensitive to the problem of population explosion and how it affects the happiness and well being of their own.

Smaller Concepts Distinguished

Distinction from Sex Education : Though there is considerable overlap and area of agreement between the two population education is sex education. Sex education has been defined as an educational programme, designed to provide the learners adequate and accurate knowledge of the biological, socio-cultural and moral dimensions of human sexuality. It embraces the biological, socio-cultural and ethical aspects of human sexual behaviour. Its real purpose is the unfolding of a boy-child into manhood and of a girl-child into womanhood. It includes knowledge about our maleness and femaleness. Its stress is on heightening sexual pleasure, on prevention of sexual diseases and on family planning. Family planning is the theme of population education though population education is not a counterpart of family planning programmes for the younger generation.

In Asia and the Pacific region there has been a cultural and religious resistance to include any kind of family planning or sex education in school curricula. Sex education is still considered "untouchable, in many countries in Asia including India. However, some countries such as the Republic of Korea and the Philippines have included family planning and sexuality as a part of population education curriculum in schools. Sex education is a major component of family life education in Fiji.

Because of the need felt for the individual to understand himself or herself as a sexual being, which is a prerequisite to the development of responsible parenthood. Some countries of Latin America lay major emphasis on sex education. In Latin America and to a lesser degree in Francophone Africa, the term sex education is used to suggest a broader range of activities which have been called 'Population Education' in Asia.

Distinguishing between Population Education and Sex Education, says D. Gopal Rao, "The need for population education mainly are because of the consequences of the imbalance between population and world resources. Family life education in the West grow out of growing evidence of disintegration of family, whereas sex education developed as a reaction to an increase in veneral diseases and out of wedlock pregnancies. Secondly, in sex education, the stress is on individual whereas in population education, it is the interaction between individual, family, society in national context that is important." Population education is not an alternate term for sex education, The area of sex education is entirely different.

Solan Rayland of Teachers' College, Columbia University, USA, introduced the term population education. He noted that term like sex education and family life education in the West were insufficient while population education is the proper term as its scope and functions were different.

Some countries which do not openly accept any kind of sex education or family planning education in school do realise the need for including some content related to these areas in the population education curriculum. A number of studies recently conducted in some countries in Asia have noted this change in the perception of and acceptance to include sex education related contents in the framework of population education.

Family Planning Programme Differentiated

Meaning: It is purely an educational programme in order to create awareness and develop understanding. It is neither prescriptive nor directive. It is purely a clinical approach and a medical job.

Scope: The scope of population education is very wide and comprehensive. It includes programmes like sex education, environmental education, family life education, family planning programme, etc. The scope and area of the family planning programme is narrow. It is only a part and aspect of population.

Comprehension : Population education is a programme meant not only for married couples but also for young pupils in schools and out of schools and adults. It embraces a large segment of population. The family planning programme is for married couples. It has less value and meaining for the young ones in schools.

Techniques : Population education programme has adopted many modern innovative techniques to create awareness. The family planning programme has been the earliest measure to curb the growth rate of population.

Objectives : The purpose of population education is to study the population phenomenon in a family and community with a view to take decisions. The family planning programme is a means to planning the numbers of children and spacing the birth in a family.

Curriculum : Population education is an exploration of knowledge and attitude about population, the family and sex. The family planning programme intends to create an idea about the "small family as happy family." It also intends to adopt many clinical measures to control the family size.

Discipline : Population education is multi-disciplinary in character. The family Planning programme is unidisciplinary in character.

Nature : Population education is an educational programme. Family planning is a medical and clinical programme.

Population Education : It is sociological and philosophical in nature. Family planning is scientific in nature.

Education of Population, with a Departure

Education of the population is a vague term having no broader meaning. Population education is an educational programme which intends to develop an understanding among the youth within and outside the schools. Population education is sociological and philosophical in nature, whereas education of the population is a concept which conveys only general concept of education to the common population (people).

Family Life Education, a Different View

The family life education is an educational process through which every society as its young members for adulthood. Most elements of family life education are informal and take place in the home, place of worship, education and work, and in everyday contact with other people. Children and adolescents become thoroughly familiar with the norms, customs and values of their society through the process of education and socialisation, through observation of people's behaviour and the ways in which others respond to it and through their own experience. These provide the guidelines for their own behaviour. After people acquire the knowledge they need to lead an adult life, they learn the consequence of transgressing accepted codes of conduct. The young child learns about life, society became life itself educated.

According to the national source book of population education: "Family life education may be defined as education for human development which seeks to ensure that each individual approaching adulthood is equipped with the skills and personal reserves to cope with the challenges of everyday life in society, within acceptable societal structures, and to adapt to change with experience and equilibrium."

Family life education is concerned with learning about living family and personal development and social relationships. It is not simply concerned with the transfer of information and values. It aims at assisting people in developing the ability to understand themselves and the society in which they live. It seeks to assist people in developing the ability to learn, to think independently, to work out and clarify their own values and to evaluate and use information effectively in making responsible decisions about their lives, Life education is not family planning education or sex education, although few are its important components. In family life education the focus is primarily on the family as a group of people with complementary roles and needs. Family planning education is concerned with the concept of planning in relation to childbearing and parenthood.

Contraception Education, with a Difference

Contraception education can be defined as education in the techniques of conception control and birth control that makes it possible for an individual to have no more children than he desires. Its aim is essentially one of immediate practicality. Its targets are the married couples and those about to be married. After the ground work of receptive attitude has been created by population education, birth control and family planning education becomes more relevant to the individual and to the society. The role of population education is long-ranged in comparison to family planning education, birth control, family life education and contraception education. Its approach is inter-disciplinary, multi-level and continuing.

Population Policy Deferred

Population policies and programmes highlight various steps taken by the government administration to reduce the growth rate of the population. Thus, population policies include the measures taken by the government to meet the challenges of population growth, population policies consist of two approaches:

Clinical Approach : The clinical approach includes the family planning programme which covers hardly 37 per cent of the population. In comparison to the educational approach its prospective is not so hopeful.

Educational Approach : The educational approach covers 42 per cent of the population in the age group of up to 14 years. It acquires important dimensions because it is this group which will decide about the population trends in the next one or two decades. Therefore, necessary population awareness is to be created in them.

Population Education Defined

Regional Seminar on Population and Family Life Education: UNESCO, Bangkok, 1907 : "It is an educational programme which provides for a study of the population situation in family, community, nation and the world, with the purpose of developing in the students rational and responsible attitude and behaviour towards that situation."

Population Reference Bureau, Washington, 1971 : "Population Education is an attempt to create a deep, universal action guiding perception of the consequences of demographic change. It seeks to bring about a realization of the individual, family, social and environmental effects of the explosive increase in human population, the rapid shift in the construction and distribution of people, the implications of changing age and other demographic patterns and the conceivable options that may be opened to mankind to cope with the consequent problem. While it is confined exclusively to a particular group, it is focused primarily on students, who will become the principal child bearers within one or two decades."

Prof. Noel David Burleson : "Population education or population awareness refers to factual knowledge about population dynamics required to understand the nature and magnitude of the burden imposed by rapid population growth."

Gopal Rao: "Population education may be defined as an educational programme which provides for a study of the population phenomenon so as to enable the student to take rational decisions towards any problem arising out of rapid population growth."

Dr V.K.R.V. Rao: "Population education should not be treated merely as a quantitative phenomenon or just an essay in numbers, it is the quality of the population that is most relevant, both as a factor of growth and an end product of growth, and numbers have to be treated in terms of the effect they have in quality either by way of deterioration or improvement. Population education therefore, is essentially, related to human resource development. Thus, population education is not only concerned with population awareness but also with developing values and attitudes so that both quality and quantity be taken care of."

Viderman : The purpose of population education is to develop awareness and understanding of the relations between population growth and national development, both in short and long run, and to develop an understanding of the consequences of individual decisions in the important area of reproductive behaviour. A population awareness programme, therefore, should provide the fact of population dynamics, of family life, of human reproduction that children will need. It should also show how the actions of each individual of the society affect the others. This is the moral and ethical purpose of population education which is in addition to its informational and attitudinal goal."

Hurbson: "Population education is an exploration of knowledge and attitudes about population, family and sex. It includes population awareness : family living, reproduction education and basic values."

Prof. Sloan Wayland: "Regardless of the term used, we were concerned about the inclusion in the education system of instructional settings in which young people will come to understand the circumstances which have led to the adoption of family planning as public policy and to understand that for the family and the nation, family planning is possible and desirable. This would include an understanding of the relationship of population dynamics to economic and social development of the country and the implications of family size for the quality of life of the individual family. The particular instructional activities at any given school level and in any particular subject field would of course be devised in a manner which would be pedagogically sound and appropriate for the particular society."

3

Basic Issues

Population Education is relatively a new discipline. The credit for introducing the term Population Education goes to Sloan Rayland of Teachers College, Columbia University, U.S.A. He had noted that terms like sex education and family life education were in use in West but none used this. Population education which was the proper term and its scope and functions were different. Population education is not the alternate term for sex education. The area of sex education is entirely different.

This is one of the recent topics that we have introduced in our courses. In fact, population education is need of the hour if we want to save ourselves from starvation and extinction. Being of recent origin, much literature has appeared on this topic. The author has drawn heavily from the wonderful book, 'Population Education' by D. Gopal Rao (published by Sterling Publishers). Students are strongly advised to go through the said book for a very detailed study.

Coming back to Population Education. How do we define it? How does it differ from sex education? Many attempts have been made to define population education, yet no clear and commonly accepted definition has emerged. Population education is a new concept as stated earlier and as such without a proper definition. However, various authorities have defined it in their own way. We shall presently see a few of these.

Dr. V.K.R.V. Rao views population education as a part of human resource development programme.

Population education should not be treated merely as a quantitative phenomenon or just an essay in numbers. It is the quality of the population that is most relevant both as a factor of growth and an end product of growth and numbers have to be treated in terms of the effect they have in quality either by way of deterioration or improvement. Population education, therefore, is essentially, related to human resource development. Thus population education is not only concerned with population awareness but also with developing values and attitudes so that both quality and quantity are taken care of.

Viderman emphasizes the moral and ethical purpose of education: "The purpose of population education is to develop awareness, and understanding of the relations between population growth and national development both in short and long run and to develop an understanding of the consequences of individual decisions in the important area of reproductive behaviour. A population awareness programme, therefore, should provide the fact of population dynamics, of family life of human reproduction that children will need. It should also show how the actions of each individual of the society affect the others. This is the moral and ethical purpose of population education which is in addition to its informational and attitudinal goal.

Tylor, Daniel in his book, "Developing a Foundation for Population Education—The Nepalese Case" (1968) stresses the motivational relationship between a population education programme and the practice of family planning.

Population education has a double task: it is both motivational (trying to encourage people to adopt family planning) and it is instructional (teaching people the facts about population problem, its probable consequences and what the possible alternatives are).

Burbson considers it relevant to include both sex education and family life education within the scope of population education.

Population education is an exploration of knowledge and attitudes about population, the family and sex. It includes population awareness, family living, reproduction education and basic values.

There are other definitions also. Above is a representative sample each stressing different aspect of the population education. None is final. We give below quoting Gopal Rao, a comprehensive definition of population education.

Population education may be defined as an educational programme which provides for a study of the population phenomenon so as to enable the students to take rational decisions towards problems arising out of rapid population growth.

In simpler words, population education means educating the students about large population or ever increasing population and the problems which this population creates.

A New Trend

We should not be satisfied with the definition of Population Education. We should understand that Population Education is an innovation in Education. This is primarily so not because it wants to bring in an additional subject or extra contents of knowledge in school curricula, but because it strives for bringing about a significant change in the goals of general education at the school stage.

The characteristics of innovation are the universality, specificity and functionality followed by its ability to galvanize the basic system of apparatus itself.

Population education is an innovation which is almost universal in nature. The universal goal of population education is to stabilize the human population on a somewhat continuing basis probably with some scope for marginal growth if necessary.

As against this universality of population education, it should be more fruitful to trace its specificity—an essential element of innovation. We are to be specific to stabilize the population at a reasonable level with a view to raising appreciably the current standard of living which are dismally low. The population problem has got to be solved. This is the specificity in the innovation.

It is an innovation in strategy also, Strategy by definition is a means, usually involving a sequence of specified activities enabling an advocated innovation to become successfully installed in an on-going educational system. Perhaps the most striking feature of the strategy of population education is its wide range, variety and multiplicity of approaches.

We are not implementing it in our schools. But state departments of education and agencies like SCERTs have facilitated initiation of innovation. Some symposia, workshops are being held.

Teacher Training colleges and University Departments of Education are doing something to supplement the work done by Departments of Education. Voluntary organisations are also doing something in the field.

NCERT has adopted integrated strategy. The NCERT textbooks in social sciences and biology which incorporate population ideas have also helped states to take necessary cue while preparing their own textbooks. Orientation of teachers is yet another dimension of this work, NCERT has a Population Education unit. It has developed a draft syllabus on Population Education for classes I to XI so that states can take up cues from this. Materials such as Readings in Population Education have been prepared NCERT has published many books/pamphlets on population education. The strategy thus is integrated one.

There are arguments for and against innovation. Urge number of children in the schools can well understand the population problem. The topic of population education has also been introduced in teacher training institutions. There are arguments against this. There is resistance to population education. The parents are conservative. The teachers are conservative. They do not want to discuss this topic.

Some observations on Population Education by Professor Sloan R. Wayland are as follows.

1. Population Education is a different kind of activity from family planning. It is essentially an educational response to a felt need for a problem, a major concern of very great magnitude. The problem before the educators is not to indoctrinate children but to help them systematically to understand the problems within their mental framework. We want to help them to understand their family circumstances, the consequences of belonging to a big family and a small family, the

economic well-being of their own families and ultimately the relationship of their would-be actions to the welfare of the nation as a whole.

2. The population educators must realise the difficult nature of the problem they are tackling. They must understand the long-term nature of the problem, their work and the impossibility of getting any immediate returns. This is indeed very difficult situation and fraught with frustration, if we expect immediate returns. It indeed a long-term and a continuing process.
3. In Population Education the role of the teacher is highly important because we may not forget that the teacher also has an affective domain. We do not know what the teacher feels about population problems. It is, therefore, necessary that all our activities should be based upon a due recognition of the teacher's role, his conviction, his will and his abilities to bring about a significant change in the attitudes and understandings of young children.
4. The relationship of Population Education with the rest of the school curriculum was one of the important problems that came up very vigorously everywhere in the early days of Population education. In this regard I think that the emphasis to be given and the relationship of Population Education to other subject areas of curriculum is going to be worked out much better once we get into the field, by virtue of field experience. We should move with an open mind, on the pattern of working, the teaching methods, research findings, field experience, and the points of views of various groups including teachers and school administrators.
5. Let us not isolate Population Education from the rest of the education or the totality of the school curricula. It would be worthwhile if we look at Population Education as one of the innovations that we have to bring about in our educational system. The strategies through which this innovation could be brought about should enable us to usher in many other innovations more effectively and speedily. We have a fascinating chance in this regard

when in 1973 the Education Satellite may start working in India. As a result of our work in Population Education, let us hope that we would be better prepared to handle educational experiments to be undertaken through the new mass-media of satellite communication. We should gain experience as to how contents of education can be changed and also be in a position to appreciate the changed role of the teacher with the introduction of educational technology in a big way.

Effect on Sex Education

Population education is not sex education. There is some difference. Whenever we talk of sex education, the stress is on heightening sexual pleasure, on prevention of sexual diseases and on family planning. Here it is family planning which is the theme of population education. At the same time population education is not to be considered a counterpart of family planning programmes for the younger generation. It is not sex education as stated earlier. In the words of D. Gopal Rao, the difference is in the following words, "The need for population education mainly arose because of the consequences of the imbalance between population and world resources. Family life education in the West grew out of growing evidence of disintegration of family, whereas sex education developed as a reaction to an increase in venereal disease and out of wedlock pregnancies."

Secondly in a sex education, the stress is on individual whereas in population education, it is the interaction between individual, family, society in national context that is important.

Education in Demand

B. S. Parakh in his book "Population Education-Inception to Institutionalisation" (1985-NCERT) advocates the introduction of population education in India on the following grounds.

Attack an Blind Faith

Population education at school and teacher education level has great educational potential as an instrument to inculcate rational humanism, imbued with the spirit of scientific inquiry that lies at the very heart of population education. It can act as an effective spearhead in a frontal attack on blind faith, superstition, dogma, fatalism and inaction, so rampant in our society.

Establishing Equality of Sexes

Population education if rightly perceived, can go a long way in establishing equality of sexes by helping women to acquire their rightful status and become equal partners in overall goal of accelerating the pace of socio-economic development. Let us hope that population education can be a small step towards enabling "men to participate freely in decision-making in various walks of life and at every level—individual, family, community and society at large.

Planning as a Way of Life

Population education lends itself very effectively to nurture the basic concept of planning as a way of life. We know that our country has accepted planned development as the national goal. This goal cannot be attained if a competitive or unplanned behaviour in the domain of personal or family life, particularly in the contest of population issues, continues to operate. The concept of planning is likely to succeed only when it is followed at both macro and micro levels, *i.e.,* at the state or societal and family or individual levels.

Dignity of Individual Freedom

Population education believes in the dignity of the individual and freedom of his choice in respect of the size of his or her family. But simultaneously it also believes in dovetailing it with the social good and the legitimate concerns of the society as a whole.

Understanding Society

Population education has the potential to become the vehicle through which socio-economic fabric of the society can be understood, the socio-economic, cultural and political factors and their interplay can be studied and social values, norm and behavioural patterns may be appreciated.

Better Quality of Life

Population education provides an opportunity as well as a challenge to the how best and through what means we can succeed in creating an urge in every individual to aspire for a better quality of life. We know that the majority of our population does not have proper perception of such a quality of life.

Producers of National Wealth

Population education helps us to look at the population not only in term of its number or mere as consumers of goods and services or natural resources and wealth, but also as the producers of national wealth. When the population is treated as a means of production, it is the quality and not only the quantity that matters. It is in this context that the role of population education becomes vital, as it leads us to appreciate productivity, conservation and maintenance of environment.

Comparison of Lifestyles

At the global level population education helps us to study, compare and contrast various life-styles, consumption patterns and inequitable distribution of resources—natural and human. Any meaningful and functional curriculum in population education will have to wage a war against wasteful and mindless consumption patterns without any rare for the teeming millions of the deprived humanity and the generations that are yet to be born and that have the same rightful claims on the riches of this indivisible earth to which they would belong as we do today. This global and futuristic concern about the destiny of the human race, which population education highlights, would not be hopefully passed over very lightly.

Value-oriented System

Pedagogically, population education, being behavioural and multi-disciplinary in nature, has a great potential to learn or to find out how best can we impart value-oriented education and ensure that children do develop a value system, inculcate socially desirable attitudes, widen their cognitive map, and imbibe the spirit of human affiliation. Population education is growing as an area that may promote such meaningful research which would enrich and hopefully even revolutionalise our pedagogical insights, perspectives and techniques. It has also a potential to extend the existing network, if any, of the education technology to the neglected area of our limited human and financial resources.

The need for population education arises from following reasons.

The Population Explosion. In almost all countries of the world, there is an unprecedented population growth. This can be because of two factors : (a) death control, and (b) no control over births. To limit population, birth control programmes have been launched and are directed towards couples with a child and the couples in reproductive age groups. There is no other evidence of any serious attempts to launch population education programmes; for the younger generation. We do not think that children have to be flooded by millions.

The impact of mass and communication efforts the national family planning programme. India, like other developing countries has a national policy and programme for birth control. The state conveys ideas about family planning and birth control to people through paintings, pamphlets, etc. The government thinks that this way children are also educated. This is in fact incidental information and incidental learning can be harmful. As such, population education need to be systematically imparted through a well-planned programme.

The age composition of population in developing countries. A characteristic feature of developing countries to quote D. Gopal Rao that about 45% of its people are below 16 years of age. They will soon be adults. The reproductive behaviour of this critical mass is of crucial importance in controlling the rate of population growth. Hence, the need to develop population education programme.

Education as preparation for citizenship and effective contemporary living. The need for introducing population education in school transcends the urgency of the problem of over- population. We do study population in S.S. and Economics and thereby we realise the magnitude of the problem. Unless we give proper population education, India will remain backward. In a broad sense, population education is a means for preparing the younger generation for effective citizenship through educating them to face realities of contemporary living.

Population education is a mutilations process. It is not to be stopped after educating one generation. Successive generations have to be educated. As such it is a continuous process.

In simpler terms, Population Education is needed because of the following.

To check population explosion. In almost all countries of the world, there is unprecedented growth. This is because of two factors : (a) Death control, and (b) No control over births. Thus, we have to give population education right from the beginning.

To check the effects of over population. We have already discussed these in the beginning of this book—it is unemployment, infection, poverty, illiteracy. So population education is a must to check these.

Education as preparation for citizenship and effective contemporary living. Unless we give population education, India will remain backward. In a broad sense population education is a means for preparing younger generation for effective citizenship through educating them to face the realities of contemporary living.

Need of Democracy. It is clear that lesser the population better the democracy.

Moral responsibility. It is rightly said that the welfare, health and fuller development of every citizen is the moral responsibility of the state. If we want all these developments to take place, we have to check our population through population education.

Need of the hour. Why not control population for better living? It is need of the hour.

Aims and Objectives

Let us see what various authorities say.

AB. Wadia in "Population Education for Younger Generation" (1969) has analyzed the objectives of population education thus:

1. Creating among the younger generation an understanding of one of the most important phenomena in a

modern world, namely, rapid growth of population, its causes, trends, and some factors affecting it, and ways of regulating it.

2. Studying the influence of population trends on various aspects of life and in particular, the close interaction of population growth and the development process, with particular reference to the national programme to raise standards of living.
3. Controlling unplanned births.
4. Realising the significance of population growth on individual and family life, and encouraging attitudes of responsibility and mutual help and cooperation in all aspects of personal and family living.
5. Appreciating the fact that for preserving the health of the mother, the welfare of children, the economic stability of the family, the Indian families today and in future should be small and compact, and not more than 2 or 3 children should be there in the family.

The national seminar on population education held at Mumbai in 1969 laid the following two objectives :

1. The objective of population education should be to enable the students to understand that the family size is controllable, that the population limitation can facilitate the development of A higher quality of life in the nation and that a small family size can contribute materially to the quality of living for the individual family. It should also enable the students to appreciate the family to ensure the economic stability of the family and to assume good prospects for the young generation the Indian families of today, should be small and compact, with only 2 or 3 children.
2. Students at all levels have a right to get information about the effect of changes in family size and in national population on the individual, the family and the nation so that this body of knowledge is utilised to control family size and national population with beneficial impact on the economic development of nation and welfare of the individual families.

When do we Start giving Population Education? Population education is to be given in the schools because : (i) Schools are exclusively meant for teaching younger generation, (ii) Schools have a tradition of being future oriented, (iii) Schools promote social changes, and (iv) Schools are already engaged in adopting new innovations and changes.

4

Significant Features

Educational Process: It is an educational process to create an awareness in the people regarding causes and consequences of population growth.

Creates Attitudes and Behaviour: It creates rational and responsible attitudes and behaviour in the learners about desirable family size and quality of life.

Multidisciplinary: Multidisciplinary in nature it borrows its contents from disciplines like sociology, anthropology, geography and biology.

Comperentative: It refers both to the qualitative and quantitative aspects of human population.

Provides Learning Situation: It provides learning situation for understanding population situation in family, community, nation and the world at large.

Man Environment Relationship: It helps to understand the relationship of man with his environment with due respect to his quality of life.

Welfare: It helps in the implications of population factors for the welfare of the individual, the family and society.

All Aspects of Population: Population education implies the nature, causes, changes, characteristics and distribution aspects of human population.

Fundamentals

1. An educational programme to develop in the teacher.
2. Understanding of interrelationships between population and quality of life.
3. Responsible attitude and behaviour towards population issues.
4. Skills in making rational decisions about population matters.

Basis, Nature and Scope

Population education is relatively a new field of study. Its concept and scope has been made explicit through the various objectives which laid down for the population education programme. Thus, population education implies a change in the attitude and behaviour patterns of the individual. It enables him to make rational decisions on population issues involving the family, the nation and the world at large. San. Avabai B. Wadia has said, "One has the strong feeling that population education seems to be one of those areas of knowledge where definitions will probably follow the empirical programme evolved rather than the other way round. It is therefore, quite possible to move on the action programmes without spending too much time on perfecting theories.'

The Characteristics

In her inaugural address at the first conference of the Asian Forum of Parliamentarians for Population and Development held at New Delhi from 17 to 20 February 1984. Mrs Indira Gandhi the then Prime Minister of India said.

"Young people must be in the vanguard of the movement to restrict population growth and to promote sustained development. In school and colleges and through non-formal education they must be made conscious of the dynamics of population growth and its implication for their own further well-being and that of the nation. Properly planned population education programmes need to be introduced at various levels so that when young people marry, they may fully aware of their responsibility to themselves, to future generations and to society. Every occasion and festival, be it religious or otherwise, where people get together, affords excellent opportunity to reach out to them to explain the importance of these programmes."

Due to the great potential of education in alleviating the problems arising from increasing population, many countries of the world have launched population education programmers a different levels of education in both formal and non-formal sectors during the past decades. Education in population dynamics is quite necessary for a well-rounded system of education to prepare young people for adult roles in future. As social institutions schools existence is justified in so far as they satisfy social requirements. The children of today are the future citizen of the country. Hence, they must be made aware of all the hazards of life they may have to face in futures. To quote T.S. Mehta, "The opportunity to decide the number and spacing of children is a basic human right. Hence, it is the decision at the individual level which is going to make any difference, and not the scientific discoveries. The values of a small family and the hazards of a large family are the two options before us. In this regard the educational programme can help to develop right attitudes among the vast population which has yet to enter the fertility age group." The following is the importance of population education :

Population Situation Explained

"The population situation is defined as the interrelationship between births and migration and other aspects of life." In almost all countries of the world there is an unprecedented population growth relative to the limited resources of the society. Because of death control, there is a rapid growth of population, which seriously affects a country's welfare, economy and values. Therefore, family planning education is necessary to lower the high rate of population growth. Its purpose is to create an awareness that the number of frequency of births would be controlled, especially by using modern contraceptive techniques, to present the advantages of this reduction in births, etc. The aim of family planning is to ensure the equilibrium of the individual and the family. It has been defined as an attempt by the individual to choose the number and spacing of his children, and to make his reproductive behaviour correspond with his goods, values and personal circumstances. By birth control is implied the large scale use of contraceptive methods, and perhaps, abortion. It is therefore of a much more systematic aware than family planning. Birth control programmes have been launched and were directed towards couples with a child and where the couples were in the reproductive age group. There is no other evidence of my serious attempts to launch population education programme for the younger generation. We were to start with children otherwise we shall be flooded by millions.

Need of Starting from Grassroots Level: The common people wrongly believe that population education is meant only for the adults, not for the children. The problem of population growth are grim and need to be remedial quickly at the grassroots level. The younger generation should be fully informed and exposed to the dangers of the future. Small children should be properly educated in order to lead a planned adult life. They should be well-informed about the consequences of population growth on the national, political and economic human life. The strategy of population education should start from the foundation education of school-goers. The children of today are the future citizens of the country. They must be well aware of all the hazards of life that they may have to in future.

Preparing the Future Generation: Over 50 per cent of our population is below 18 years of age. It is this group that shall strongly influence the demographic scene of the country for the next few decades. The reproductive behaviour of this section of people shall make the progress of the country. The future growth of Indian population will depend on the attitudes and behaviour pattern of the people of this group acquired during the period of their education. To quote John Edlefsen "These young people will constitute the major portion of the adult population of the world in the next three crucial decades." Therefore the need for introduction of population education in the school curriculum.

Promotion of the Quality of Life: Countries like India with a large population and a high rate of population growth have to invest a greater share of their resources in meeting the basic demands of the increasing population. Hence very little resources were left for improving the quality of life of the people. India's rapid growth in population has set to nought most of the planned development, and nullified economic and other gains. More than half of the Indian population is hungry and live in squalor, filth, disease, ignorance and sub-human conditions. It is a vicious system which allows a rich people to get richer. While the millions upon millions of poor people go on getting poorer and poorer though producing more and more children and creating more and more mouths to feed and bodies to clothe. Thus, the quality of Indian life has got down beyond expectation. Population education programme is the only means and alternative to solve the problem.

Creating Population Awareness: In the government family planning programme mainly directed to spread the message of family planning. Through these media the mass media like radio, films, public posters, banners, leaflets, etc. the messages were sent to the remotest corner of the country reaching the target groups of married adults. The mass media cannot be an exclusive way to boost the programme. As the educational system has both an opportunity and responsibility to integrate the non-school experiences in a constructive manner, it should take cognizance of the fact that the students who complete the school education should have some sort of population awareness. In creating further awareness about population issues population education has much to impart.

Understanding Population Components: Population education may help people recognise and define the nature of problem which have population components. It may help them realise better, how problems arise and what consequences of their decisions and action will have. Within a developmental contest, it may be designed to help people comprehend that social and economic development is to some event influenced by population process and that their decisions may depend upon the social and economic status of a society or nation.

Making Education Learner-centred: Population education programmes may contribute in many ways to innovation and renovation and to the general development of education. Since most population issues have economic, social and political components, population education seeks to deal with their interactions. It contributes to the recognisation of curriculum along interdisciplinary lines. It adds to selecting content relevant to the lives of learners. It contributes to the development and use of learner-centred methods of instruction.

Remedies to Population Problems: Programmes of population education may contribute to solve the population problems faced by individuals and nations. Remedies to these problems depend upon social changes leading to greater equity and social justice, greater interdependence and self-determination. This potential of population education as an instrument of change has not been exploited in most of the Third World Countries including India.

Progress of Family Planning Programme: India's family planning programme has failed to produce the desired results because we have made no effort to understand the various issues connected with the problems. Without the spread of population education among masses and substantial improvement in their standard of thing the rate of population growth cannot decline. The slow progress in our family planning programme is due to arbitrary, uninformed and unimaginative nature of the decision-making at the highest level of organisation. The importance of population education is felt for this reason.

Restriction on Early and Universal Marriage: In India, the practice of marriage is both a religious and a social ceremony which is the potent cause of the rapid increase in population of India. The population education will create awareness among the people about the marriageable age.

Removal of Ignorance and Superstitions: Indians consider a child to be a gift of God. Hindu religious books say that no man can achieve heaven and salvation unless his last rites were performed by his son. People do not want to interfere with God's wish. They have no idea of family planning. A person is supposed to be richer and luckier if he had a number of sons and grandsons. Population education may remove the superstitions and check ignorance.

Check on Widespread Poverty: At the root of the acute poverty of the Indian masses lies a high birthrate. India is a country of villages where people are poor and illiterate. They do not understand the economic value of birth control and family planning. They welcome further additions to their families to supplement their income. Population education shall check poverty by giving a boost to family planning.

To Fulfill Educational Needs: India's educational system needs improvement. Persons who have been trying since long to improve the present educational system agree that a new type of educational system should be introduced, to provide an opportunity to promote other educational changes. "Relevance of population education may be expressed either in terms of the developmental needs of the society as a whole or in terms of the personal needs of the individuals." The population education fulfils both these criteria. The knowledge of the rate of growth of population is important factor for individual and family welfare. Therefore, the programme of population education is highly relevant to the lives of the people to achieve the following objectives in education:

To Improve Teaching Methodologies : Population education is necessary to introduce better teaching methodologies. The most appropriate teaching methodologies we those which encourage learning that last for a long time. The learning process should be interactive. It should discourage lecture and memorisation and introduce problem-solving. It should stimulate activities, group discussion and other enquiry promoting methods. The use of better teaching methodologies will improve many aspects of education.

To Promote Lifelong Education : Population behaviour goes on over a long period of time. Between her teens to her late 40's a woman can give birth at any time. People may migrate from one place to another at any time of their life. To make the people understand their population situation, we should arrange different types of educational programmes aimed at different ages. Population education cannot be confined to schools only, rather it should be given at all stages of people's life. Important structural changes in the educational system are very much essential to cultivate this idea. It is important to develop curriculum and training programmes through cooperation among people from several subject areas.

To Promote Values : Population education as a powerful device for promoting changes with regards to values. In our school system, one of the implicit values is that the teachers and adult members are considered the masters of all wisdom. They give decisions and advice. However so far as "Population decisions" is concerned, things we done in a different way. While taking a decision to marry or to have a number of children one makes decisions himself. The teacher should focus his attention on the student's learning rather than his own teaching. He is not the source of all information and ideas. He should help and guide the students to learn. Information and ideas should be supplied by him. This new approach to both teaching and learning can influence the existing value system of the society.

Preparation for Citizenship and Effective Living: India will remain backward unless we gain proper population education. Population education is a means for preparing the younger generation for effective citizenship through educating them to face realities of contemporary living. Thus the need for introducing population education in schools transcends the urgency of the problem of over-population.

Mass Communication in the National Family Planning Programme: Like other developing countries, India has a national policy and programme for birth control. Through paintings, Posters, etc. the state conveys ideas about family planning and birth control to people. The government thinks that children are also educated this way. This is incidental information which is insufficient. Population education should be imputed systematically through a well-planned programme.

Population Education : Mottos

Dr. Simmons observes: "Population education holds promise not only as means of diffusing information about population problem more pervasively in a given country that can be done by the channels ordinarily available to family planning programmes, but as a means for bringing about the desired changes in attitudes, behaviours and values in the next generation (which is almost here)." Dr. Sloan R. Wayland has given the following list of possible goals of population Education for the individual's own personal behaviour-pattern and attitudes:

(a) Acceptance of the small family norm.

(b) Understanding that the size of the family can be controlled.

(c) Acceptance of marriage at a mature age as a desirable pattern.

(d) Appreciation of the advantages of planning, including health and economic plans from spacing and limitation in total number of children, and of the health, education and other opportunities for children that may be more adequately provided for in all the family.

Aims and objectives are prime necessities in every type of educational policy. Unless the objectives are specific and practical no definite programme of education can be laid down. Population education necessitates spelling out objectives for its teaching.

The members of National Seminar opined that the growth of population is a major challenge before the country. They decided that population should be an integral part of education at all levels. Kamla Rao and D. Gopal Rao felt that there is a great necessity for developing systematic objectives of population education. They suggest that such objectives can be spelt out at three different levels:

(i) Policy level objectives;

(ii) Implementation level objectives; and

(iii) Instructional objectives.

Policy level objectives emphasise the general objectives of population education stage. Following are the aims and objectives of population education :

To Develop Methodologies: The policy level objectives of population education lay emphasis on developing methodologies by influencing the young through schools and adults through other educational agencies in order to create awareness and consciousness on population growth. These objectives adopt educational strategies both inside the school and outside the school. The implementation and success of population education depends on the methodologies and strategies that it adopts population education thus aims at developing different educational policies for educating and imparting the learners. It undertakes different educational programmes, methods of teaching, curricular and co-curricular activities for the regular school-goers and those who are out of schools.

To Understand Population Education: Prof. To. Mehta (UNESCO) wanted to develop some important understandings among the young generations through population education :

To Understand Demography : The population education aims at developing understanding of demographic transitions of population growth. It enables a learner to understand the population growth in different stages, from ancient times to the modern periods. It facilitates to understand different causes in the rise and fall of the rate of population growth in different periods.

To Understanding Different Causes of Population Growth: The population education programme aims at developing understanding of the rapid growth of population and its multidimensional causes. It not only formulates educational strategies but also roots out different causes of population growth. As growth of population is the product of different factors like society, early marriage, remarriage of widows, literacy, presence of superstitions, poverty, preference for sons, universality of marriage, belief in large family, joint family system, etc., the location of different causes help the younger generation to understand how can any factor contribute to the high birth rate in a particular society.

To Understand the Impact of Population Growth : Another objective of population education is to develop an understanding of the impact of population growth on the social, political, economic and cultural life of individuals. Population education enables the young generation to understand the serious effects of population growth on vitality of our economic life. It highlights impact of population growth on, environment pollution, quality of life, quality of education, economic development, national income, labour and employment, food problems, agriculture and health problems.

To Understand Impact on Environment: An important objective of population education is to understand the evil effects of over-population. Its purpose is to know the impact of population growth on air pollution, water pollution, noise pollution, thermal pollution, radioactive pollution, food and soil pollution, etc.

To Understand Medicinal Advancement : Population education creates an understanding of scientific and medicinal advancement in the present decade. Its knowledge enables us to get an increasing control event family diseases, and deaths and the imbalance thus created between death rate and birth rate. Different programmes of population education make the learners aware of the contribution of medical sciences and technological development towards the human lives.

To Understand the System of Reproduction : The population education creates an understanding of the mechanism and physiology of reproduction, responsible for the continuation of the species. It is highly marooned with the biological factors relating to the reproduction of the human child.

Population Aspects

Population Growth and Quality of Life : The population education enables the learners to have an appreciation of the relationship between population size and quality of life. Unchecked population growth creates economic problems and political tensions. In view of the ever-increasing population whatever economic progress is made goes in vain. If it is not checked, our five-year plans will remain a mid-summer night's dream.

Population Dynamics : It is one of the factors in the whole process of the improvement of quality of life. A variety of factors affect the achievement of the desired quality of life. These include population dynamics, socio-political system, process of development, availability of resources and the existing levels of living of the people. Population dynamics is one of the factors of quality of life which affects other factors and is in turn affected by them.

Population Explosion : The programmes of population education makes the learners conscious of how population explosion affects the standards of life and leads to a number of evil consequences. It tries to makes the people poor. It creates undue pressure on land. It creates serious food problems. It results in unemployment. It leads to crime and corruptions.

Impact of Small Size Family: Population education programme creates an appreciation of the relationship between small size family and its good effect on the preservation of the health of the mother and the welfare of the children. Population education should be made an integral part of general education. It should impart education relating to family life. Its objective should be to enable the students to understand that family size is controllable and population limitation can facilitate the development of a higher quality of life.

Family Planning Programme : Within the last three decades vast changes have occurred in many aspects of life in every country of the world. Population policies are therefore, rapidly becoming an accepted part of developing programme. In 1932, the All India Women Conference, Lucknow, passed a resolution that men and women should be instructed in the methods of birth control in recognised clinics. It would create an appreciation of the fact that for preserving the health of the mother, the welfare of the children, the economic stability of the family and the future prospects of younger generation, Indian families, should be small and compact with not more than one or two children.

Government Policies : Through population education the learners will definitely appreciate and understand the government family planning programme in relation to the country's need. Its whole objectives are—

(i) To reduce the population growth rate not necessarily to zero.

(ii) To stabilise the size of population by achieving a zero population growth rate.

(iii) To achieve a negative growth rate with a view to reducing the size of population.

Trends in Population

Population Trends : The population education seeks to study the influence of population trends on various aspects of life. It will faciliate the study of close interaction of population growth and development process with particular reference to the national programme to raise the standard of living.

Impact of Population Education on Society : The aim or objective of population education is to assess or study the broader implication of its introduction on parents, teachers, school pupils and society.

Population Education : Practical Aspect

To Involve Formal Educational System : According to Kamla Rao and D. Gopal Rao population education should aim at involving the formal educational systems-its curricular activities, teacher training programme, etc., in imparting a systematic content on population education at the different stages of school and college education.

To Involve Teachers and Society : A teacher is the model and the ideal in population education programme which invites teachers and social workers to get involved actively and understand the gravity of the situation.

Demographic Phenomenon : Retaliation

Population education must enable individuals to recognise the causes of the demographic phenomenon, social, economic, political, biological, ethical or religious and to enable the people to make changes in order to remove these obstacles for social progress.

Views of Dr. Edlefsen. While explaining population edμcation in terms of objectives Dr. Edlefsen cites the following 10 specific objectives :

1. To understand the basic principles of demography.
2. To learn about the causative factors of rapid population growth.
3. To understand the impact of rapid population growth.
4. To understand the close relationship between the pupil well-being and socio-economic development.
5. To understand the meaning and significance of environmental harmony.
6. To learn that family size can be controlled as opposed to fatalism.
7. To understand the significance of small family norm and its relation to the quality of living.
8. To understand the far-reaching consequences of population density and rapid growth to one's self and one's environment.
9. To realise that human behaviour has a direct influence on the social structure and on social change.
10. To change attitudes and instill a sense of responsibility towards the welfare of the nation and the world.

The above objectives of population education were not mutually elusive. The interaction among the various facts of population dynamics is such that it is not possible to identify them with a defined border. The objectives listed above outline an operation framework of population education.

Sphere, Scope and Area

Family Life Education : Growth is a normal, physical, emotional and social process. Somewhere between the ages of ten and nineteen the youngers reach a stage in their lives when they begin to leave childhood behind. Their bodies grow and change. They begin to look and feel different. They were given the rights and responsibilities. They are expected to behave in a more matured way. They become more aware of themselves. They also learn how to get on with others and to cope with the situations that a part of everyday life.

As growing up is not always easy, almost every society has found ways of helping young people through this period of change and development. The process of education assists young people in their emotional, physical and social development as they learn to be adults and prepare themselves for important changes in their lives such as marriage, parenthood and work. It helps them to develop the knowledge and skills they need to cope with the challenges of adult life, with personal relationships and belonging to a family and a community.

Family life education must be based on the needs of those to whom it is to be imputed. It is vital to know the educational needs of young people in their preparation for an adult life that will be as satisfying as possible for themselves and for others with whom they come in contact. Young people's education for family is traditionally provided informally by members of the family or religious and community elders. From them, young people learn the customs and beliefs of their community, the approved patterns of behaviour and the practical knowledge required for everyday living. They also learn through watching and listening to other people, by experimenting, making choice and taking risks. The family life education is largely based on the experience of several generations. It includes : the family as a basic social unit, functions of the family, role of the family, factors strengthening or weakening family life and the best though not the least the reproductive process.

Population Policy: UNESCO defines population policies as "measures and programmes designed to contribute to the achievement of economic, social, demographic, political and other collective goals through affecting critical demographic variables, namely, the size and growth of population, its geographical distribution (national or international), and its demographic characteristics." Consisting of both the formulation of and articulation by the government of some population objectives or a set of objectives that maximise the public welfare and levels of living 'Population Policy involves the commitment and manipulation of resources in pursuit of these population objectives.

Thus, a population policy is not purely an instrument of fertility regulation. It implies affecting population size by net migration, or by changing certain demographic characteristics such as marital status, educational attainment, work participation etc.

In India, during the First Five-Year Plan (1951-56) a population policy committee was set up in April 1952. Subsequently, a Family Planning Cell was created in the Directorate General of Health Services. The family planning programme means to plan the size of the family. It implies limiting the number of births in each family as well as proper spacing between the birth of the first child and the second child. For planned parenthood one should beget a child by choice and not by chance. This may be achieved through various birth control measures, such as moral restraints, contraception-such as medicines, chemicals, loops and other devices, sterilisation of males and females, medical termination of pregnancy of the married men, etc.

Children should be aware of the nation's policy and programme on population. The population policies and programmes have not been very effective in the less developed countries like India, Nepal, Indonesia, Pakistan, etc. In developed countries like America, Russia, England, etc. go through population policies and programmes. Indian students should be aware of different programmes and policies of our country. They should go through steps taken by five-year plans. India National Population Policy should comprise of marriage age of male and female, promoting two-child family norm introducing a variety of contraceptives providing population programme for all children in the 11-15 year age group providing population education to those who are out of educational institutional through adult education and non-formal education.

Population education will create an appreciation and understanding of different family planning programmes of the government.

Physiology of Human Reproduction: Physiology of reproduction has great significance for mankind. The continued process of human reproduction has institutional itself under the most significant social institutional, the family. Males and females are given the social sanction through marriage to live together, establish a sexual relationship and procreate in a family as a unit of the larger society. There may be instances of couples living together, having sexual relationship and procreating without entering into wedlock, particularly in the Western countries.

However, such cases tend to generate complex social implications. The human reproduction has critical sociological and psychological ramifications. Influenced by socio-cultural and behavioural factors it has significant socio-economic and men political implications. Male and females have different reproductive organs. The knowledge of male and female reproductive system is essential.

Population education aims at providing insights into (i) the physiology of man reproduction, (ii) fertility regulation, and (iii) sexually transmitted diseases, including AIDS. The overall objective of education of these three aspects is to assist teachers in preparing adolescents with adequate knowledge and values about their own bodies for dignified and responsible interaction with the opposite sex, for a healthy and better married life and for responsible parenthood.

Population Explosion and Status of Environment: Explosive population growth upsets the natural balance between the human population and its environment. The rapid growth of human beings greatly reduces certain animal and plant population. Man kills animals and cuts down forests. He fills up swamps and reclaims seashores that form this home. He pollutes the lakes and streams. He poisons them with chemicals. He hunts and traps many living beings to destruction.

Consequent upon unimaginative interference of human beings with nature mounting problem of pollution have been adversely affecting the quality of life. Pollutants are reserved at the wrong place. As such they represent a continuous drain on resources. They have disruptive or degrading impact on air, soil and water

Environmental Education: It includes deforestation, soil erosion, flooding, excessive ground water exploitation, threat to wildlife, excessive use of chemicals and pesticides unimaginative mining water pollution, ocean pollution, air pollution, acid rain, greenhouse effect and ozone depletion.

Environmental education is an educational programme to create the consciousness and awareness of a good environment, the causes and the consciousness of environmental pollution. It concludes a suggestive measure that a step should be undertaken to include environmental education as an integral part of the general education.

Population Dynamics: It refers to the statistical explanation and description of the historical development of population sceneries. Through population dynamics the students are able to understand the statistics of population growth in the past, the present and the anticipated future.

Sex Education: In India both teachers and parents are hesitant and reluctant to provide adolescents with sex education. This attitude deprives adolescents from acquiring a proper understanding of sexuality of their responsibilities as growing individuals, and of ways to know and communicate with opposite sex. Adolescent boys and girls lack the requisite knowledge about their own physique, sex organs and their functions. The adolescents develop emotional and other psychological problem during pubic period, when physical, physiological and psychological changes occur in them. Changes occur not only in their body and particularly in their sex organs, but also in their feelings towards the opposite sex. A proper guidance and counselling in sex education may equip them with coping skills, and help them to best adjust in life and live successfully in society.

Different Views

As view of the Asian Regional Workshop (1970), following are the important components of population education ;

Causes of Population Growth: The causes of population growth are important factors. These should be known by the students in order to make them understand the different aspects of the population problem. In many societies the social norm tends to favour development of large families. Similarly, determinants of fertility, mortality and migration behaviour should be clearly comprehended. Because the knowledge of population is to be imparted and attitudes to be developed in students so that they may base their own more rational population behaviour on them. The Regional Workshop considered the inclusion of the determinants of population growth as an important component of population education content.

The factors of population growth have their room in tradition or culture of place, in their religious beliefs and even in economic conditions of the people. Thus the knowledge of determinants of population growth must be an essential part of population education programme.

Consequences of Population Growth: In its final report the Asian Regional Workshop (1970) stated : It was discovered that the most pervasive elements of existing definitions or objectives were the consequences of rapid population growth."

Population growth directly affects both the individual and the nation. The consequences of the population growth can be studied at macro and micro levels.

Micro Level : This includes factors such as food, health, employment opportunities, homing, education and recreation may be emphasised.

Macro Level : This includes the effects of rapid population growth on economic and social development may become vital components of population education.

Demography : Demography is a link between the causes and consequences of population growth. Demographic scenarios comprise the tools such as mass reports, birth and death rates, population density, marriageable age, etc. In order to understand the current situation with references to the past the students must be acquainted with this basic demographic tool. They could also have some idea of the future. Demographic aspect will help the students to analyse local, national and worldwide trends of population growth. The students can understand the meaning of population explosion in true perspective.

Sex Education : According to the Asian Regional Workshop on Population and Family Education, sex education consists of :

- Human physiology and reproduction;
- Contraception, and
- Social interactions associated with human sexuality.

According to this Workshop the goals of population education programme and sex education differ substantially.

Human reproduction has been a part of biology courses for many years, much before the advent of sex education. Therefore "Human physiology and reproduction" can be safely included in the school curriculum as a non-controversial subject. It will facilitate children to learn the phenomenon of reproduction in a more scientific way than to learn it accidentally through exposure to outside influences. A respective place should be given in population education to knowledge about human physiology and reproduction. But it should be taken in the way it is handled by teachers in the classrooms. Human reproductive systems can be imparted to children unhesitatingly.

Prof. Jayasurya has stated broad areas of population education as follows:

Collection and Analysis of Population Data : Under this area, are included methods of collecting population data on :

- The demographic processes of birth, death and migration.
- Calculation of birth, death and growth rates.
- The age structure of a population.
- The muses underlying different kinds of age structure.
- Determinants of fertility, morbidity, and mortality trends in population growth; refined indices of fertility and mortality.

Population Growth and Human Development : Considered at the macro level of the nation this topic should include the relationship between population growth and natural resources agriculture, food, homing, employment, economic development, educational development and the development of health services should be included.

Problem of Urbanisation : This component should include the problem associated with housing, transportation, supply of water and other utilities, air and water pollution, urban unemployment, etc.

Family Life Education : This includes : the family as a basic social unit; functions of the family-, family roles; factors strengthening or weakening family life; psychological aspects of human sexuality, the reproductive process.

Population Planning : Strategies of planning and their implementation at regional and national levels through individual, social and governmental action are the topics to be discussed under population planning.

Smt. Avabai Wadia has suggested the following components of population education :

1. Demographic trends their determinants and consequences.
2. Trends, facts and figures of social and economic development.
3. Population growth and ecological factors.
4. Social and family organisations.
5. Subjects relating to reproduction in plants, animals and humans.
6. Family life and interpersonal relationships.
7. Basic values and quality of life, human progress.

Indian Scene

Experts believe that population education should not be made a separate school subject, but should be judiciously interwoven with all subjects. It should not smack of propaganda. No separate period need be alloted. There is no need for appointing special teachers. Necessary information should be given in a natural way. An intelligent resourceful teacher can integrate relevant population problem while teaching his own subject. Following are a few topics which automatically crop up whenever one discusses problem of national welfare in the classroom

1. Population growth-census figures.
2. Economic development and population.
3. Social development and population.
4. Impact of population growth on environment.
5. Nutritional standards and population.
6. Education, social justice and population growth.

Objectives of Instruction

1. To develop an understanding of some demographic concepts and process.
2. To develop among younger generation an understanding of the most important phenomenon of the modern world viz. rapid growth of population and its causes.
3. To develop an understanding of the influence of population trends on the various aspects of human life, political, social cultural and economic.
4. To develop an understanding of the close interaction of population growth and development process with particular reference to developmental programmes for raising the standard of living of the people.
5. To develop an understanding of the evil effects of overpopulation on the environment and the concomitant dangers from population.
6. To develop an understanding of scientific and medical advancement enabling them to get an increasing control over famines, diseases and untimely death and the imbalance thus created between death-rate and birth-rate.
7. To develop an understanding of biological factors and phenomenon of reproduction which are responsible for the continuation of the species.
8. To develop an appreciation of—
   (i) the small family norm as proper and desirable;
   (ii) the relation between population size and the quality of life;
   (iii) the fact that family is a matter of deliberate choice and human regulation rather than of accident or forms beyond human control.
9. To develop an appreciation of the relationship between the preservation of the health of the children and the small size of the family.
10. To develop appreciation of the fact that the actions of each individual member of the society affects others as

well and personal and national decisions concerning family size and population have a long range of consequences for the whole world.

Teaching Points at Secondary Level

Lower Secondary Level

Understanding	Content
1. Food, shelter and clothing are basic necessities of life.	Per capita requirements of basic necessities -malnutrition and chronic illness.
2. Availability of the basic necessities varies from place to place.	Rapid population - lack of availability of basic necessities - high prices.
3. Standard of living differs from country to country depending upon the stage of economic development.	Nutritional requirements of several groups - per capita availability of essential commodities in a few select countries.
4. Relation between production and population.	(i) Both are subject to human control. (ii) Depletion of natural resources.

Higher Secondary Level

1. Increase in production is nullified by rapid increase in population.	Rate of growth of population and production - Gross National Product Contribution of Agriculture and Industry to national income.
2. Rapid growth of population adversely affect the economic life of country.	Natural resources allocation exploitation of nature by man. Unemployment.
3. Standard of living - relationship between production and population.	Standard of living is relative - minimum need programme.
4. Low Standard of living results in lower production.	Vicious circle - low production, low standard of living decrease in production.
5. Effective ways to check population explosion.	Agencies involved in arresting population.

Enrichment Activities in Population Education

Following activities may be emphasised in the subjects taught to bring home the messages of Population Education after modifying them to suit the school needs :

1. Language	(i) Precis-writing-condensing a passage -which describes the population situation in India. (ii) Comprehension—Let the students silently read an article or an instructional material prepared by you and answer a few questions to test their understanding. (iii) Essay-writing—An essay on a relevant social or economic problem and its links with the country's population growth.
2. Mathematics	(i) Growth of population in the school, town or village - comparison of census figures. (ii) Family budgets in relation to size and income of the family. (iii) Comparing national income with those of other countries.
3. General Science	Man and his- physical environment- sanitation and health conservation of natural resources - pollution - protecting the environment. These topics may be explained through suitable illustrations. Discussions may be held on the above themes to develop the skill in scientific analysis.
4. History	(i) Citizenship training. (ii) Overpopulation-migration wars. This relationship may be illustrated from history. (iii) Preparing a chart to show the growth of population of the world from the dawn of history.
5. Geography	(i) Studying the density of population in different countries. (ii) Using suitable shades to make the population density in all the States of India. (iii) Comparison of natural and human resources in select countries. (iv) Scarcity and famine conditions where they exist? Why?
6. Arts	(i) Songs and dances to depict the effects of unchecked population growth.

(ii) Simple diagrams—to illustrate population growth, availability of accept-commodities and the need to accept the small family norm voluntarily.

Material for Instruction

1. Printed Text and Reference Materials—Illustrated work-books supplementary books, comic etc.
2. Inexpensive Supplementary Materials.
3. Projected Material-Films filmstrips, transparencies, TV. presentations etc.
4. 3-D Materials-Dolls, models etc.
5. Displays-Flannel boards, display boards, cutouts etc. Some of the above mentioned aids are available with the Health and Family Welfare Department. Press clipings and pictures can be effectively used in all schools.

Teacher's Responsibility

Teachers not only serve the cause of education, but also lend a helping hand to all nation-building activities. Many teachers are real 'opinion-leaders' in their villages and command much respect. In their informal chat with the people in the community, they can stress the concept of the 'small family norm'.

In the words of Dr. Chandrasekhar, "The teachers are the backbone of this educational movement and the success of this innovation will depend largely on the ability of these pioneers to put across the concept of all family norm to the young intelligently and effectively. This means that the teachers themselves must learn a great deal about the dynamics of population problem and what is equally important, most master techniques of imparting such information in an attractive and compelling manner."

QUESTIONS

1. Define Population Education and discuss its goals.
2. Distinguish Population Education from similar concept.

3. Discuss the aims and objectives of Population Education.
4. Describe the importance of Population Education.
5. Explain the scope of Population Education.
6. Write an essay on Population Education in India.

5

Various Theories

A theory of population is an explanation of the phenomenon of population growth. It tries to explain the rise and fall, the growth and decrease of population in different countries. It surveys the trends and analyses the muses of the various stages in the curve of population. Based upon data in one or more particular countries, a population theory seeks to generalise about the laws of population. It tries to unravel the first principles of demographical process. Though systematic theories of population have evolved very recently, theorising about population is sufficiently old. In ancient times statesmen and thinkers tried to control population according to the availability of means or to encourage it if required. The criteria for encouraging or discouraging were the military, political, social and economic issues. This is true about population theory even now. The problem of population is not worked out in vacuum. It is always considered in the context of economic, social and political issues. Of these the economic issue is the most important, since the most important problem concerning population is to meet the needs of the growing population. The history of population theories has been classified on the basis of before or after the advent of Malthus, the celebrated demographer. Thus, the periods are classified as Pre-Malthusian, Malthusian and Post-Malthusian periods. These periods show thinking about population theories. But even before these some early thinking can be discerned about population problems.

Early Scholars

Most of the thinking in the West started with the Greek thinkers, in the Greek scheme of life, the individual was a part of the state. The purpose of marriage was procreation. Wins required a continuous demand of soldiers. Therefore, procreation was encouraged and even rewarded by Greeks and the Romans. The Spartans and the Athenians encouraged population due to expansionist policy. They also tried to avoid overpopulation and encouraged abortions and even infanticides.

The idealist Greek thinkers tried to estimate optimum population. According to Plato (427-347 BC) a city state should have 5040 citizens so that highest good may be achieved. In his ideal population Plato did not include women, children and slaves. Including them the total population of an ideal city state in Plato's time was about 50,000. Plato also did not overlook the possibility that the demographic ideals may not be followed. Therefore, he recommended infanticide on the grounds of Eugenics in order to control population and maintain its highest quality. Plato recommended selective breeding among human beings. He recommended that the age of marriage for the girls should be between 16 and 20. Marriage was made compulsory. The peculiar number of 5040, according to Jowett, is based upon numerology. According to Hutchinson, "it was simply to aid in maintaining an even division of property."' Plato's ideal on population, as expressed in his Laws, were based on the ideal of city state.

After Plato, Aristotle (348-322 BC) maintained that fast population growth leads to increase in poverty and suggested abortions and infanticides, in order to control the size of the city state. He also proposed family planning to be prescribed by the state. Thus the Greek thinkers insisted both on proper quantity and quality of population.

Besides Greeks, the Romans also thought over population issues. They encouraged procreation and the marriage compulsory. Those who did not marry were burdened by several disabilities.

Teachings of Great Religions

Most of the ancient thinkers were influenced by their religious. Religion had a hold on thinking in ancient time. Therefore, in order to understand the early thinking on population issues it is necessary to cast of glance on the prescriptions of great religions on population issues. This is particularly true about early Indian thinking. Hindu thinking on population issues was guided by the Dharmasastras.

Hinduism. Hindus have prescribed marriage at almost compulsory. According to the Dharmasastras, no one can go to heaven without procreating a son. In order to conduct religious activities every man needed a wife by his side. The household Ashram was considered the basis of the entire social structure. Thus, most of the males and females centred Grahstha Ashram after completing Brahmacharya Ashram. The Hindu marriage aimed at the three fold ideal : fulfilment of Dharma, procreation and sex enjoyment. Of these, procreation was considered most important. The birth of a son was the ideal but sometimes one finds prayers for the birth of a daughter since Kanyadan was also a source of religious gains. Fertility was praised and encouraged so much so that the newly married couples were blessed for having eight sons and five daughters. From the political and economic viewpoint, the Arthasastra of Kautilya has recommended large population for military and economic gains. Thus, the Hindu Shastras have everywhere encouraged growth of population. Therefore, there is hardly any wonder that in India population multiplied fast.

Judaism. One finds an oft quoted injunction to Adam and Eve in the sacred books of Jews, "Be fruitful and multiply and replenish the earth." Thus Judaism deplores childlessness and admires fertility. It is true about the Jews even now considering the large number of their followers as compared to the number of followers of the great religions.

Christianity. In the world today, Christianity commands maximum number of followers. This is not only due to the greatness of Christianity but also their encouragement of fertility like any other great religion. From the moral viewpoint the Christian saints eulogised celibacy like the Hindu thinkers and marriage was sometimes regarded as a necessary evil. However, as a general rule marriage was blessed by the priests.

Islam. The most populationistic great religion is the Islam. It is both because it prescribes polygamy and also encourages procreation. According to the Fatwa of Sheikh Abdullah Al-qualquili, "Marry the affectionate prolific woman, for I shall be proud of you among the nation."' The ideal of marriage was procreation. It is interesting to note that Ibn Kuldoun (1332-1460 B.C.) was of the opinion that a densely settled population helped to achieve more division of labour, more utilisation of resources and ensued military and political security. He, however, also pointed out that the vicious circle of population growth leads to luxurious living which in turn causes economic depression and ultimately depopulation. The Muslim tradition recommends marriage with four women at one time, and the fifth could always be married by divorcing one of the four at short notice. Therefore, the economically well of section procreated at a high rate. The Muslim population has grown fast in almost every country, including India due to Islams encouragement to population growth.

Pre-Malthusian Theories

This period is calculated from the beginning of l6th century to the end of 18th century. It was a period of rapid thinking in all aspects of human life. Thinking on economy and population was particularly influenced by exploration of routes from West to East, discovery of America, rise of Capitalism, collapse of feudal system and the emergence of Imperial powers like British, French, Portuguese and Spanish. The following landmarks can be traced in pre-Malthusian period :

The Mercantilist School. This has been considered as a link between medieval and modern economic thought. It aimed at increasing national wealth and power resulting in rivalry and competition. Therefore the size of the population was considered an asset from the point of view of war, supply of labour and utilisation of national resources. Hence, as Eli Heckscher has pointed out, "An almost frantic desire to increase population prevailed in all countries."The general opinion during this period favoured increased birth rates. The increase of birth rates was to be gained by procreation on the one hand and, on the other hand by the adoption of such measures at; (a) placing various disabilities on celibates; (b) encouraging marriages directly, (c) encouraging fertility, (d) making punishment for illegitimate births less severe or abolishing such punishment entirely, and (e) encouraging immigration and preventing emigration." The most important mercantile writers included Niccolo Machiavelli (1469-1527) and Giovanni Botero (1540-1617). Of these Machiavelli has been hailed as one of the precursors of Malthus. Botero was one of the first to study population scientifically. He was convinced that food for subsistence was necessity for any population. He, however, regarded large population a source of strength.

The Physiocratic School. As a reaction against the mercantilist ideas and policies, the physiocratic school of economic thought evolved in France about the middle of the 18th century. This school considered land as the source of all wealth. They did not favour population increase at the cost of standard of living. They approved only such increase which may be useful to expand agricultural production. This school was founded by Quesney (1694-1774). He maintained that a large population may be desirable only if it could be comfortably maintained. Another French economic thinker Mirabeau (1715-1789) maintained that agriculture must be encouraged to feed large population desirable for the state. Similar views were expressed by Merier de Is Riviere and Cantillon.

The Beginning of the Malthusian Theory. During this period it was more and more realised that population increases more rapidly than food supply. Therefore, the earlier optimism was gradually replaced by a pessimistic view resulting in the benevolent faith in means to control population. Among the most important writers during this period were Mathew Hale (1677), Robert Wallace (1687-1771), John Bruckner (1726-1804), James Steurt (17124780), and Joseph Townsend (1739-1816).

Malthusian Theory

Historical Review. To meet important theory in the history of demography was presented by Thomas Robert Malthus (1766-1834). Among his most important works was his famous Essay on Population entitled : An Essay on the Principle of Population as its Affects the Future Improvement of Society; With Remarks an the Speculations of Mr. Godwin, M Condorcet And Others. This essay was published anonymously. It, however, became one of the most controversial books of modern times, and brought both honour and criticism to the author. Its importance as a landmark in the history of population cant be judged by the fact that the year of its publication is reckoned as the base year for the study of population doctrines.

As is clear by the title of the Essay, it was mainly directed against the optimistic views of William Godwin, an English philosopher and Marie learn Aromatic Condorcet, a French mathematician, economist and philosopher. Therefore, it is necessary to understand the view of these two persons before understanding Malthusian theory. According to Condorcet, 'All inequalities of wealth, of education, of opportunity of sex, would soon disappear. Animosities between nations and laws would be no more. All persons would speak the same language. The earth would be bountiful, without stint. All diseases would be conquered, "if they not become immortal, the span of his life would have no assignable upper limit. The question whether production would always suffice to satisfy the people's wants could not be answered, for the problem would not have to be faced for ages to come by which time man would have acquired new types of now still unimagined knowledge. In the rational age to come, men would recognise their obligations to those not yet born and to the general well-being both of their society and of all humanity and ... not to the puerile idea of filling the earth with useless and unhappy beings. At the time, a limit could be set to the population other than by premature death of a portion of those born.

William Godwin published his book 'Enquiry Concerning Political Justice', in 1793, which presented a Utopian ideal of perfect society. In this society, according to him, "There will be no war, no crimes, no administration of justice as it is called, and no government." Besides this, there will be neither disease, anguish, melancholy nor resentment. Every man will see with ineffable ardour the good of all.

This Utopian thesis was challenged by Malthus. He pointed out that the tendency of the population to grow faster than the means of subsistence gradually leads to human misery and creates impediments in the path of progress. He laid more emphasis on criticism of the Poor Laws in the 2nd edition of his Essay published in 1803. This edition contained substantial statistical data in support of arguments. It proposed moral constraints as a preventive against rapid growth of population. Next five years in the life of Malthus were devoted to collection of further statistical data and study of the writings of other authors. In 1826 was published the 6th edition of the work of Malthus now entitled : An Essay on the Principle of Population or a views of its Past and Present Effects on Human Happiness, Kith an Inquiry into our Prospects Respecting the Future Removal or Mitigation of the Evils which it occasions. In 1872 was published the 7th edition of the essay.

Central Theme. Malthus started his essay by laying down two postulates : "First, that food is necessary to the existence of man ... " Secondly, the passion between the sexes is necessary and will remain nearly in its present state." He argued, "Assuming then my postulate as granted, say that the power of population is definitely greater than the power in the earth to produce subsistence for men. Population, when unchecked increases in a geometrical ratio. Subsistence increases only in an arithmetical ratio. A slight acquaintance with numbers will show the immensity of the rust power in comparison with the second. The following propositions were put forth by Malthus, to establish his theory. "(1) Population is necessarily limited by the means of subsistence; (2) Population invariably increases where the mews of subsistence increase unless prevented by some very powerful and obvious checks; (3) These checks, and the checks which repress the superior power of population and its effects on a level with the means of subsistence, are all resolvable into moral restraint, vice and misery." Therefore, Malthus concluded, "Taking the whole earth - the human species would increase as the numbers 1, 2, 4, 8, 16, 32, 64, 128, 2,56 and the subsistence as numbers 1,2,3,4,9,5,1,6, 7,9 8, 9. In two centuries, the population would be to the means of subsistence as 256 to 8 ... "2 Malthus recognised that the growth of population does not go unchecked. Pointing out powerful checks on the growth of population, he said, "The first of these checks may, with propriety, be called the preventive check to population, and the absolute necessity of their operation in the case supposed is as certain and obvious as that man cannot live without food." Now in order to check the preventive checks such as epidemics, wars and famines, Malthus suggested moral restraints as the best preventive check. He describe it as, 'Abstinence from marriage, either for a time or permanently, from prudential consideration, with a strictly moral conduct towards the sex in the interval. And ' this is the only mode of keeping population on a level with the news of subsistence which is perfectly consistent with virtue and happiness. Vice was described as, "a sort of intercourse which renders some of the women of large towns unprolific," such as prostitution and extra-marital sexual relations. The preventive checks were necessary in order to avoid positive checks which (ended to shorten human life. These positive checks have been described by Malthus: "Such as unwholesome occupation- severe labour and exposure to the seasons-bad and insufficient food and clothing arising from poverty-bad nursing of children-excesses of all kinds-great towns and manufactories-the whole train of common diseases and epidemics-wars, infanticide, plague, famine." Malthus was against poor laws since he considered poverty as an evil. He classified positive checks also into two categories : "The first were those brought about by natural carises and labelled as 'Exclusively misery,' such as epidemics, famines etc., the other positive checks were those which mankind brought upon itself by itself such as wars and all types of excesses which could have been avoided."'

Evaluation of the Theory. Malthusian Theory, as we have already pointed out, has been acclaimed as an Epoch-making theory. It was a landmark in the history of population which divided the history into two periods : before it and after it. Though wine of the ideas were known earlier, Malthus presented them in a larger framework. He examined the interrelationship between population growth and economic and political developments. His style of writing was polished and authoritative with a philosophical touch. He never claimed originality but only more systematisation. According to Kenneth Smith, the success of Malthus may be attributed to the opportune circumstances and the political climate prevailing in his time? Disillusioned by the French revolution, the intellectuals of his time supported his theory. His economic message was welcomed. The optimism of his predecessors paled before his realistic pessimism. According to Kenneth Smith, "Malthus- offered a scientific pessimism which, gloomy and fatalistic though it was towards the hopes of the working classes, absolved the ruling classes from the need to make futile efforts on their behalf." His plea for the Abolition of poor laws naturally appealed to many persons. His doctrines were convenient to the rulers who were always afraid of the growing poverty.

Criticism. However, the theory of Malthus was subjected to harsh criticism as well. Kautsky, one of his bitterest critics, accused him of plagiarism and said, "It was as correct to name the new population theory after Malthus as to name America after Amerigo Vespucci. Both did no more than to spread the news of what others had discovered." It is undeniable that many of the ideas put forward by Malthus were already anticipated by Machiavelli, Sir Walter Raleigh, Francis Bacon, John Graunt, William Petty, Sir Mathew Hale, Benjamin Franklin, Store, Joseph Townsend, Sussmilch, Sir James Stuart, Hume, Robert Wallace, Arthur Young Archdeacon, Paley and others. Some writers even used abusive language and more bitter criticisms. While criticising Malthus very harshly, Karl Marx referred to him as one who, "have taken the monastic now of celibacy"'. It may be noted in this connection that Malthus was married and had three children. The criticism such as this were obviously based upon misconceptions and ignorance. However, the weakest point in the theory of Malthus was the ratio between the arithmetical and the geometrical progressions. According to Kenneth Smith this ratio was never really proved. It was pointed out that the theory that the population would double in a period of 25 years was based upon the evidence of doubtful American statistics in which the role of lemmigration in the North American population was completely rejected.' According to E. F Hutchinson the idea of arithmetical ratio concerning the growth of the means of subsistence was unanimously rejected by scholars. As a general rule the following points were raised as criticism against Malthusian theory :

1. As has been already pointed out, the ratio of arithmetical progression of means of subsistence and the geometrical progression of population growth was never proved.

2. In so many cases the theory of the growth of the means of subsistence in arithmetical ratio was not proved.
3. Malthus did not clearly distinguish between fecundity and fertility or the physiological capacity to reproduce and the actual reproductive performance.
4. The classification of checks on population growth as preventive and positive were cited as an example of poor classification, since they were not independent categories.
5. Malthus did not succeed in connecting positive and preventive checks with his theory.
6. Malthus placed undue emphasis on the limitation of the supply of land. Agricultural production tremendously increased through agricultural revolution in the 19th century.
7. Malthus painted a too gloomy picture of the future growth of population. According to Ralph Tholardinson, his predictions did not come out to be true due to agricultural revolution.
8. Malthus underestimated the importance of industrial development in increasing means of subsistence.
9. The religious belief of Malthus, according to Ralph Thomlinson prevented him from understanding the possibility of the widespread use of contraceptives.
10. According to Eversley, Malthus did not utilise the 1831 census data of England.' According to him, Malthus did not make any significant contribution to social thought.
11. One finds a contradiction in the twin role of Malthus as a scientist and as a moralist. His role as a scientist was vitiated by his attempts opposing birth control.
12. He invented postponement of marriage and even total abstinence.

In spite of the above mentioned criticisms, Kingsley Davis has rightly maintained that though not empirically valid Malthusian theory was theoretically significant. His time occupies an important place in the history of population thought.' He was the first thinker who systematically and thoroughly applied inductive method to social science. Though by 1900 his main thesis was almost completely rejected, it was revived in the second decade of the 20th century. The wave subsided by 1934 but again revived after the second World War. In evaluating the status of Malthusian theory in the history of demography, it will be best to conclude with Charles Emil Stangeland, who remarked: "Malthus's work was a great one written in an opportune time, and though it cannot lay claim to any considerable originality as far as the theories presented are concerned, it was successful in that it showed more fully, perhaps more clearly, and certainly more effectively than had any previous attempt, that population depends on subsistence and its increase is checked by want, vice and disease as well as by more restraint or prudence."

Neo-Malthusianism

Neo-Malthusians are the successors of Malthus. They were keen supporters of family planning movement. According to them Malthus was the fast thinker who established that controlled increase of population will lead to poverty and therefore birth control must be popularised. Among the most important neo-Malthusian thinkers may be mentioned Mary Stopes of Great Britain and Margaret Sanger of U. S. A., besides so many supporters in Western Europe. These people popularised chemical and mechanical methods of birth control. The family planning movement gradually extended not only to the entire Western World but also to the countries of Asian and African continents.

According to Neo-Malthusianism, Malthus did not distinguish between sex desire and desire for children. Both these we fulfilled by the same physical organs. The sex desire also involves desire for reproduction. Neo-Malthusians however, do not accept this view. They reject the Malthusian theory that sex desire is identical with the desire for children. According to them sex desire is a natural and biological desire. It is the most powerful physical and psychological desire among the adults. Its repression leads to so many mental and physical evils. Desire for children, on the other hand, particularly depends upon social, moral and cultural values. It is not inherent but a product of socio-economic conditions. Fulfilment of sex desire is must for normal and healthy life. The desire for children however, should be adjusted according to favourable or unfavourable circumstances. Only that woman should reproduce who is physically and mentally fit for the purpose. Males and females should be allowed to satisfy their sex desire without procreation. There is no moral evil in using chemical or mechanical means of birth control to satisfy sex desire.

Neo-Malthusians acclaimed Malthus as their leader in family planning movement. However, the French economists did not agree with this idea. They pointed out that Malthus would have called modern means of birth control, "Unmitigated conjugal fraud". He would have declared them as anti-Christian and un-Godly. In his essay on Population Malthus has pointed out that artificial mews of birth control are much inferior as compared to natural restrictions such as self- control. The Neo-Malthusians, on the other hand, maintain that in the second edition of his essay, Malthus concluded that population cannot be controlled by moral restraint alone. Moral restraint is a mews which cannot be expected to be practised by ordinary people. Therefore, in spite of himself Malthus was prepared to allow artificial means of birth control. The Neo-Malthusians have advanced the following arguments in favour of their artificial birth control movement.

1. Birth control is necessary to limit the family sin in the contest of available economic means, otherwise the standard of living will fall down considerably. Without limiting the family, it is impossible to bring up children properly and pay attention to their physical, mental and moral development.
2. Birth control is equally necesssary to limit the burden on world economy. This has already reached its saturation point. Therefore it has no more capacity to feed the additional growing number of world population.
3. Birth control is necessary on the ground of health and medical as well.
4. Those who oppose the Neo-Malthusian approach maintained that birth control is unnatural. It is an undesirable interference in the working of the natural process. The sexual intercourse aims at child birth. Restriction upon child birth will therefore restrict the

very aim of marriage. In answer to this objection Neo-Malthusians point out that if birth control is unnatural, the same can be said about wearing clothes since man is born nude and that is his natural condition. Then, why do we wear clothes ? On the same grounds artificial birth control may be supported.

5. Another argument advanced against birth control is that it is immoral. To this Neo-Malthusians point out that morality is a relative concept. Ethics is man-made. Human principles are never categorical and fixed. If a principle is useful from the social viewpoint, it may be accepted from the moral viewpoint as well. Birth control is today a social necessity. It should be accepted as desirable without any sense of immorality.

History records that in spite of criticism and vehement opposition to the Neo-Malthusian theory of birth control, the message gradually spread in the West and also in the East. When Mary Stopes declared in England that women have a right to enjoy sex without child birth, she was threatened by the English Lords for what they called the misguiding of their women. Mary Stopes however, won her point. The feminist movement starred by her not only spread over the entire British Island but also in Europe. Today, there is no controversy about the artificial birth control to check population growth. On this other hand, most of the governments in developing countries like India are doing everything within their means to popularise the methods of artificial birth control. The feminist movement, spread all over the world, has also encouraged artificial birth control.

Classical School

The classical theory of population was based upon the idea that the production, consumption and distribution of wealth are determined by economic laws. This school was founded by Adam Smith, followed by David Ricardo, Thomas Malthus, Nassau Senior, John Stout Mill and J. B. Say. They were political economists and believed that economics functions better under a free and private 'initiative with keen competitions.

Neo-classical School

This school of thought placed more emphasis on mathematical economics and the analysis of the psychological background and consumer demands, decisions and actions. It was founded by William Jensons, Carl Manger and Leon Walrus. Among its notable leaders were Alfred Marshall, John Bates, Clark, Irving Fisher and Vilfredo Pareto.

Both the classical and neo-classical schools were concerned with an examination of the inter-relationships between population and production. This was a serious point of discussion. While according to some, increasing population resulted in increasing production, others maintained the opposite view. None of these views was conclusively proved due to lack of empirical and theoretical evidence. The issue appeared to be resolved by the formulation of the economic principle of diminishing returns in the second decade of the 19th century. This principle supported Malthusian theory. The Classical economists accepted it as a natural law. In 19th century it was observed that the general being of the people and the population growth went hand in hand. This was contrary to Malthusian theory and the principle of diminishing return. John Stuart Mill and Henry Sidgwick pointed out that many countries would be better off with smaller numbers since their population had already reached the point of diminishing return. The economists Gray, Chamers, Burn and Wirth pointed out that increasing number of people stimulate production. Godwin, Ravenstone, Sadler, Almond, Scrope and Ricardo disapproved the principle of diminishing return. According to Marshal, a neo-classical economists, this law was applicable particularly to agriculture and not to industry. It was realised that the total and the per capita production not only depend upon population but also upon resources, labour, capital and technology. It was pointed out that per capita income was inversely related to the number of population. It was the factor of capital which influenced the size and growth of the population. Thus, by the end of the 19th century, it was concluded that population variable was only one variable in the total economic system. The importance of population growth was therefore considerably diminished. It was even ignored by some writers. Economic growth in the West kept pace with the population growth, negating the gloomy picture painted by Malthus. In this ferment of thinking about the relationship of population and production, the following points emerged :

1. Population is only one of the several factors affecting production, distinction and other human affairs.
2. The socio-economic phenomena in general and the effect of population phenomena in particular are far from simple.
3. A more cautious appraisal of the socio-economic role of population is required. It has been recognised that productivity is affected by so many factors depending on the stage of economic development and the demographic situation.
4. The law of diminishing reform is applicable more to agricultural production and seldom to industrial production.
5. The population question cannot be considered only in relation to economics. It is also influenced by cultural factors. Therefore, it is a dependent variable, a product of so many influences.
6. The theory of optimum population has resolved the old debate about the consequences of large and growing population.

Optimum Theory

The optimum population theory had its beginning in the writing of Karl Winkelblech (1810-1865), a German Professor who classified nations into three categories according to the size of their population:

1. Under-populated nations, 2. Over-populated nations and, 3. Normal-populated nations. It was Edwin Cartoon (1861-1935), an English economist, who used the concept optimum population, as synonymous with the best possible population. According to him, at any given time, the population which can exist on a given extent of land, consistent with the greatest productiveness of industry at that time, is definite United Nations have defined the concept of optimum population, to mean the size of the population

which results in the highest per capita income, the highest productivity as measured in different manners, or the highest level of other less well-defined economic indicators such as economic welfare, level of living, real income and in some cases employment." While some writers have considered the concept too restrictive, most of the writers have accepted the idea. However, later developments provoked a critical re-examination of this theory. This theory implied that the growth of population was beneficial upto a certain point, after which it becomes harmful. The following criticisms were levelled against this theory :

1. It is doubtful that the optimum point in the growth of population can ever be determined. The demographers have never agreed over this point.
2. The concept of optimum population is essentially a static concept, based upon the assumption that there is an optimum limit of technology, resources, foreign trade and social structure.

This theory was very popular in the second and third decades of the present century. It has been rightly concluded by survey that this theory may be accepted net as an absolute theoretical concept but as a convenient tool.

Marxist-Socialist Theory

As has been already pointed out, Karl Marx-completely rejected Malthusian theory, as it did not fit in a socialist society. According to Karl Marx, there can be no natural or universal law of population. According to him, 'An abstract law of population exists for plants and animals only, and only in so far as man has not interfered with them.' Again, "Every special historic mode of production has its own special laws of population, historically valid, within its limit alone. Thus, the population theory is peculiar to the capitalist system of production. It is inherent in the capitalist system and not in production. Engels maintained that under the capitalist system surplus population was linked with surplus capital. This state of affairs, according to socialist view, can be changed by social reorganisation. Communist Manifesto laid down the fundamentals of a socialist society. Origin of the Family emphasized the need for emancipation of women. The need of conscious control was emphasized. It was maintained that due to the superior status of women there will be slower growth of population in a socialist society. Later socialists however, supported responsible parenthood. According to them reproductive behaviour should be based upon complete harmony between the individual and the society. Since birth control contributes to the emancipation of women, it is accepted. Even abortions are permitted. The Marxist socialist theory of population is applicable to modern socialist countries of Europe where it is being practised and supported. Criticisms of this view have been obviously advanced by the thinkers of the capitalist society since in the capitalist countries the views of Marx and Lenin are not accepted.

Biological Theories

Biological theories of population include : The Density Principle, The Diet Principle and other Theories. Though these theories have not been accepted by the demographers, however, a brief reference to them will not be out of context here.

Density Principle. This principle was laid down by Michael Thomas Sadler (1730, 1835), an English political economist in his work entitled 'The Law of Population.' This book presented the principle that fertility varies inversely with the density of population. The contradiction found in countries like Netherland, where both fertility and density were high, explained by Sadler by pointing out a direct relationship between fertility and mortality. According to him, increasing fertility increases mortality which in turn decreases fertility. This principle, however, has not been accepted by most of the demographers.

The Diet Principle. This was propounded by Thomas Doubleday (1790-1870), an English political economist in 1841, in his essay The True Law of Population Shown to be Connected with the Food of People. According to Doubleday poverty stimulates population growth since the diet of the poor is inadequate. On the other hand if the diet is sufficient one finds less fertility. It was pointed out that due to this principle one finds high fertility among Chinese, Irish and the Scotch and low fertility in France. Similar conclusions were reached by Josue de Castro in his book, Geography of Hunger in 1952 based upon the negative correlation between the protein content of the diet and the birth rate in a country. Most of the demographers, however, rejected this theory. Thomlinson remarked about Castro, "He might as well have considered the correlation between national fertility and consumption of ice cream, soda, use of washing machine or watching of television."

Herbert Spencer's Theory

Herbert Spencer presented a theory of population on biological basis, in 1880. He pointed out that fertility increases in response to the progress of society. It is a great agency for the advancement of mankind. However, when population becomes excessive, it threatens the very existence of the human species. This requires control of population.

Corrado Gini's Theory

The Italian biologist Corrado Gini has recently presented a biological theory of population, known as the cyclical theory. According to Gini the population tends to follow an evolution similar to the life cycle of the individual. As the individual passes through the successive stages of development, maturation add involution, similar is the case with the evolution of the human being. The biological theories have not been accepted the sufficient explanations of population since, as has been pointed out by social and cultural theories, social and cultural factors are equally important in the growth of population. Fertility is not a mere biological phenomena but very much influenced by social and cultural factors.

Mathematical Theories

Development of mathematical techniques has encouraged formulation of mathematical laws of population growth. The mathematical approach to the study of population was first adopted by a Belgian astronomer Quetelet. Among the mathematical theories, the theory of logistic growth of population was developed by Verhulst. In United States it was propounded by Pearl and Reed. According to them the growth of population occurs in cycles. It was maintained that, "Within the cycle and in a specially limited area or universe, growth in the first half of the cycle starts slowly, but the absolute movement per unit of time increases steadily until the milk point of the cycle is reached. After this point, the increment per unit of time becomes steadily smaller until the end of the cycle." According to this theory, the total population follows all S-shaped curve. The law of logistic growth of population was declaimed everywhere. It was found useful for estimating and projecting future population size. However, it was gradually widely questioned since it neglected socio-cultural and economic factors. It did not take into account the changes in the population growth which permit the population exploit its resources effectively. It did not consider the changes in the aspirations and motivations concerning various patterns of fertility behaviour.

Demographic Transition Theory

Demographic transition mean the progress from one demographic condition to a different stage, for example in Western countries it was found that the population moved from a condition of high mortality and high fertility to conditions of low mortality and low fertility: Thus, the stage of high expansion of population itself leads to the stationary stage and vice verse. Several demographers such as Landry in 1909 and Warren Thompson in 1929 attempted to construct a typology to describe demographic transition from conditions of high mortality and high fertility to the conditions of low mortality and low fertility. None of these demographers, however, made an attempt to explain these changes. In 1947 C. P. Blacker identified five phases of the demographic transition as follows:

1. The high stationary stage characterised by high birth rates and high death rates.
2. The early expanding stage with falling birth rat but rapidly decreasing mortality.
3. The late expanding stage with failing birth rate; but rapidly decreasing mortality.
4. The low stationary stage with low birth rates balanced by equally low mortality.

5. The declining stage with low mortality and deaths exceeding births.

It was Frank W. Notestein who, for the first time presented a theory of demographic transition in 1945 in a matured form with explanations for the changes in fertility. John Caldwell has therefore credited Notestein with expounding the theory of demographic transition. According to Notestein, the rapid growth of population during the past three centuries was particularly due to the decline in the death rate, this decline resulted from the process of modernization.

Modernization involved high standards of living, high incomes and advanced level of sanitation and medical knowledge, with the result that fertility registered a decline. By the middle of 1930 birth rates reached very low levels in Western countries. This was the result of widespread acceptance of contraceptive methods due to the ideal of small family prevalent in urban industrialised society. According to the stage of demographic evolution the population in different countries may be characterised into the following three types :

Incipient decline. In this stage fertility falls below the replacement level. This stage could be seen in populations of Europe, The United States, Australia and New Zealand.

Transitional growth. Notestein has explained this stage where, "birth and death rates are still high and growth is rapid, but the decline of the birth rate is well established."[1]

High growth potentials. Notestein has defined this stage of population in these words : "Mortality is high and variable and is the chief determinant of growth, while fertility is high and thus fair had shown no evidence of a downward trend. In these populations, rapid growth is to be expected just an soon as technical developments make possible a decline in mortality." Examples of this stage of population were pointed out in most of the countries of Asia, Africa and Latin America. According to George J. Stolnitz, "All nations in the modern era, which have moved from a traditional, agrarian-base economic system to a largely industrial, urbanised base, have also moved from a condition of high mortality and fertility to low mortality and fertility."

Demographic transition has been also studied from the point of view of economic development. According to Ansley J. Coale and Edger M. Hoover, the agrarian peasant economy is generally characterised by high death rate and high birth rates. The death rates fluctuate according to the variations in harvests and the incidents of epidemics. Due to poor diet, lack of sanitation and medical and public health programmes, the death rates are usually high in peasant societies. On the other hand, the birth rate is high due to the prevalent ideals of prolific fertility reinforced by the economic advantages of having a large number of children. As the agrarian economy changes into industrial economy, levels of production and urbanisation rise, with the result that death rate falls due to better diet and medical care. Due to the acceptance of the ideal of small family in urban society the birth rates fall. This decline occurs after a time to the decline in the death rate. The birth and death rates pursue a parallel downward course, though the decline of birth rate lags behind. As further deductions in the death rate are difficult to achieve, the birth rate again approaches the level of the death rate with the result that population grows slowly. While the death rates do not fluctuate, the birth rates fluctuate due to social and cultural reasons.

Some other thinkers have pointed out different stages in demographic transition. According to Donald Olen Cogwill, the population passes through the five stages known as : Primitive Cycle, Modern Cycle, Future Cycle or Baby Boom period, Probable Cycle and Population Cycle in the long run. According to this view population increases in S-Curve. Karl Max has categorised the above mentioned stages into four stages only. According to him the second and the third stages in population growth are the stages of population explosion. Landry has divided demographic changes into three demographic regimes on the basis of the theory of Cantillon : A Primitive Regime, An Intermediate Demographic Regime and A Modern Epoch.

Criticism of the Transition Theory. Generally speaking, the following criticisms have been advanced against the theory of demographic transition :

1. This theory was based on the experience of population changes in Western countries. But since the population

growth in different countries does not follow identical patterns, therefore no theory can explain population growth everywhere. One finds so many exceptions to the rule. Thus, this theory is only a broad generalisation.

2. This theory fails to explain the phenomenon of 'The Baby Boom' in Western countries after the Second World War.
3. This theory does not provide a theoretical explanation of fertility as a force in demographic transition.
4. In fact this theory cannot be called a theory in the real sense since it neither extracts fundamental processes from a phenomenon nor identifies crucial variables.
5. This theory does not provide explanation of fertility decline nor does it identify crucial variables in it. Therefore it has no predictive value.
6. This theory cannot be applied to developing countries since the demographic stages in the Western countries are not necessarily explicit in the population growth in developing countries. In the face of the above mentioned criticisms, it may be concluded that the demographic transition theory at the best provides a framework and means for wider empirical generalisations. It cannot be considered a theory in the strict sense of the term, particularly for the explanation of the demographic growth in the developing countries.

Social Theories

The social theories of population, as is clear by the title, explain population growth on the basis of social factors. The most important among these theories was the theory of Karl Marx: which we have already discussed. Therefore, we will only present a brief outline of some important social theories of population.

Theory of Single Tax. This theory was presented by the American Economist Henry John. According to him, "The law of population accords with and is subordinate to the law of intellectual developments and any danger that human beings may be brought into a world where they cannot be provided for arises not from the ordinances of nature, but from the social maladjustments that in the midst of wealth condemn men to want." Therefore, the principle of population is subordinate to the principle of mental growth. Fecundity and fertility decrease with mental growth. There is no contradiction in the growth of population and the means of subsistence, provided the latter are controlled by the state. Therefore, the government should directly charge single tax from the users of land.

Theory of Social Capillarity. This theory was presented by Dumont (1849-1902) on the basis of his study of the growth of French population. According to Dumont, "The development of number in a nation is in inverse ratio to the development of individual." In other words, as the individual develops, birth rate decreases. Dumont has called in theory of social capillarity since capillarity means the will for social progress. According to Dumont, this theory of population applies to a well developed society based on rational thinking and idealism. He says, "From the moment when the imagination and the attraction of the ideal enter the scene, we find ourselves in the presence of a new principle of population." Thus, a theory of population is directly related to the stage of the growth of a society. Malthusian theory of population applies only to undeveloped and primitive societies. There is an inverse relationship in social capillarity and rate of birth. Since this force is inactive due to caste system in India, the birth rate is high. In France, on the other hand, due to political freedom and democracy, the birth rate is low. According to Dumont, "Just as a column of liquid must be thin in order to rise under the force of capillarity so must a family be small to rise in the social scale." The birth rate, due to the same reasons, is high in the villages and low in the cities. According to Dumont this theory does not apply to India where capillary power is inactive due to caste system. Thus, a rigid social structure retards social progress. Birth rate in the cities is always less than that in the villages. The reason of this distinction is the urban urge for a high standard of living. The thinking and conduct of urban people is more rational since they have better knowledge. Other factors influencing lower birth rate in the urban areas include : democracy, middle class, will to progress and higher standard of living. On the other hand, the factors leading to higher birth rate in the rural areas include casteism, old style thinking, illiteracy, ignorance and poverty, etc. According to Dumont this theory is not applicable to the societies having socialistic economy since in it an individual has limited scope of rising high. "The socialist principle of equality of function, if entirely applied, would necessarily imply the destruction of social capillarity and cause a high birth rate."

Criticism. The theory of population advanced by Dumont was an improvement upon Spencer's theory. However, the rise of a society does not depend upon nearly on lower birth rate but also upon so many social, economic and political factors. Therefore, Dumont's principle cannot be accepted as a rule.

Voluntarism Theory

This theory was presented by Frank Fatlar in the end of the century. According to Fatlar, the main defect of Malthusian theory was its being confined to sex motive among human beings. Man, on the other hand, is a complex being very much influenced by ideals, experiences, ambitious and desires, etc. Therefore, the behaviour of a group is influenced by so many factors. Hence, no theory of population explains all the social phenomena. The demographic changes should be explained on the basis of factors influencing society. Several psychological tendencies influence man's reproductive behaviour. Different classes exhibit different types of family environment. The poor do not pay much attention to restrict reproduction since the additional child will further add to the family income. On the other hand, the rich do not want such increase since it will further divide the family income and property with the result that the standard of living will fall down. Therefore, Fatlar concludes that economic progress retards birth rate since the incentive shall be considerably less. Voluntarism seeks to remove lack of far sight and economy. Similar theories had been presented in U. S. A. by Arthur Hadley in 1896 and Weber in 1899. According to Arthur Twinning Hadley, "Intellectual man is more capable of birth control then emotional person. He can exercise more self restraint."

Individuality Principle

This theory was advanced by the Italian economist Francesco S. Nitti in his book Population and the Social System. Nitti pointed out defects of other demographic theories including that of Malthus, Spender, Marx and Dumont. According to him demographic progress has also led to the progress of civilization. Pointing out the factors influencing growth of population he said, "The influences of the Psychical moral order and the influences of the political order, are but slight compared to influences of an economic kind. But for a true understanding of the law of population the biological factors play important parts."

Prosperity and Pleasure Theory

This theory was presented by Brenton. According to this theory the ideal of human life is pleasure. Reproduction rate increases among persons who have better means of pleasure. The poor class does not have so many options in pleasure seeking. They have no access to books, art and spiritual pleasures. Therefore, the only means of pleasure accessible to them is sexual intercourse. Consequently, they reproduce more children. On the other hand, since the rich have so many options to enjoy pleasure, therefore birth rate among them is lower.

Rationalism Theory

This theory was presented by Ungern-Sternberg. He, for the first time, admitted that birth rate may be lower even among poor. The real cause of birth rate, according to him is not biological but psychological. As he pointed out, "The women too become masculinized (when infected by the capitalist mentality) in their search for equality Love relationship becomes business-like and matter of fact."' Advancing examples from Norway, Finland, etc., he maintained that the wealth or poverty itself is not the factor determining birth rate nor is it urban or rural environment. The real factor determining birth rate is mental, it may be both among males and females. There is a correlation between economic development and lower birth rate. It is the capitalist mentality that induces; low fertility. This, however, may be equally found in rural areas. Therefore, rural or urban, rich or poor do not necessarily determine birth rate.

Besides the above mentioned social theories, some other comparatively less known theories of population have been advanced by some other thinkers. They are however, susceptible to the same objections as have been already pointed out.

QUESTIONS

1. Trace Pre-Scientitive thinking on population.
2. Discuss Pre-Malthusian theories of population.
3. Explain Malthusian theory of Population.
4. Describe Neo-Malthusianism.
5. What is Optimum Theory of Population ? Explain.
6. Describe Biological Theories of Population.
7. Write short note on Theory of Demographic Transition.
8. Discuss Social Theories of Population.

6

Issues at Stake

Ethical Values

Ethics is the science of right and wrong, good or evil. This raises issues regarding population education—Is it right to give population education to young children? Will they not laugh in their sleeves? Will it keep them morally healthy? What values will population education generate in small children? There are an ethical questions which we are trying to answer.

All of us know that the world faces population explosion. And if this is not stopped, we will die of hunger. We will live like ants. Hardly any space will be left to build houses. Is it ethical to go on producing children? This is the other side of the same question.

Population education thus becomes a very complex question in the light of ethical issues. Population education is not a fashionable trend. It calls for action and action raises ethical questions.

Population education aims at limiting the number of humans so that we can live in harmony with other creatures of nature. He is not to eat away all the flora and fauna. Thus, it is ethical to limit the family. There is nothing ethical about it. It is the principal of "Live and let live". It is right.

And then while teaching population education, the question that arises is—Which language is a teacher to use so that children do not start blushing and do not suffer from shame? What technique a teacher is to use to drive home the point? It all depends upon the teacher. It is a difficult task and we concede. His approach has to be a rational approach. He is to create new value commitments and therein lies his success.

Population education is to strengthen the values of family and stable marriage. Happiness of marriage is to be strengthened. Social fabric of society is to be strengthened. And it is also to stress the point that the slogan of small family has the sanction of the society. It is more socialistic in approach.

Population education means limiting the family. Small family means better quality of life. The value of quality stands generated. Children are looked after better. The health of mother will improve. Our resources will stand stabilized.

The ultimate goal of a society according to population educator is one largely based on "recycling technology"—a technology that is based on making the last use of replenishable resources in the first instance, e.g., hydroelectricity. Wherever non-replenishable resources are involved, the technology would strive to minimise its consumption, try for readily available substitutes and where necessary would work on wrap and waste materials recycling them into further use.

Another value is about having a fresh look towards marriage. Marriage is not to be looked as institution for blind satisfaction or blind passion only but it is to be considered as something more noble, responsible and dutiful. The "Grahistha" ashram has to be nicely lived. We have to survive. That is the point that we are trying to drive home. It is survival that is at stake.

These are the values-social values, freedom, fraternity, dignity of individual that we want to instil in our students.

Parents' Responsibility

A large number of studies have been conducted to know the attitudes of parents towards population education. Yes, about the conclusions, your guess is as right as mine. Most of the parents are averse to the idea of population education. Their opinion is negative. This can be due to several reasons. They are not aware of the concept of population education or they think that children will automatically learn about it when the time comes. There the story ends.

National Policy Implemented

The National Policy on Education, 1986 states:

Para 3.4: (P.U.). NPE document:

"The National System of Education will be based on a national curriculum framework which contains a common core along with other components that are flexible. The common core will include history of India's freedom movement, the Constitutional obligations and other content essential to nurture national identity. The common core will conclude history of India's freedom movement, the Constitutional obligations and other content essential to nurture national identity. These elements will cut across subject areas and will be designed to promote values such as India's common culture heritage, egalitarianism, democracy and secularism, equality to sexes, protection of environment, removal of social barriers, observance of the small family norm and inculcation of scientific temper. All educational programmes will be carried on in strict conformity with secular values."

It is thus clear that National Policy on Education 1986 believes in small family norm and wants to promote it. The future of population Education in the country appears to be bright.

The National Policy on Education 1986 further states:

"The growth of our population needs to be brought down significantly over the coming decades. The largest single factor that can help to achieve this is the spread of literacy and education among women."

We have already said that population education aims at population control. Even when we give general education to women, population council must automatically come in.

We have already discussed environmental education with population education. And National Policy rightly believes in, To quote from it para 8.15, page 23, NPE document.

There is a permanent need to create a consciousness of the environment. It must permeate all ages and all sections of society, beginning with the child. Environmental consciousness should inform teaching in schools and colleges. This progress will be integrated in the entire educational progress.

Environmental education and population education will go together and this has been stressed by NPE and we have already done a chapter on it.

In anticipation of the NPE, perhaps we started working on Population Education much earlier and have considerable literature on it in the form of conceptual framework to implementation. We do not need literature now on it. We have understood it, the need is to implement it. It is to be ensured that the teachings/goals of population education are understood by each and every citizen of India. Therein lies our future.

Various Levels

Primary School Stage: We know that education between 6-11 years of the child is primary education. It is in the primary school that maximum number of children are found and certain very important attitudes toward life are formed. Children are also free from sex inhibitions at this stage.

T. S. Mehta and B. S. Parakh state that it should be possible at this stage to give very simple ideas regarding family size and happy family life. The ideas like "a small family is a happy family' are to be concentrated upon. If we are to provide food, shelter and clothing to every individual in such a large country, we shall be exhausting our limited resources. This is to be drilled in the minds of children.

In their book on social studies or in their book on language test, some interesting lessons on the topic can be incorporated. And while teaching health, nutrition and environmental study relevant and simple concepts regarding population growth and pressures should be taken up.

Middle School Stage: Children at this stage (12-14 years) are in a better position to understand things. Further, it is from this section of population that much of our leadership in rural area is likely to emerge. Naturally, we should be very serious about population education at this stage.

The teacher at this stage is also better equipped professionally and academically and further all subjects are compulsory. All can talk about population problem and the pressures which the children are likely to face. Children will better understand the population problem. Teachers of Geography, Civics, Social Studies, Biology, should in particular, talk of population problems and population dynamics. Topics on population education can be related to actual syllabus.

Secondary and Senior Secondary Stage: Now we are dealing with adolescents and potential parents. They have now understood the problems arising out of population pressures. They can feel this in their own lives and they are eger to discuss these and arrive at their own conclusions. A general awareness of population dynamics —determinants and consequences would develop in them desirable attitudes on population matters when they come of age. You may not talk of contraceptives at this age.

T. S. Mehta and B.S. Parakh suggest a two-pronged attack on this issue. An intensive work on Population Education will have to be undertaken in subject areas like Geography, Civics, Social Studies, General Science and Biology. Manuals on Population Education can also be prepared. Specific teaching units can be put in manuals focussed on population dynamics and its various social, political, economic repercussions. Handbooks can be prepared by training colleges and SIE's. This also ensures their involvement. Extension lectures ran also be introduced. Graphics can also be made of use. Films can also be shown to X, XII class students. They will appreciate all these.

Non-school Stuff

Population education is not to be confined to schools and colleges. There is another and larger segment of population who do not go to school, they also marry and produce children. We are worried about them. How can we educate about population, this segment (out of school segment) or society.

Practical Application

Dr. A. K. Sen writes about the need of population education for the out-of-school youths. The need arises out of the following factors:

(1) The out-of-school youths constitute a sizeable percentage of our population and add to the eligible couple groups every year.

Their reproductive behaviour in the married life would he crucial to the control of population growth. Population education to the youth would supplement the efforts of family planning.

(2) This group of population has not been covered under any programme of population education or family planning. Family planning programme tackles the married individuals.

(3) Family planning programme could be successful when it is supported by the community. Population education would help the community in building up a positive attitude to family planning.

(4) Population education to the out-of-school youths would enlighten the parents who would supplement and complement the efforts of school imparting population education to the school going children.

(5) The youth are receptive, do not have any fixed attitude and are susceptible to changes and adjustments. Hence, programme like population education has a reasonably good chance of success.

A Different Education

Population education includes population dynamics and the problem created by rapid population growth, the advantages of small family norms, late marriages and other closely-related topics. It does not include sex education and family training. That is the normal concept.

But for the out-of-school youth, the population education will have to include three different areas of education—family life education, sex education and family planning in view of special needs of this group.

The family life and social life in our country today are rapidly changing their pattern. An individual is to be assisted in making proper adjustment in the family and society. He has to understand what makes for a happy family and to realize the responsibilities towards the same. Family life education would prepare the youths for satisfactory and effective membership in his family and society.

Sex education would help the youths to develop rational attitudes with respect to sex. This would be useful to the individual and to the society. The ignorance about facts will stand removed.

The youth need to be told about family planning which is very crucial to them and to society at large. They should have an adequate information as to how to space children and to limit the size of the family. They are also to develop healthy attitude towards family planning.

Population education has to be presented in a package together with the above three areas of education for these illiterate youth. That is why we call it population education with a difference. The real issue which needs to be decided is how much of the three areas should be included at what stage, in which form and by whom.

Agencies in Adult Education Area

Population education which essentially involves changes in values and behaviour of the youth is essentially an adult education programme. As such population education for the non-school going youths should be integrated with adult education programme. The adult education agencies will effectively carry out this programme.

In adult education classes, the atmosphere is informal. The point can be driven home better.

Ordinary School versus Community School

School can make a positive contribution towards the population education for the out-of-school youths, although it has its own limitations. The school can be developed in a pattern so that it serves the entire community and not merely school children. The school can play its role in the following way in the words of Dr. A.K Sen.

(i) It can render extension services to the community by way of demonstration, study session, organized population education classes, library facilities and field visits in close co-operation with various community agencies.

(ii) It can work with the local community agencies and voluntary organizations and can encourage them to participate in the population education programme.

(iii) It can present suitable topics on population education through radio broadcasts and can stimulate the local organizations to form listeners' groups. Members of the group can discuss among themselves the topic after the broadcast.

(iv) It can design the school curriculum in such a manner so that it not only meets the need of the school-going children but also that of the out-of-school youths, the young adults and particularly the parents. The out-of-school youth, parents and other adults are involved in planning and in actual carrying out the curriculum. They can be involved in the survey of the needs, interest and resources of the community, development of teaching units, formulation and carrying out of action project and the evaluation of the teaching-learning activities to population education.

QUESTIONS

1. What is the ethics of Population Education ?
2. What is the role of parents ?
3. What are the stages of Population Education ?

7

Rising Population

In India, the birth rate is not above the average for the Third World countries it is higher than what the Indian economy can sustain at the existing level of development. During the past four decades the birth rate has not declined significantly in India because a number of economic and social factors continue to favour high fertility.

Economic Factors

The economic environment of a country influences human behaviour. Fertility has its basis in the economic life of the country. The occupational distribution of the population, the extent of urbanisation and the spread of poverty, have considerable bearing on the birth rate of the country. In India these factors have not allowed any significant decline in fertility.

Agricultural Economy. India is an agricultural country 70 per cent of population is dependent on agriculture. There is an unchanged occupational distribution of population. In an agricultural economy, children find work easily in farms, especially during the time of harvesting amid sowing seasons. Therefore, in agrarian societies children are never considered an economic burden. Thus such countries have bigger families on economic grounds. Agricultural countries are generally backward, overpopulated, and faced with the problem of disguised unemployment. Therefore, there is an economic rationale for a relatively bigger family in a predominantly agricultural economy with precapitalist relations of production as India. In an industrial society, parents have to support their children for a much longer period. Therefore most people prefer to have a small family on economic grounds. As the pace of the process of industrialisation in India has been rather slow over the past four decades, the decline in fertility that accompanies industrialisation has not happened here.

Adverse Occupation at Pattern. The fertility of those women whose husband is in a white-collar job, generally in the professional category or as manager, supervisor, administrative head, etc. of a firm or organisation, is much lower than the fertility of those women whose husband is engaged in a blue-collar job as an unskilled or skilled labour or as a production process worker. Is the wife is employed in a white-collar job, her job itself forces her to have fewer children which means a lower fertility for her, on the other hand, the women who are either not working or who are working in agriculture or in households as maid-servants show frequent child-bearing as it does not adversely affect their work.

Slow Urbanisation Process. In 1991 the proportion of urban population in India was 25.72 per cent as against 17.62 per cent in 1951. Thus the pace of urbanisation in this country has been rather slow. In European countries the urban population amounts for 70 to 80 per cent of the total population. City life has its own problems. Housing is the biggest problem in cities. Upbringing of children in cities is far more costly than in villages. The mobility of labour contributes to disintegration of joint family system. All these factors reinforce each other in bringing down the birth rate. As the process of urbanisation has been slow in India it has failed to generate social forms which usually bring down the birth rate. Fertility differentials between cities and rural areas are not very significant in India. It is somewhat lower in cities than in the countryside, but that is a consequence of the high male-female ratio in cities.

Low Income. The number of children born per couple decreases with the increase in the per capita monthly income or expenditure of the household in both rural and urban society. A high per capita income of the household implies that the children and mother have better nourishment in the family and that medical care can be provided more easily and more often in case of sickness of the child. This in turn prevents infant and childhood mortality. Once the couple is sure about the survival of those children who are already born in the family, they may no longer attempt to have more children. In the higher income groups, the son normally does not follow the occupation of the father, and hence, for a long time, the child remains a consuming unit instead of becoming a 'producing' unit at the very young ages of 8 to 14 years. All these factors show that low income is a significant use of high fertility in India.

Widespread Poverty. Widespread poverty another factor responsible for the rapid growth of population in India. Presently per capita income is very low and nearly 40 per cent of the population is below the poverty line. Even those above the poverty line are denied nutritious food and other amenities of life. This economic millieu provides an incentive for having more children. The birth of an additional child hardly matters even to those poor whom a child neither provides income nor security. Cynical indifference to the size of the family is inevitable when life is already miserable and there are virtually no stakes in it. Thus, poverty is a major factor which works against the acceptability of family planning programme by the poorer section of the Indian society. To quote an eminent sociologist, Mahmood Mamtani "While rich farmers invest in machines, poor villagers invest in children." In one of its report the World Bank has stated, "There are good reasons why, for poor parents, the economic costs of children are low, the economic benefits of children are high and having many children makes economic sense." Hence, family planning is not an accepted norm among the young couples especially among the low income groups. Illiteracy and ignorance along with poverty add fuel.

Social Factors

Contribution of social factors to the high birth rate is tremendous in India. Universality of marriage, relatively lower age at the time of marriage, religious and other superstitions, joint family system, lack of education and a very limited use of contraceptives are a few important social factors arresting significant decline in fertility in India.

Lower Age at the Time or Marriage: In India the relatively lower age at the time of marriage is very much responsible for high fertility. On the basis of an empirical study N.C. Das has claimed that women marrying between 20 and 24 have the same fertility, as those marrying before the age of 20. Some reduction in fertility occurs when the marriage age reaches 25 or over. Since the average age of women at marriage is still around 18 years in India, the fertility is bound to remain high, particularly when other factors which could bring it down are non-existent. After the passing of the Child Marriage Restraint Act (CMRA) in 1929, the frequencies of child marriages decreased. This Act raised the minimum age limit for girls to 14 years and for boys to 18 years. The Act was amended in 1949 to raise the minimum age of males to 18 years and female for 15 years. The National Policy on Population announced by the government in 1976 enhanced the age to 18 years for females and 21 years for males. Thus in a period of 100 years -the female age at marriage increased by six and half years and that of males by 4 years 2 months. The mean age at the marriage of females has a direct bearing on the birth rate. When the age at marriage is low the females will begin to bear children early and their reproductive span is larger. S.N. Agarwal says, "It has been calculated that an increase in the mean age at the marriage of females by six and half years during the period 1891-1901 to 1981-1991 in India has resulted in a 4.3 per cent decline in the birth rate over the period."

Remarriage of Widows: Though a matter of social reform, this has been one to pro-natality factor influencing the increase of Indias population. A legislation permitting the remarriage of widows was passed in India as early as in 1891. According to Dr. Chandrasekhar, "There are about 24 million widows of all ages (including virgin widows) who normally do not marry. Even widowers do not marry widows as a rule. But India is in fact changing and, of late there are very men who are willing to marry eligible and unencumbered widows. This welcome modern trend which negates the traditional custom of banning widow remarriages and withdrawing these women from participating in reproduction is contributing its small share to the population problem." According to S.N. Agarwal (1972), "Studies conducted in the rural part of the country establish that nearly 25 per cent of those who get widowed are remarried. There are chances of widow remarriage before the age of 20 and when they have no children. A few number of men who got widowed after the age of 30 are remarried.

Duration of Fertile Union: Fertile union starts with the age of effective marriage and it continues up to death, separation or with the crossing of the maximum fertile age which is taken a 50 years. In case of India, when marriages are taking place at an early age the duration of fertile union is longer.

Universality of Marriage: In India marriage is both a religious and a social requirement. The custom of arranged marriages results in near universality of marriage. Only 5 out of 1,000 Indian women remain unmarried. About 80 per cent girls are married during the most fertile period of 15 to 20 years of age. Dr. Chandrasekhar says "...everyone in India, sooner or later, usually sooner, gets married. Marriage is not merely a necessary social institution but a quasi-religious duty ... spinsters; and bachelors are a true phenomenon in India and newly every adult male and female in the country participates in reproduction."

Social Action System: In India, the bearing of children is considered to be the most important function of a newly married bride. Her own status in her new home basically depends on the success in her reproductive career, and particularly her ability to give birth to male children. The spacing of children in Indian family is largely determined by traditional and family norms regulating the duration of breast-feeding of the new born, post-partum taboos, abstinence from intercourse on certain specified days and certain other practices. In Indian society the couple is not really free to chat its own reproductive career. It is the concern of the extended family, and perhaps even of the community. The woman who postpones having children, will surely be the object of criticism, as will be the one who conceives in quick succession, or who continues to have children even when grandchildren have started being born. In fact different segments of our village society have different norm and practices in regulating the fertility behaviour.

Ignorance and Religious Superstitions: Indians consider children as gifts of God. The Hindu religious books say that no man can achieve heaven and salvation unless his last rites are performed by his son. A person is supposed to be richer and luckier if he has a number of wives and daughters. Simple people do not want to interfere with God's wish. They have no idea of family planning. The use of family planning techniques is not known to many people. On account of their religious and social superstitions, most Indians desire to have children, having no regard for their economic conditions. They also wish to have a daughter as the giving of a daughter in marriage is an act of "high religious merit". These irrational social religious attitudes, get reflected in the present cultures. Describing the situation in Indian villages, Mamdani writes, "In India it is considered ones dharma (religiously sanctioned social obligation) to have children to desire as many children as possible is not only in the natural order of things but also for indication of virtue. Marriage vows and blessings put emphasis on the good fortune of having many children. Folk songs usually sung on occasions such as marriage, childbirth or the harvest praises sing of the prolific mother and fertile soil. Sanctions against childless women further underline the necessity of children." In India different religious sub-groups display varying fertility level because of the fact that they have wide differences in their socio-economic backgrounds which do find their expression in their age at marriage and other critical determinants of fertility.

Low Standard of Living: Indian standard of living is low as compared to their counter-partners in well-educated and advanced countries. In backward areas, people are not in a position to educate their wards. As soon as they are able to earn something, they are married. Besides, they consider it a means of entertainment. As a consequence, there is a rapid increase in population.

Joint Family System: The joint family system, reduces or even eliminates the responsibility of bringing up children, for there are ones own parents to look after them it provide for them. The joint family system is advantageous for parents to give birth to children more quickly, while their own parents are alive and active so that these children can be very well looked after by the old people. This is a kind of social insurance against old age and unemployment. The children in the joint family live in an atmosphere of cordiality and affection and the whole family reacts in adverse as well as in happy circumstances as one man, under the custodian care of the head of the family. Thus, the joint family system has acted as a pro-natality factor. S.P. Jain opines that the joint family system is one of the factors which encourages child marriage. He remarked, "There are a number of reasons why the Indian society favours child marriage. The most important is the joint family system. In this system, a woman's place is in the home. The bride easily adjusts to her husband's home and follows the customs and traditions of the new family." Thus, the joint family system is to a great extent responsible for the increase in the population especially in rural mass of India.

Ideal of Large Families: In India, many couples and safety in large numbers of children. The norm of high fertility is, still prevalent in Indian society. In spite of all efforts at industrialisation and urbanisation, India continues to be an agricultural country. In most Western countries the change towards small family norm has been brought about by widespread education and large scale urbanisation. According to Prof. Jaya Suriya, "in a society which practised agriculture of the traditional type, a large number of children were in advantage. Even if a few of them did not survive beyond ten or twelve, they fulfilled at these and younger ages as well, certain functions of economic nature, tending cattle or sheep, or carrying out simple tasks in the field."

In developed countries the democratic spirit of partnership between men and women has led to complete absence of early marriage. Economic freedom for men is at the very roots of emancipation of men in those countries. To quote Margaret Sainger, the pioneer in the field of planned parenthood, "No woman can call herself free will she can choose whether she will or will not be a mother."

Preference for Sons: In India the birth of a male child is always welcome because it is expected of the sons to help and support their parents in old age and also perform all the religious duties. The sons also carry on the family name after the death of the father. The greater the number of sons, the larger will be their addition to the family income. The preference for sons is so deep-rooted in the minds of people that even educated and conscious people, crave for more and more sons. Persons having two or three daughters do not go for family planning methods till they beget a son. Dr. Chandrasekhar says it is bad Hindu manners to expect financial aid from daughters or sons-in-law."

Less Number of Working Women: In comparison to non-working men working women display lower fertility. They have higher educational level, higher age at marriage, higher incidence of contraceptive use, greater economic independence, much wider sphere of social interaction. All these factors together increase women's participation in the decision-making process. Moreover, the constraint of being a worker the limitations of being an employee by themselves restrict the number of confinements among working men.

Absence of Sex Education: Lack of sex education is a hindrance to population control. Sex education helps an individual adolescent to play a healthy and desirable role in his/her later life. Sometimes lack of sex education and sex mechanism determine the reproduction of human babies in an illegal way. The students need right direction and guidance.

Infant Mortality: High infant and child mortality is one of the deterrent factors in the adoption of a small family norm in developing countries because successful reproduction requires high fertility to offset high mortality. Couples do not merely want liable but surviving offspring. The demographic transition theory states that mortality declines first to be followed by fertility, as parents realise that a large number of children will also result in economic pressure in order to raise an unprecedented number of surviving children. Following five mechanisms by which infant mortality may affect the fertility level :

Biological Effects : These operates through shortened breast-feeding periods leading to a more rapid return of ovulation following the infant's death. A woman after delivery of a child usually suffer from temporary sterlity. This post-partum sterility varies positively with the duration of breast-feeding. The probability of conceiving again is high for a woman who experiences and infant death; because if breast-feeding is discontinued ovulation is likely to resume sooner.

Replacement Effect : In order to replace the actual death of child or children parents may strive to have additional birth. Hence, decline in child mortality should lead to a decline in fertility.

Insurance Effects : Insurance effect operates in anticipation of perspective high child community mortality rather than in response to actual mortality. In high mortality societies parents may feel the loss of children and may, therefore, produce more children than they would otherwise.

Societal or Community Effect : All high mortality societies develop a wide range of social norms, beliefs and practices either explicitly or implicitly designed to deal with the problem of child loss. For example, through one means or other pre-industrial societies evolved normative practices maturing a high average level of fertility to offset prevailing high mortality, for without them the society was doomed to extinction. One method was the extended family system which removed many of the costs of marriage and child-bearing. Family supports like looking after the pregnant woman in her parent's house also ensured greater infant survival.

Dependency Burden : As the number of surviving children raise economic pressure upon parents and total resource increase.

Thus, reduction in infant and child mortality may lead to reduction in fertility by means of increasing the duration, location, amenorrhoea, etc.

Illiteracy and Lack of Education: According to the 1991 Census, 52.11 per cent of the population was literate in India. The percentage of literacy among women was 39.42 per cent as compared to 63.86 per cent among men. Moreover, female literacy is largely concentrated in urban areas. The incidence of female illiteracy is the highest in large Uttar Pradesh, Bihar, Rajasthan and Madhya Pradesh. Education alone can change the attitudes of the people towards family, marriage and birth of a child. A mass of illiterate population cannot be exposed to rational ideas. People will not shed irrational ideas and religious superstitions, and will continue to have bigger families even if it muses deprivation and a low standard of living. In India, there is enough evidence for the inverse correlation between education and fertility. While the impact of primary school level education on birth rates is not very clear, there is no doubt that fertility declines with education at higher secondary and college levels. Education and fertility have been found to be negatively correlated. Even a few years of formal education bring a perceptible change in the reproductive behaviour. Education is capable of changing people's perceptions, ideas, aspirations, etc., much more significantly than even the micro economic realities. More than the purchasing power education determines the attitude towards disease, hygiene, nutrition etc. Education influences fertility in following two different ways :

Education of Parents : Higher levels of parents education is associated with higher age at marriage, better communication between spouses, greater participation of females in labour form, development of attitudes and values favouring small-sized family, wider spacing between children, greater use of birth control measures and greater participation of women in the decision-making process.

Education of the Mother : Various studies have revealed that the mother's education is more strongly correlated with the couple's fertility intentions than the education of her spouse.

The Level of Educational Attainment : Several studies have reported that a lower educational level has very little effect on fertility. Chatterjee observed that the fertility of women with only primary education is sometimes greater than that of illiterate women. It is only at the secondary level of education that the female's education begins to play an effective role.

Education of Children : Education of children also influence the parents decision with regard to their family size. The education of children has a two-way economic impact, one of increasing the cost of upbringing of the children and, two, of making them non-available for participation in economically gainful activities.

The teaching unit deals with several social problems caused by unprecedented population growth in the recent decades. The general aim is to acquaint the pupils regarding the impact of the population explosion on their day-to-day life.

Through this unit, they are expected to understand that human population does not exist apart from the social order. The unchecked population growth creates shortages of various resources which eventually lead to various social evils, Viz, poor ethical behaviour, black marketing, adulteration, cheating, etc.

Objectives in General

The general objectives of teaching this unit are:

(i) To enable the students understand that population growth itself is a social problem;

(ii) To enable the students understand that population growth leads to many social problems; and

(iii) To educate the students as to how problem grow and the social problems arising out of it can be solved through a proper programme of education.

Objectives Specified

Information and Understanding

To enable the pupils to understand:

(a) facts relating to the growth of population in their locality, district, state and country as a whole;

(b) difference between birth rate and death rate of population of their state and country in the last few decades;

(c) impact of the growth of population on supply of various goods and services;

(d) advantages of a small family in relation to food supply, clothing, shelter and happy life; and

(e) social and mental strains vis-a-vis unproportionate population growth.

Skills and Attitudes

To develop in pupils:

(a) skill for locating information about population growth of their locality, district, state and country from various sources available to them;

(b) an attitude for collection of information pertaining to various social problems;

(c) good hygienic habits so that they keep both their person and environment clean; and

(d) skill to prepare relevant charts and graphs of population growth of their state and country.

Detailed Study

Our country is rich in many ways. It abounds in rich resources in its mountains, rivers, flora and fauna, agricultural production and forests, etc. and most of all its people and culture.

India has one seventh of the world's population but has only 45th of the total land area. Population, if manageable and efficient, is an asset to any country. It works as an index of strength. It promotes better and fuller exploitation of the natural resources. But if it becomes unmanageable, it eats into the vitals of the nation and becomes rather an unmixed evil.

Population growth operates in low ways to retard the betterment of man's development.

First, because of increased population, pressure upon the country's land and resources increases tremendously;

Second, it tends to accentuate the rate at which the store of exhaustible and non-replaceable natural resources are spent up;

Third, the prolific growth of population creates considerable proportion of the dependent group of population which is rather young; and

Fourth, lack of adequate supplies and services give rise to various social evils.

It will be noted that the population growth upto 1921 was not much. The population even decreased slightly during the years 1911-20 due to wide-spread influenza in 1918. During the years 1961-70, growth of the population had been the highest.

Rapid Growth Determined

An important factor which has hitherto been instrumental for an explosive birth rate in India is the high figures of illiteracy and blind faith in superstitions and customs. Birth of a son is essential to keep the family line as also to discharge various religious ceremonies. This implies that until a son is born in the family the process of births will continue unchecked. Although such customs which regulate the behaviour of individuals in the society have lost much of their significance, their grip is still holding fast among the major portion of illiterate population which lives in village.

It will be observed that the death rate has come down remarkably. Corresponding birth rate has also declined but at a slower pace. Hence growing gap between birth rate and death rate has caused high rate of growth of the population in the recent decades. The decline in the death-rate has been brought about through phenomenal expansion of medical facilities in the country.

Immigration also affects population growth. But in case of our country the act migration per year to other countries during the past half century was less than 0.05% of the total population.

The prime objective is to promote among the pupils understanding of the adverse effects/impact of the resultant unproportionate growth of the population. For illustration, mention is made hereunder of some of the social maladies, emanating from the unchecked population growth:

(a) Overcrowding;

(b) Unemployment;

(c) Shortage of services and supplies, viz., inadequate housing, transport and medical facilities, insufficient supply of food and clothing, and low standard of living; and

(d) Social and personal disorganisation.

We have seen that unabated increase in the population leads to various social problems. If no measures are taken to check the most causes of uncontrolled population growth, a vicious circle sets in and pollutes the whole social environment. For the sake of a better understanding of the situation, the genesis of social problems listed above is analysed in the following paragraphs.

Density on Rise

It has been mentioned earlier that India has only 1/45th of the world's total land area and that every seventh man is an Indian. On the top of this, at the present growth rate, population of one Sweden is being added to India's population every year. Besides, the distribution of India's population is very different to that of an advanced industrial society. Almost 80% of the population lives in about 5,70,000 villages of India and the remaining 20% lives in about 3,000 towns, Of these, only eight have population exceeding 10,00,000. When land area at our disposal has limits, it is all the more necessary to set limits to the population growth. Another drawback of this staggering growth of population is that people cluster around certain centres of industries in order to earn livelihood. Women-folk and small children are also employed in order to supplement family earnings.

The excessive concentration of population gives rise to various social evils, viz., development of slums, insanitary living conditions, exposure of children to deviant social behaviour, insufficient supply of goods and services, etc.

Problem of Unemployment

It perhaps appears strange that in our country which has inadequate supply of goods and services, should at the same time suffer from insufficient employment opportunities, still strange part of it is that India has also colossal under-employment. This inevitably results in low national income, poor standard of living and miserable plight of the people.

Unemployment is absence of work for the able-bodied persons who are willing to work. The failure of demand to equal supply may be the result of an increase in the number of workers or a decrease in the number of positions or both. Both these forces area at work at present in India.

The National Sample Survey attempted an assessment of employment and unemployment in rural areas from July 1964 to June 1965. Its report (No. 1173) published in 1970 reveals that the working force in rural areas constitutes 40.15% of the total population of which gainfully employed forms 38.40% while persons unemployed and available for work constitutes 1.75%. However, persons working for four days, or less and upto one day form 10.24% of the total population.

The National Employment Service which consists of a network of employment exchanges render assistance to all employment seekers. Besides, it also acts as a centre for collection and dissemination of employment information.

It may be emphasised that the staggering growth of population is further aggravating the problem by way of increasing the number of employment seekers.

Shortage of services and supplies, inadequate housing and medical facilities and insufficient supply of food, clothing and low standard of living.

Housing. Shelter is one of the three basic needs of man, the other two being food and clothing. The need for an adequate housing facilities is, therefore, very vital. Apart from this, the houses should be reasonably comfortable and hygienic possessing essential amenities. Unfortunately, the housing conditions in India are extremely unsatisfactory. Leaving aside the considerable rural population, the conditions in the cities and industrial towns are worse. Most of the industries grow up without any plan and hence cities have grown haphazardly. The result is that innumerable slums exist in the country.

Because of the acute housing shortage, workers are compelled to leave behind their families in their village homes. Consequently, sex disproportion in the industrial cities has increased immensely. In his Indian Working Class, Dr. Radhakamal Mukerjee points out that the number of women per thousand males in Kolkata and its suburbs is 500, in jute mill towns of Bengal 526; in Mumbai 524 and in Kanpur 698. This wide disparity has naturally regrettable effect on workers' morale.

Medical Facilities. Like all other under-developed countries of the world, India has poor levels of health which are reflected in low vitality and a short span of life of its people. This fact is proved by high death rate—both infantile and maternal—although of late improvements have definitely taken place in this direction due to increased control over diseases and epidemics.

Judging from the enormity of the growth of population, above figures of personnel available to cater to the vast requirements are very humble. On the top of this, there exists a wide imbalance in regard to the availability of these personnel. Almost 80% of India's population living in villages, gets an insignificant proportion of such trained personnel to serve. Most of the trained personnel cling to the cities shirking the inevitable responsibility to serve the ailing.

The compelling necessity for adoption of governmental measures in order to bring the benefits of modern medical science within the easy reach of every member of the society both rural and urban cannot be overemphasized.

Food Supply. A rapidly increasing population and slow increase in agricultural production has resulted in a conspicuously decreasing per capita consumption of food in India. That our per-capita consumption of food is below the minimum standard.

Food consumption in terms of calories intake is far short of 3000 calories recommended by the nutrition experts. The average Indian gets a lop-sided diet primarily because of its extremely high cereal content.

The increase in food production and growth in population have to move in a balanced way. In case of latter outstripping the former, the position becomes unmanageable and adversely affects the per capita consumption of food by existing population.

Clothing. Ours is a hot country and people generally use much less clothing than is normally required in cold countries. Our clothing standard is very low. On an average, one does not get annually even cloth equivalent to two dhotis of 5 yards each to cover all the clothing needs. The lot of masses is even worse than this. At the end of Third Plan, consumption of cloth per head worked out to only 18 yards in contrast to average consumption of cloth in USA which is over 64 yards. In all probability, the needs of masses in regard to bare necessary clothing will remain a dream.

Disorganisation at Personal and Social Levels

It has to be recognized that there is a reciprocal relationship between the population and social structure, i.e., Social structure influences population changes as well as is affected by them. Primarily our domain is social influences on population.

In India, the transition from the rural to urban economy; from handicraft production to the machine industry has been too brisk and disintegrative to permit slow and gradual adaptation of the habits and attitudes of the people. Vast changes have accompanied severe economic pressures, such as changing pattern of joint family, status and roles of the people in general and the individual has been greately effected by the impelling changing foxes. It has to be emphasised that failure of the mental and social adaptation accounts for the prevalence and increase of diseases as T.B., hysteria, insanity and suicide among the urban middle classes in India. The continuous city-ward drift due to increasing pressures on land and the overcrowding at the industrial centres have introduced new problems of moral and social determination unknown before. A pessimistic account features the isolation of the individual, frustration and sense of futility as disintegrative causes of disorganisation.

The desire to limit family size has now been ushered by many other causes; among them are the resentment by women against excessive childbearing declining importance of the joint family system; increasing economic burden of children; rising standards of parental care and especially the desire of parents to give their children best possible start in life.

Tips for Teaching

The topic population growth vis-a-vis problems will be mainly at the communicative level. Hence, the teacher will have to make an effort to place the relevant materials and information in a very systematic and logical order. Some vital questions as suggested below will be raised in the class. Discussion of these questions, it is expected, will lead to the understanding of the major issues involved in the lesson. Students will be encouraged to handle reference materials available to them. They will be guided by the teacher to observe social phenomena like population growth, undertake survey work, collections of data, etc. Students will be asked to prepare charts, graphs etc. with the help of collected data.

How can Teachers be Prepared? Some attempts have been made very recently to think on this problem and device a syllabus on the subject of population education for the use of teachers colleges.

But the controversy has been raging hard on the approach which should be adopted by the colleges. There are three approaches which could be adopted with some advantages and some limitation in each. They are as follows.

1. 'Integrated Teaching Approach' which attempts to incorporate the concept of population education within the present curriculum on Principles of Education General Methods and Special Methods of Education areas offered by the colleges.
2. 'Special Study Approach' which consists in having a separate course an population education to be added to the total curriculum where special time-table, teaching staff, test procedures and instructional materials are to be provided by the college.
3. 'Extension Lectures Approach' which consists in arranging series of relevant lectures on Population Education during the year without disturbing the usual curriculum. They can be organised in the extra time as a part of co-curricular activities and need no permanent staff except a few resource persons occasionally.

During May 1970, the All India Federation of Educational Associations (AIFEA) in collaboration with the Indian Association of Teacher Educators (IATE) organised a workshop on Population Education to formulate a special study course on Population Education for the teachers colleges of India. The workshop adopted the second approach and outlined the following major areas and sub-areas for such a course.

Scope and Sphere

Population: The Problems and the Challenges

1. Population in India
2. Dynamics of population growth
3. Indian population situation in the world perspective.

Population Growth and Food Supply

1. Food is our basic economic problem.
2. Foodgrain production in India.
3. Malnutrition due to over-population.

Health

1. Health of people related to population growth.
2. Over-population leads to overcrowding.

Standard of Living

1. Meaning of standard of living and how it is affected by the size of population.
2. Economic growth and population growth.

Small Family for Better Living

1. Modification of family size is a family responsibility.
2. Family size: factors affecting size.
3. Population control: need and methods.

Population Growth and Education

1. Over-population and its implications for education.
2. Education for desirable changes in social values.

This approach is relevant but the drawback in this outline is that it contains more information material for a trainee on the subject but fails to provide him with the more understandings and skills he will need to use in his class-room after training. In other words, it is a subject-oriented course in population rather than methodology course in education for population.

In contrast to the above, the Population Education Centre established in the Faculty of Education and Psychology at the University of Baroda in June 1970 has attempted to device a course of special field for trainees as follows.

Introduction to Population Education: Its Aim and Objectives

— The problem of population in the world and in India

- — Programmes at national state and district levels (both the Government and the non-Government programmes).
- — Need for special educational programme through purposeful involvement of secondary schools.
- — Introducing population education concept in school curriculum.
- — Population education as a means of social change geared to national development and progress.
- — Population education versus sex-education, population education vis-a-vis family planning education, population education versus education about birth control.
- — Major areas of population education: demographic, social and economic.
- — Aims and objectives of population education:
- — To create 'population awareness'.
  - — To correlate school curriculum with life situations.
  - — To impart relevant information.
  - — To prepare responsible citizens.
  - — To prepare proper attitudes and new values for small family.
- — Need and significance of the course in the schools of modern India.

Relationship of Population Growth and Education

- — Population explosion and its adverse effects on quality of education.
- — Its impact on education measured in terms of:
  - — Adverse student indexes
  - — Adverse teacher indexes
  - — Adverse material indexes
  - — Adverse organisational indexes

— Population education as a phase of progressive education meant for developing: -
  — Imagination
  — Innovation
  — Creative thinking
  — Problem-solving
  — Social change and planned living
— Population control as a key means of quality control in education.

Methods and Approaches of Population Education

— Direct versus indirect approach
— Integrated versus specialised approach
— Methods of correlation of the concept of population education through:
  — Curricular activities
  — Co-curricular activities
  — Extra-curricular activities
— Planning lessons in different subjects with a bearing on population education.
— Debates, essay-writing, symposia, group discussions, visits to centres working on population programmes.
— Projects on population indexes, such as, food, housing, education, medical cue and health provision, entertainment including recreation, employment, opportunities to learn skills in various trades and leisure time activities.

Curriculum for Population Education in Schools

— Identification of the areas of curriculum for integration of the concept of population education.
— Preparation of teaching units with a bearing on population education.
— Reinterpretation of the present curriculum with reference to the population problems.

- Some important areas of learning in population education like: (a) population dynamics; birth the death rates, rates of fertility, mortality and migration, (b) health, food and nutrition, (c) standards of living, economic development including employment opportunities, and (d) civic amenities.
- Incorporating ideas on population studies and problems as a bias in textbooks of social studies and languages.
- Elaboration of topics related to human reproduction in science subjects in a simple manner.
- Development of instructional materials with stories, essays, poems and other language components with a focus on population explosion.

Evaluation in Population Education

- Testing of pupils' knowledge and information about population dynamics and problems included in the course.
- Various types of tests useful in population education.
- Observation and assessment of the relevant attitudes and values of pupils.
- Interviews with pupils to evaluate the outcomes of the course on population education.
- Identifying area of improvement in approach, methods and curriculum of population education.

Teacher's Role in Population Education (Teacher as an agent for social change).

- Teacher's faith in national development through proper planning.
- Teacher's conviction and basic belief in the need for checking further growth in population.
- Teacher's faith in education as a strong tool of social change and development.
- Teacher's firm belief in population education programme as a sound measure to achieve national goals.

— Teacher's knowledge of population education areas.

— Teacher's basic understanding about population education concept.

— Teacher's knowledge of socio-economic problems of the country.

— Teacher's knowledge of sex and human reproduction system and its relation to social function of life.

— Teacher's skill in disseminating information according to age and intellectual capacity of students.

— Teacher's characteristics, e.g., being intelligent, liberal creative, imaginative, innovative and interested in social needs and problems.

Controversies and Issues

— Conceptual differences in meanings (sex education, family planning propaganda, or education about birth control).

— Types of population education for different levels.

— Age-level to be exposed to population education.

— Competence of teachers to deal with the subject.

— Adverse reaction of pupils with different family backgrounds.

— Objection from parents and sections of the society.

— Cultural, religious and political issues against population education.

Assignments for Practice

— Drawing lessons for practice teaching with a bias on the theme "Country and its Population."

— Giving population education oriented lessons in the school.

— Gathering data and other demographic information about population of the local community.

— Collecting data on school-going population with regard to the number of schools and enrolment figures.

— Reporting on the visits to
  — Hospitals and family planning centres
  — Foster homes
  — Beggar homes
  — Employment exchange bureau, etc.

Now, it is the challenge before teachers colleges to try out a course in population education as an optional special field for those trainees who are genuinely interested in this area of special study. This also means the staff who is interested and competent can render their services for the worse. It has to be interdisciplinary, as the subject of population come across several social and biological boundaries.

Causes Based on Nutrition

Rapid population growth is hindering the achievements of our efforts in almost all areas of development. The green revolution has enabled the country to increase food production substantially, but the per capita availability of food grains has only increased marginally. Malnutrition and undernutrition is a serious health problem among our children of 0-6 years and school-going population in 6-11 years age group. Such conditions in many cases are the result of lack of knowledge relating to nutrition and not always due to the non-availability of food items. There are many inlets which influence the nutritional status of individuals. Besides the availability of food, these may include their eating habits, cooking practices, physical and emotional environmental conditions, etc. An approach to solve the problem of nutrition is to be made not only by striving to produce more through improved methods of cultivation and developing high yielding varieties, but also through efforts of population control, various types of nutrition programmes and education in relation to nutrition.

Geography syllabus presents a very good scope to integrate some important concepts on nutrition at various levels of school education. An effort has been made to develop a sample unit on nutrition through the teaching of Geography at High School stage. The Unit consists of general objectives of the unit, key concept of health and a major concept related to nutrition, which is further broken into 10 subconcepts which may be integrated in the

Geography curriculum at the school stage. Further for each subconcept, detailed outline of content to be organised under each concept has been worked out and suggested teaching-learning activities have been listed. Teachers may develop their own instructional objectives for day-to-day teaching depending upon the local resources and their competency in terms of methods. Regarding evaluation it has been recommended that the same procedure will be followed which is required to evaluate the teaching of Geography beside the day-to-day questions by the teacher in the classroom and feedback from students and parents through discussions with them.

General Objectives

1. To develop an insight into the influence of land-population ratio on nutrition and development.
2. To develop an understanding of the influence of economic and social constraints on nutritional status of people in a country facing rapid population growth.
3. To develop an understanding of the differences in foods of people living in various geographical and cultural environments and their effect on physical and mental development.
4. To develop an understanding of the relationship of nutrition with human performance—physical and mental.
5. To develop an appreciation of special nutritional needs of infants, children, and pregnant women and lactating mothers.

Key Concept of Health

Health is an ecologic resultant involving the interaction of many factors and conditions.

Major Concepts

A variety of factors emerging from physical, economic and socio-cultural environment of individuals may be responsible to malnutrition and under-nutrition of people leading to poor health and ultimately affecting the prosperity of a nation.

Suggested Content and Activities for Developing the Concepts

Subconcepts	*Content to be Organised under the Subconcept*	*Suggested Teaching Learning Activities*
1	*2*	*3*
1. The green revolution without check on rapid population growth is only a partial solution for our food problem writing out of rapid population growth.	Food needs of the country (plan wise). Crop land under cultivation, Measures to increase food production in the country and at local levels. Problem of unequal distribution of food	Visa to nearby farm to intent themselves can local rose production. Visit to market places inverse fees availability and cost comparison. Display on bulletin boards; of materials related to local and national problems of food.
	Relationship of population control with nutritional status of people.	Diagrammatic representation of statistics on food production and requirement for the preceding five year, plot.
		Discussion on topics related to contemporary food problem. Panel discussion on food problems involving government and public personnel.
		Visit to small and big families from same socio-economic strata of Society and follow-up discussion about the observations or the quality of life in those families.
	Discussion on population growth since 1951, Implication of large families on (i) Mother's health (ii) Children's growth and development	Display of nutrition profiles and diet profiles of different socio-economic groups and states.

Subconcepts	*Content to be Organised under the Subconcept*	*Suggested Teaching Learning Activities*
1	*2*	*3*
	Incidence of nutritional deficiency, diseases at national, state, and local levels over a number of Relationship of nutritional status and work efficiency. Per capita availability of food gains over a period or time in relation to total increase in food production. Relationship of nutrition to health and health to national prosperity. Functions of food satisfies hunger, provides energy, helps in growth and maintenance and provides body resistance against diseases. Factors influencing food requirements of various categories of people.	Visit to MCH centre to learn about problems related to health. Visit to centre of special nutrition programme in urban and rural areas and discussion/ interview with expects involved in the programme. Preparation of diagrams supporting are message with the help of available smashes. Self analysis by students of their diet intake for its nutritive contribution. Evaluating school snack or meal programme and its contribution dietary arms.
	General classification of local fruits based on their nutritive value.	Collection of food beliefs and superstitions existing in the Rival community
	Detrimental effect of food beliefs and superstition on health-physical, menial, and social Seasonal variation in local diets and its implication oil nutrition.	An Analysis of local food availability from quality point of view, (Milk, Pulses, vegetables—leafy, and others, and fruits etc.)
4. Overeating is at health problem.	Health and nutrition implications of overeating.	Discussion by health nutrition aspects. Discussion on usual liking for specific food items which students

Subconcepts	*Content to be Organised under the Subconcept*	*Suggested Teaching Learning Activities*
1	*2*	*3*
		might have or have observed in others and implications of these habits on health and nutrition of people.
4. Overeating is at health problem.	Food components of an adequate diet.	Collection of live samples or models of seasonal foods and displaying them according to their food values in the school museum and inviting community to view.
5. All nutrients needed for growth and functioning of the body are available through a variety of foods.	Cost-nutrient value of various food items of similar food groups. Salient parts required in diet planning.	Preparation of charts giving cost and moment contribution of selected common food items.
6. Many kinds of foods are available to be selected for an adequate diet from foods produced under local climatic conditions.		Plan menus for breakfast, snacks, lunch, and dinner from locally available seasonal food items to provide adequate food requirements.
7. Food practices are an integral part of socio-cultural patterns.	Socio-cultural influence of diets of people in different parts of the country and around the world.	Display of regional foods and discussion on it. Collection of recipes from different parts of the country.
	Influence of cultures and food practices on nutrition of vulnerable groups.	Collection of a list of food habits of local mothers which adversely effects child. Talk by family planners MCH/ social workers on the

Subconcepts	*Content to be Organised under the Subconcept*	*Suggested Teaching Learning Activities*
1	2	3
8. Storage and processing practices can improve food availability, variety, palatability and higher nutrition quality of food.	Traditional and indigenous two storage facilities in respect of grain loss and foul value. Measures to prevent loss of food value during processing.	effects child. Talk by family planners MCH/ social workers on the effect of their programme on changing the dietary practices. Visit to a village to collect facts about prevalent food storage facilities and discussion with villagers on the advantages and disadvantages of them. Discussion with farmers on innovations. Demonstration by Home Science teachers on food processing practices. A Home project on propagating improve food processing practice in their homes and report to their class about their experience.
9. Growth and development of human beings and plants can be affected by nutrition and its interplay with heredity and environment.	Influence of heredity an human growth. Influence of nutritional status of parents, especially (if mother on doe newborn child and him potential for development Influence of the environment on the growth and development of children).	To visit urban slum an rural communities to see sanitary conditions, water facilities, drainage and their influence on the health of the inhabitants. Microscopic examination of water and food-born soil-born, and air-born pathogen in laboratories. Field visit to observe soakage pits, RCA latrines. Discussion by an expert on measures taken by the Government to prevent food adulteration and food contamination.

Evaluation of this Unit may be done in accordance with the evaluation of Geography unit. No separate procedures exclusively for this Unit are suggested.

Trend of Urbanisation

Some urban centres in India flourished from time to time though the country has always been predominantly rural in character. For example, Varanasi and Prayag were good centres of learning for so many ceramics. In 19th and early 20th century Mumbai and Kolkata were famous industrial centres. The process of urbanisation however has particularly grown in the twentieth cetury. The definition of an urban unit was fixed first of all in 1961, according to which the term included all municipalities with 5,000 or inhabitants. A place with less than 5,000 inhabitants could be considered urban if the Census Superintendent believed to be so Since the 1961 Census the criteria for urban localities are : (i) Urban density of not less than 1,000 per square mile (ii) at least three-fourth of the working population should be engaged in non-agricultural activities. However, all the localities with the municipal local self-government were included in urban class irrespective of the fact whether they fulfilled the above criteria or not.

Urban Population on Rise

Indian censuses have classified the towns in six classes on the basis of population sizes as follows : 1-1,00,000 and over, 11-50,000 to 99,999, III-20,000 to 49,999, IV-10,000 to 19,999, V-51000 to 9,999, VI-below 5,000.

In 1960 there were only 111 cities in the world with a population of more than million. Today their number is 280. Of the two-third and in developing countries.

Metropolitan Cities Getting Overcrowded

In 1971 the sequences of the first 10 largest cities in India was as follows : Kolkata, Greater Mumbai, Delhi, Chennai, Hyderabad Ahmedabad, Banglore, Kanpur, Pune, Nagpur. According to Registrar General of India the urban population increased to 205.1 million by 1991 and to 278.3 million by 2001.

Life in Indian metropolitan cities like Kolkata, Mumbai, Delhi and Chennai is becoming a nightmare for a majority of the People and if the present trends continue, there will be a total failure of the urban system by the end of the century, according to environmentalist Rashmi Mayor. Dr. Mayor points out that while there is an appreciable decline or stabilisation of large cities in industrialised countries, the pace of urbarnisation is increasing significantly in the less developed nations, Mexico, India and Egypt being prime examples. Dr. Mayor lists the present urban growth rate at four per cent yearly, approximately twice the rate of population growth, half the growth being natural and, the rest due to migration from rural areas. The present rate of urbanisation, he says, will be accelerated after 1985 and by the end of the century, the approximate number in various urban centres all over India will reach 335 to 350 million people.

According to Press Trust of India, Mumbai's population is expected to almost double during the next 20 years, making it the second most populous city in the world after Tokyo, according to projections by the United Nations.

Mumbai is at present the sixth largest urban agglomeration with a population of 14.5 million. It is expected to gain 12.9 million residents to tally a population of 27.4 million by 2015.

Kolkata with 11.5 million people is also among the top 15 urban agglomerations.

Tokyo is currently the largest agglomeration with 26.5 million people, none than one and half times as large as the second largest agglomeration, New York with 163 million inhabitants.

Urbanization at Slow Pace

The growth of urban population in the country during the last decade (1981-1991) has surprisingly slowed down by about ten per cent, as compared to the earlier decade of 1971-1981. This is also an index of the new trend of a comparative slowed down migration of people from rural to urban area in the country during the last decade.

This interesting aspect has been brought out in the latest report of the Registrar-General and Census Commissioner on "Rural-Urban Distribution" of the country's population (Paper-2) on the basis of the 1991 census. During 1971-1981, the growth of urban population was recorded as 46.14 per cent, and between 1981-1991, it went down to 36.19 per cent.

This is notwithstanding the fact that the number of cities and towns has been consistently increasing. There were 3,126 cities and towns in 1971, and the figure went up to 4,029 in 1981 and it now stood at 4,689. The urban population in the country was now 25.72 per cent of the country, more than 84.43 crore population.

With the change of growth pattern, the big four cities, which were earlier classified as metropolitan cities, were no longer metros; they have "graduated" into "mega cities" now. The four megacities with a population of more than five million are Mumbai, Kolkata, Delhi and Chennai. Then comes metros, which are now 23, with each having a population of between one and five million. These included Hyderabad, Bangalore, Ahmedabad, Pane, Kanpur, Ludhiana, Baroda, Patna, Varanasi and Nagpur.

The growth of urban population has, however, been uneven. If no one extreme is Haldia, where the population growth recorded during the last decade was about 374 per cent, Vanparai in Tamil Nadu represented the other extreme with a minus eight per cent in growth.

Big cities (Class 1) in 15 States like West Bengal Andhra Pradesh Maharashtra, Madhya Pradesh, Uttar Pradesh and Tamil Nadu had more than 50 per cent of urban population. Again, in the two States of Maharashtra and West Bengal, the share of population was very high, viz- 77.85 per cent and 81.71 per cent, respectively. About two-thirds of the urban population in Gujarat, Karnataka and a few other States lived in class-one cities.

In terms of levels of urbanisation in various States, the position is rather perplexing. In several States like Gujarat, Tamil Nadu, Karnataka and Punjab, the level of urbanisation has been higher than the national average of 25.72—varying between 26 and 34 per cent.

Another interesting point brought out in the just released census report (which is follow-up of the one on population released a few months ago) is that the "tempo" of urbanisation has slowed down. The annual growth has declined from 3.09 per cent during the next decade (1981-1991).

Among the States, Mizoram has recorded a growth rate in urban population of 160.27 per cent.

Delhi has, however, shown a rapid increase in its population over the years. In 1911, its population was about 2.38 lakh, the year when Delhi became the national Capital. By 1951, it recorded a very large growth of 106.58 per cent. But later the tempo of the growth rate started slowing down from 1961 onwards—from 54.57 per cent during 1961-1971 to 46.18 per cent during 1981-1991.

Factors of Migration

The most important source of data concerning migration in India are the decennial population Census reports. In the Census 1881 a question was asked from the respondent about his or her place of birth and the period of residence at present place. This provided data concerning internal migration in India. Since then this question was repeated in every Census operation. The scope of Census operation widened in every decade. In 1961 Census information was collected on the duration of residence at the place of enumeration. In 1971 Census a question was asked about the place of last residence. Information was also asked about the district and State of the birth place. Another important source of data concerning migration in India were the National Sample Surveys. The Just National Sample Survey was concluded in 1951 providing data about migration. Since then so many surveys have provided important data about inter-State migration, rural-urban migration and international migration in the Indian contest.

Migration Trends

In the Census 1931 the number of persons born outside India were enumerated as 7,30,546. It was estimated that roughly 2.5 million Indians were living outside the country. This gives a lifetime migration balance of 1.75 million persons. According to Census 1961, 9.5 million persons living in India were born outside the country. Of these 8.3 million came from Pakistan and Bangladesh. Thus, 1.2 million foreigners were living in India. According to 1971 Census, the persons born out of India numbered 0.9 million including 0.81 million immigrants from Pakistan and

Bangladesh. The number of foreigners was therefore 0.9 million in 1971—0.4 million males and 0.5 million females; 0.6 million urban and 0.3 million rural. According to 1971 Census and most of the Census reports in India it has been established that Indian population is virtually immobile. In 1961 Census, 68.6% of the population was enumerated at the place of birth. In 1971 this percentage was 68.8%. This shows that the percentage of the immobiles was almost double thom that of the migrants, though the percentage of the immobiles was almost double in 1971 Census. Another important trend in migration in India is that most of the migrants move to only short distances. According to 1971 Census, 65.84% of migrant population was born outside the district of enumeration. The Census operation from 1891 to 1931 indicated that the percentage of persons enumerated in the province of their birth was almost static. Thus, the tendency of inter-State migration has not changed in India. According to kingsley Davis, the most important factors determining the immobility of Indian population were predominance of agriculture, the caste system, early marriage, joint family, diversity of languages, variety of culture and lack of education, etc.

A third important trend in internal migration in India is the predominance of females among the migrants. It is due to the custom of married women migrating to the place of their husbands. However, female migrations is generally at short distances. Village exogamy has been an important factor in female migration in India.

In the history of Indian Demography, the problem of migration became complicated in 1947 due to the influx of refuges from both the wings of Pakistan. Another important factor was the reorganization of States, Union Territories and delimitation of district boundaries. The economic development and industrialisation of several areas in the country was another important factor in the increase in migration. Migration in India can be studied as Cummulative Lifetime Migration, Net Migration, Rural Urban Migration, Marriage Migration, Lifetime Migration and Migration by Age. This will be now discussed in more details.

As a result of inter-State migration during 1951-1971 the following States gained in population: West Bengal Maharashtra, Delhi, Madhya Pradesh, Assam, Punjab, Mysore (Karnataka) and

Gujarat. The following States were the losers: Uttar Pradesh, Bihar, Kerala, Rajasthan, Andhra Pradesh, Tamil Nadu, Orissa, Jammu and Kashmir. According to the estimates of net migration during 1961-1971, however, Tamil Nadu, Jammu and Kashmir, Bihar, Orissa gained in population. On the other hand, Karnataka and Punjab lost in population. The States of Uttar Pradesh, Kerala and Andhra Pradesh remained among the losing States. In nearly all the States the net migration of males has been greater than that of the females. The overall direction of population redistribution through internal migration during the period 1951-1961 has been from areas of comparatively low economic development to areas of higher economic development.

Cumulative lifetime migration is not a satisfactory index of migration. Therefore, internal migration has been estimated by the Census; survival method. United Provinces, Bihar and Orissa, Rajputana, Chennai, Hyderabad, Punjab, Bengal and Jammu and Kshmir lost their population due to out-migration whereas Assam, Mumbai, Central Provinces, Central India, Travancore-Cochin and Mysore gained. United provinces, which in 1931 had 14 per cent of the population of the country and 6 per cent of the total land areas lost 760 thousand people during 1901-31. During 1901-11, 1,57,000 males moved out of United Provinces and 40,000 moved in. Thus, the net loss was 1,17,000 males. But 64,000 females moved out and 67,000 moved in so that there was a net gain of 3,000 females. The combined net loss, however, was 1,14,000. Likewise in the 1921-1931 decade 274,000 males and 1,65,000 females moved out, while 68,000 males and 87,000 females moved in. The net loss was of 2;06,000 males and 78,000 females the total being out-migration from United Provinces has been mostly to Bengal, Mumbai and Punjab.

Bihar and Orissa lost about 88,000 persons to Bengal and 14,000 to Assam during 1921-1931. But Bengal, in turn, lost 2,66,000 persons to Assam during the same period. 1911-1921, Bengal gained 2,98,000 persons from Bihar and Orissa and lost 2-,2,000 to Assam. Assam gained 5,75,000 persons during 1911-1921 and 3,28,000 during 1921-1931.

Analysing the data of inter-State net migration in India as given by different Census reports, S.N. Agarwala has pointed out, "It is indeed surprising that burring Mumbai (Maharashtra), Mysore (Karnataka) and Travancore-Cochin (Kerala) all other States should have lost due to out-migration during the 1941-1951 decade. Assam, which has always been a gainer, also shows net out-migration during the decade. It appears that the assumptions which have been made for estimating internal migration by States may not be wholly appropriate."

Migration from Village to Town

Most of the studies of migration in India have revealed that the migration from rural to urban areas is very small in comparison to migration from one rural area to the other. Migration by marriage is generally from one rural area to another. It is only in the search of occupation that migrants go to urban areas from the village. The speed, however, is very slow. According to the Census 1971 among the migrants in India 70.66% were from one rural area to other. The rural-urban migration was 14.88%, the urban-rural migration was barely 4.89%. In the study of rural-urban migration, four aspects have to be particularly studied. These are : 1. rural to rural migration or rural turnover; 2. rural to urban migration or push-pull activity-, 1 urban to urban migration or urban turnover; and 4. urban to rural migration or reverse push back. According to the estimate by Zachariah, the rural-urban migration in India during the period 1951-1961 was 5.2 million. This is 8.4% of the 1951 urban population. According to a recent report India continues to be predominantly rural although its urban population increased by more than 49 million during the 1971-1981 decade. The rural-urban distribution of the population obtained from the quick tabulation of provisional totals of the 1981 Census shows that 76.27 per cent of the population is rural.

The Census Commissioner recently released figures putting the urban population in 1981 at 15,61,88,507. The balance of the total population 65,81,40,676 is considered rural. These figures exclude Assam where the Census has not so far been held and Jammu and Kashmir where the Census was taken two months after the February-March enumeration in the rest of the nation.

The 1981 urban population of 23.73 per cent compared to 20.22 in 1971,18.26 in 1961, and 17.62 in 1951 when the first post-independence Census was taken. The population was a mere 10.40 per cent in 1911. Dadra and Nagar Haveli as well as Lakshadweep entered the streame of urbanisation for the first time during the 1971-1981 decade. Maharashtra is the most urbansed State with 35.05 per cent of its population in urban areas. Tamil Nadu, Gujarat, Karnataka, Punjab and West Bengal follow in descending order. These States have a higher urban population than the national average of 23.73 per cent. At the other end, Himachal Pradesh, Dadra and Nagar Haveli and Arunachal Pradesh have more than 90 per cent of their population in rural areas.

Kerala, Meghalaya, Uttar Pradesh, Sikkim, Nagaland, Bihar, Orissa and Tripura have more than 80 per cent rural population, Nagpmr, Lucknow and Jaipur crossed the one million mark at the 1981 Census. They joined the group of Kolkata, Greater Mumbai, Delhi, Chennai, Hyderabad, Ahmedabad, Bangalore, Kanpur and Pune as big cities or urban agglomerations. Together the 12 does and urban agglomerations account for 44-56 per cent of the urban population.

Trichur in Kerala has the highest literacy rate of 81.09 per cent. Sambhal in Uttar Pradesh is the least literate city (24.84 per cent).

According to the 1971 Census, of the 548 million population in 1971, 376 million remained at their place of birth, 310 million in the rural areas, and 66 million in the urban area. Among the remaining 172 million persons, 108 million were enumerated within the district of enumeration and another 36 million within the State. Only 19 million persons were enumerated in a State outside their place of birth and 0.9 million persons born in countries other than India. Most of the 19 million persons who migrated outside the State of their birth moved short distances ınd to border districts.

1. The 1991 Census could not be held in Assam. The figures for 1981 for Assam have been worked out by interpolation.
2. Includes projected population of Jammu and Kashmir.

Migrations Due to Marriage

A sex-wise break-up of the data concerning migration in India shows that more females than males migrated. In 1961 the break-up of migration from rural to rural was 23.73% male and 7627% female. The number of females was higher even in urban to rural migration. In 1961, this was 39.15% males and 60.85% females. On the other hand, as has been pointed out earlier, among rural to urban migrants the number of males was higher being 54.03% while the per cent of female migrants was; 45.97, According to 1971 migration data in India, 22.42% male and 77.58% females migrated from rural to rural; 37.13% males and 62.87% females migrated from urban to rural areas. The percentage of migrants from rural to urban areas in 1971 was 52,07 and 47.93 respectively. These data show that among migrants from rural to rural and urban to rural the percentage of females is how in India. This is due to marriage migration. The chief causes of migration in urban area marriage, transfer of the earning member, search of employment and search of better employment. Of the total rural migration roughly 1/2 of the female migration is marriage migration. The percentage of women migrating from rural areas to urban areas in search of employment is very limited in India. Marriage migration accounts for migration of 0.6% males and 46.2% females in all the urban areas. The most important cause of female migration is marriage followed by transfer of the earning member. The most important cause of migration for male, however, is search for employment followed by transfer of the earning member.

The Age Factor

Several studies of migration in India have established male the heaviest migration in both the sexes; it is found in the age groups 15-34 and 35-39. Among males 16.6% belong to the age group 0-14; 48% to age group of 15-34; 30.7% to the age group of 35-39 and 4.7% to the age group of 60 and above. The corresponding percentage for females according to 1971 Census were 20.5; 47.3; 26.0 and 6.2. The higher number of migrants in younger age is due to the mobility of youths marriage, search fair better employment, etc. It is due to the absence of all these causes that migration is very low in upper age groups.

Migration for Life

Lifetime migration is studied by the distance of migration. Migration within the district is called short distance migration. Migration within the state is known as medium distance migration. Migration between states is known as long distance migration. All these types of lifetime migration may be rural to rural, rural to urban, urban to rural and urban to urban. In India, it has been found by the migration during the period 1961-1971 that lifetime migration was as follows: Short-distance migration was 70% of the female and 50% male migration. Long-distance migration accounted far 20% of the male and 10% of the female migration. Medium-distance migration accounted for 27.44% male migration and 19.88% female migration. There is not much significant difference in the percentage of short distance, medium distance and long distance lifetime migration during the Census 1961 and 1971. The most important lifetime migration both among males and females in India is short distance and that too rural to rural. This is followed by medium distance lifetime migration with the same tendency of maximum rural to rural migration. Long-distance migration, however, is a bit distant. While among females it is maximum from rural to rural, among males it is maximum from rural to urban.

QUESTIONS

1. Write short note on overcrowding in cities.
2. Write short note on slow urbanisation in India.
3. Describe the main features of Indian Population in 1991 causes.
4. What are the caus of fast growth of Indian Population ?
5. What is Migration ? Describe its types.
6. Write an essay on Migration in India.

8

Demographic Situation

The Indians knew the value of population studies since ancient times. The Arthashastra of Kautilya gives a detailed description of how to conduct a population, economic and agricultural census. During the reign of Akbar the great Abul Fazal compiled the Ain-e-Akbari containing comprehensive data on population, industry, wealth and traits of population. During the British period the system of decennial census started with the first census in 1872. This was particularly planned to understand the traits of Indian population based upon the census reports from 1872 to 1941. Kingsley Davis, the well known demographer, produced his monumental work The Population of India and Pakistan, which is valued even today for its contribution to the progress of population studies in India.

India will be the most populated country in the world in 2050 with a population above one and a half billion, leaving China behind.

An important contribution to the growth of demography in India has been made by Imperial Gazetteers. The first Imperial Gazetteer was published in 1881 in 9 volumes at the instance of W.W. Hunter. In 1882 a companion volume entitled The Indian Empire : Its History, People and Products, was published. Revised versions of the Imperial Gazetteers were published in 26 volumes during the period 1907 and 1909. The first volume of the Imperial Gazetteer contains discussion on matters such as nutrition, early marriages, birth rate, relationship between marriage customs and birth rate, rural urban birth and death rates, differential in mortality by sex, religion, rural urban residence, infant mortality, causes of death and health conditions in European and the native countries. This was the section of Public Health and Vital Statistics. It may be noted here that all these subjects form the subject matter of modern demography. However, before 1930, not much progress was made in India towards the growth of demography. The First Indian Population Conference was held in 1936 under the auspices of the University of Lucknow. At this Conference a paper entitled "Future Growth of India's Population" was presented. The Second All-India Conference on Population and the First Family Hygiene Conference was held in Mumbai in 1938 and a paper on differential fertility based on field experience in Cochin State was presented. An interesting controversy regarding the rate of population growth ensued at this Conference and was continued later between Professor B.R Adarkar of Allahabad University and Dr. K.C.K.E. Raja of Chennai Public Health Services (who later became the Director of Demographic Training and Research Centre, Mumbai) which kept the question of population growth alive. At about this time, Professor Adarkar started teaching an optional paper on "Population Problems" to the M.A. Economics students of Allahabad University.

The Second All-India Conference on Population and the First Family Hygiene Conference were jointly held in Mumbai in 1938. Apart from discussing the social and medical aspects of birth control and human sexuality several other subjects related to population studies were covered. These included differential fertility, maternity and child welfare, infant mortality, homing and health, nutrition, morbidity, vital statistics, logistic law of growth of the Indian population, economic problems associated with population size and growth, such as population and unemployment, poverty and population, optimum theory of population sociological analysis and forecast of population growth. Thus it is clear that Indian scholars were gradually taking interest in different aspects of demographical studies. The interest was formerly centred around the discussion whether India was over population. Among the most important books written on this subject during this period may be mentioned Food Planning for

Four Hundred Millions by Radhakamal Mukerjee; published by MacMillan (London) in 1938. This book emphasised the need for agricultural development. It was followed by another equally important publication India's Teeming Millions by Gyan Chand published by George Allen and Unwin (London), in 1939. This book discussed the population problem from the economic viewpoint.

In 1936 Enid Charles presented his book Twilight of Parenthood, which maintained that the population of India was slowly increasing. This aroused an interesting controversy between Dr. K.C.K.E. Raja, a public health worker, and Professor Adarkar, an economist, about the trend of future population growth in India. The two scholar maintained the opposite view. Other important books concerning population problem in India, published during this period include P.K. Wattal, Population Problem in India (1916), Brij Narain, The Population in India (1925), B.K. Sarkar, The Sociology of Population (1936), S. Chandrasekhar, India's Population-Fact and Policy (1946) D. Ghosh, The Pressure of Population and Economic Efficiency in India (1946).

During the period 1940 to 1956 the Government of India started taking interest in population studies. In 1944, the Department of Education, Health and Lands set up the Population Data Committee under the Chairmanship of W.M. Yeats to advise the Government of India on the available data relating to growth of population. The Family Planning Association of India was founded in Mumbai in 1949 and it started propagating population control. In 1946, the Government of India appointed the Health Survey and Development Committee (popularly known as the Bhore Committee) to study health condition in India and to make recommendations for their improvement. The Committee made a thorough study of the activities in the field of population, Vital and Population Statistics. One of the important recommendations of this Committee was that "the population problem should be the subject of continuous study." Important field enquiries were made by the Indian Statistical Institute, in pre-independent period under the able directorship of Prof. P.C. Mahalanobis. The Institute collected data on fertility through field enquiries. In 1945, the All India Institute of Hygiene and Public Health, Kolkata conducted several field studies under the guidance of Dr. C. Chandrasekharan. In 1942 Prof. N. V Sovani of the Gokhale Institute of Politics and Economics, Pune, published a study entitled,: The Population Problem in India : A Regional Approach.

Developments before Independence

The following are important landmarks in post-independence growth of demography in India.

The 1951 Census

The first post-independence census report was prepared by the Census Commissioner R.A. Gopalaswami in 1951. This report covered not only the size and distribution of the population but also change in it, Dr. Gopalaswami warned about the dangers of rapid population growth and said, "It is extremely important that the attention of the people should be focused on this factor of improvident maternity ... The occurrence of improvident maternity should evoke social disapproval of any other form of social indulgence.."[1] Hearing this warning the government paid particular attention to family planning in five year plans.

In 1952, the National Family Planning Programme was launched in India to control population growth.

The National Sample Survey

In 1949 the National Sample Survey System was established to meet the need of census data and the data for the evaluation of development plans. The National Sample Survey (NSS) collected data on differential fertility, family planning knowledge, attitude and practice for rural and urban areas, internal migration, employment, etc.

Field Surveys

Some important field surveys were made during this period. In 1952-53 was made the Mysore Population Study, jointly sponsored by UNO and the Government of India. This study brought out social and cultural factors affecting fertility in India it served as a model for other fertility surveys. A notable survey on fertility and mortality, conducted by Professor V.M. Dandekar and Prof. Kumudini Dandekar in Nasik, Satins and Kolaba Districts, also contributed to a better understanding of fertility behaviour in India.

Demographic Centrals

The Central Family Planning Board set up in 1956, appointed a subcommittee on Demographic Studies under the chairmanship of Dr. V.K.R.V Rao. This sub-committee recommended the establishment of four demographic research centres in different parts of the country, where studies might be conducted in fertility mortality and associated factors. As a result, the Demographic Training and Research Centre (now known as the International Institute for Population Studies) was established in Mumbai in 1956; the Demographic Research Centres in Kolkata, Delhi and Trivandrum in 1957; and the one at Dharwar was established in 1960.

Population Studies Institute

This Institute was established for training and research in population studies. It has few functions :, Teaching, Research, Consultative services and Documentation. According to an assessment in 1976-77, the institute trained 569 persons, out of which 355 were from India and 214 from various countries of the ESCAP region. The institute's library, perhaps the best in the world, has a stock of 27,500 books and 5,850 reprints. It subscribes to most of the periodicals on population and associated fields. Among the important studies of UPS are the following :

(i) K.C. Zachariah, A Historical Study of Internal Migration in the Indian Sub-continent 1901-1931, Mumbai: Asia Publishing House, 1964.

(ii) C. Chandrasekharan and K. Ruder, Family Planning Through Clinics, Mumbai : Asia Publishing House, 1965.

(iii) S. Kono and M. Shio, Inter-Prefectural Migration Streams Analysis, Mumbai : Asia Publishing House, 1966.

(iv) K.V. Ramachandran et al., A Survey of School Children in Greater Mumbai, Mumbai : Asia Publishing House, 1968.

(v) K.C. Zachariah, Migrants in Greater Mumbai Asia Publishing House, 1968.

(vi) K.V. Ramchandran and G. Shantakumar, Fertility Differentials in West Malaysia, Mumbai International Institute for Population Studies, 1974. Demographic Research

In 1959, the Demographic Advisory Committee was appointed by the Ministry of Health, mainly to co-ordinate research on population. The Family Planning Communication Action Research Committee was set up in 1960 to co-ordinate and promote research in family planning, communication and motivation. The two committees were merged in 1967 to form the Demographic and Communication Action Research Committee which became defunct when its term expired on November 3, 1971. This Committee was reconstituted on December 6, 1972, as the Committee on Socio-Economic Studies on Family Planning to cover the economic, sociological, educational, psychological, communicational and demographic aspects of population growth and family planning.

Institutions Engaged in Demographic Research

Name of the Centre/Institution	*Areas of Research Activities*
1. Administrative Staff College, Hyderabad.	Family planning management, health management and information system.
2. Central Statistical Organisation, New Delhi	Population projections, fertility.
3. Demograhic Research Centre, Bureau of Economics and Statistic, Trivandrum.	Family planning, fertility, migration.
4. Demograhic Research Centre, Gokhale Institute of Politics and Economics, Pune.	Fertility, family planning demographic surveys, inter-district migration.
5. Demographic Research Cetre, Banaras Hindu University, Varanasi.	Mathematical models, small-scale sample surveys.
6. Demographic Research Centre, Indian Statistical Institute, Calcutta.	Fertility family planning mortality, nuptiality.
7. Demographic Research Centre, Institute of Economic Growth, Delhi.	Migration, urbanisation, fertility changes.

Contd.

Name of the Centre/Institution	*Areas of Research Activities*
8. Demographic Research Centre, Institute of Economic Research, Dharwar.	Fertility, demographic surveys of cities.
9. Demographic Research Centre, Lucknow University, Lucknow.	Fertility, demographic surveys, population projections.
10. Demographic Research Centre, Patna University, Patna.	Demographic surveys, biostatistical studies, mathematical models.
11. Demographic Research Centre, Patna University, Patna.	Fertility, Family Planning demographic surveys
12. Demographic Research Unit, Jadavpur University, Jadavpur.	Mathematical models, metropolitan area studies.
13. Department of Statistics, University of Kerala, Kerala.	Fertility, fertility surveys, family growth study, population models.
14. Economics Department, Mumbai University, Mumbai.	Migration, economic activity analysis, sex ratio.
15. Indian Institute of Management, Ahmedabad.	Family planning management, management information and evaluation system.
16. Indian Institute of Management, Bangalore.	Family Planning
17. Indian Institute of Management, Bangalore.	Health statistics.
18. International Institute for Population Studies, Mumbai. communication and evaluation, mortality and population simulation model.	Fertility, nuptiality, migration, family planning attitude.
19. Institute of Manpower Research, New Delhi.	Area man-power surveys. man-power studies.
20. National Council of Applied Economic Research, New Delhi.	Population projections, city surveys.
21. National Sample Survey, Delhi.	Fertility employment and unemployment, births and deaths
22. Office of the Registrar General of India, New Delhi	Census operations, mortality, fertility birth registration.
23. Operation Research Group, Baroda.	Family planning and fertility surveys.
24. Planning and Evaluation Division, Ministry of Health and Family Planning, New Delhi.	Family planning programme evaluation.
25. Population Centre, India Population Project, Bangalore.	Surveys, evaluation, management studies.

Contd.

Name of the Centre/Institution	*Areas of Research Activities*
26. Population Centre India Lucknow. Population Project, Lucknow.	Benchmark surveys, family planning management studies, nutrition and family planning evaluation, family planning training, management information and evaluation system.
27. Population Studies Centre, Sri Venkateshwara University, Tirupati.	Population education, cost-benefit studies.

Family Planning Communication Action Research Centres

Name of the Centre/Institution	Areas of Research Activities
1. All India Institute of Hygiene and Public Health, Calcutta.	KAP, evaluation, communication.
2. Council for Social Development, India International Centre, New Delhi.	Infant and child mortality, fertility and marriage.
3. Demographic Communication Action Research Centre, Institute for Social and Economic Change, Bangalore.	KAP, evaluation city surveys.
4. Department of Psychology, University of Patna, Patna.	Attitude scale.
5. Department of Rural Economics and Sociology, Utkal University, Bhubaneswar.	Family planning communication.
6. Department of Sociology, University of Kerala, Trivandrum.	KAP, evaluation, communication.
7. Family Planning Research Unit, Indian Statistical Institute, Calcutta.	Evaluation, motivation, communication.
8. Gokhale Institute of Politics and Economics, Poona.	KAP, organizational aspects evaluation, communication.
9. Indian Institute of Technology.	Family planning attitude
10. Institute of Rural Health and Family Planning, Gandhigram.	Family planning training, family planning and health evaluation studies, fertility and mortality.
11. International Institute for Population Studies, Mumbai.	KAP, family planning evaluation, family planning communication, cost-benefit analysis, target setting.
12. Institute for Economic and Social Change, Bangalore	Migration, regional activities.

Contd.

	Name of the Centre/Institution	Areas of Research Activities
13.	National Institute of Family Planning, New Delhi.	KAP, Planning evaluation, family planning communication.
14.	Population Centre, India, Population Project, Bangalore.	Family planning nutrition.
15.	Population Centre, India, Population Project, Lucknow.	Family planning, nutrition.
16.	Shri V. T. Krishnamachari Institute of Rural Health, Vadodra.	Training, evaluation, KAP, organizational aspects.

Demography Taught

Many Indian universities today have provision for teaching and research in demography. At the post-graduate level demography was taught leading to M.Sc. degree in the University of Kerala for the first time in India. In 1973 a Population Studies Centre was established at Shri Venkateshwara University, Tirupati. Since 1974 Demography is being taught at JNU. Besides, it forms a part of the syllabi as an optional paper in Economics at Agra, Aligarh, Allahabad, Varanasi, Vadodra, Mumbai, Kolkata, Gorakhpur, Lucknow, Meerut, Rajasthan, Sagar and other Universities. It is a part of the post-graduate courses in Sociology at Annamalai, Gorakhpur, Lucknow, Punjab, Vikram and Indore Universities. Besides, it is a part of M.Sc. Statistics course at Agra, Annamalai, Delhi, Gorakhpur, Karnataka, Pune and other Universities. Provision has been made for lectures on demography, population problem and Vital Statistics in post-graduate teaching in Economics, Statistics and Sociology at some 14 universities. The scope of teaching of the subject is fast expanding to other universities as well. The Indian Association for the Study of Population (IASP) started publication of a journal, Demography in India, in 1972, with financial support from the Family Planning Foundation of India. The demand for demographers is gradually increasing in this country.

The Census

This provided a wealth of information in the field of demography for students and research workers.

Asian Population Conference

In 1963 India hosted the First Asian Population Conference at New Delhi which encouraged demographical research in India.

The Sample Registration Scheme

This scheme was initiated in 1964-65 by the Registrar General of India, to obtain reliable estimates of birth and death rate and the rates of natural growth.

Indian Association for the Study of Population

A significant forward step in the development of Demography in India was taken in 1972 with the establishment of the Indian Association for the Study of Population.

The above brief review of the progress of Demography in India will not be complete without mention of some eminent demographers whose work has been acknowledged not only in this country but also in the West. Among them may be named Radhakamal Mukerjee, Gyan Chand, S.N. Agarwal, C. Chandra-sekharan, S. E Jain and S Chandrashekhar, R.A. Gopalaswami P.K. Watal, Brij Narain, B.K. Sarkar, D Ghosh among others. The formulae developed by S Chandrashekhar in collaboration with Deming to estimate the missing events of birth from vital registration and retrospective surveys are now widely used. A new technique for evaluating and adjusting Indian age data was developed by Mr. S.P. Jain. A significant contribution was made to the technique of analysing migration data collected through a census by Zachariah. Dr. S.N. Agarwal made important contribution to research in the field of family planning. Mr. J.R. Retry Present Director, International Institute for Population Studies has evolved a method of estimating birth and death rates and rates of natural increase from the data. Today, a large number of studies are being undertaken in different fields of demography. There have been numerous studies covering knowledge, attitude and practices concerning family planning. These are known as KAP studies. By March 1977 newly 450 studies were completed in the field of fertility alone. Thus the future of demography in this country appears to be bright.

The latest count reveals that India is the second largest populated country in the world accounting for 15,53 per cent of the estimated world population of 3721 million. But India accounts for only 2.4 per cent of the world area.

China is on the top with one thousand million people.

The population of India is now 6,83,810,051 according to the provisional figures arrived at after the 1981 census. This shows a growth rate of 24.75 per cent which is .05 per cent less than that recorded in the 1971 census. There has been a net addition of 1,356501399 since the 1971 census.

With the exception of Kerala, men continue to outnumber women in the country-the ratio now is 935 females to 1000 males.

The density of population is now 221 per sq. km.

Over 1.25 million field workers were mobilised to carry out the census operation-the biggest in the world. Counting supervisory personnel and staff at controlling levels the total task force that was at the census operations would be of the order of 4.5 million.

The census officer had classified eunuchs as 'males'. According to Mr. P. Padmanabha, Census Commissioner "eunuchs have been classified as 'males'. The dictionary defines eunuch as a "castrated male person". Prostitutes, whenever they volunteered the information, were classified as working women.

Many people who may have complained of having been missed by the enumerators may actually be fully enumerated. Often the information required was garnered from the neighbours or the servants of persons concerned.

Assam, Gujarat, Tripura and Mizoram have the distinction of always registering average higher than the all-India averages-from the 1901 census right through to 1981.

Though their population is small, the highest growth rates have been registered by Chandigarh at 74.95; Andaman and Nicobar Islands at 63.51 and Delhi at 52.41.

Women continue to outnumber men in Kerala.

In 1971 there were 161,673 more women in the State. But in 10 years the number has gone upto 427,295, according to provisional population figures announced.

The men in 1981 accounted for 12,497,961 as compared to 100597,581 in 1971. There were 12,915,256 women by March 1 compared to 10,759,524, 10 years earlier.

The total population of Kerala as on March 1, 1981 was 25,403,217. In 1971 it was, 21,347,375.

On the adverse female ratio-which is found only in India, Pakistan and Bangladesh-there is little evidence to support the view that female infants die due to deliberate neglect. On the other hand, there are certain diseases that selectively kill more women than men.

The females now number 330,462,802 and the males 353,347,20.

The population has doubled since independence. It may again double itself by 2001 unless the present trend of a declining growth rate is not only kept up but improved upon, in which case the projections are of the order of 950 million.

Uttar Pradesh has the population with 110,858,019, Bihar has 69,823,154; Maharashtra 62,693,898; West Bengal 54,485,56), and Andhra Pradesh 53,403,619.

Delhi has the highest density of population : 4178 per sq. km. The lowest is Arunachal Pradesh with seven persons per square km. The highest female to male ratio is in Kerala at 1034 to 1000 while adverse is in Andaman and Nicobar Islands where there are 761 females to 1000 males.

The literacy rate is now 36.17—for females it is 24.88 and for males 46.74. These figures do not include Jammu and Kashmir.

While the 1901 census showed that there were 1466 literate males for every 100 females, the 1981 head-count revealed 201 literate males for every 100 females.

Kerala continues to be the most literate state in the whole country with literacy rate of 69.17 per cent.

The next seven places are taken by union territories with Chandigarh reporting 64.68 per cent rate, Delhi 64.06 per cent, Mizoram 49.50, Goa 55.86, Lakshadweep 54.72, Pondicherry 54.23 and Andaman and Nicobar Islands 51.27 per cent.

The literacy percentage has increased in all the states and union territories since the last census.

For the country as a whole the literacy has been estimated at 36.17 per cent compared to 29.45 in 1971 and 24.02 per cent in 1961.

With 9,165,650 persons, Kolkata is the most thickly populated city in the country, according to 1981 census figures.

Greater Mumbai comes next with 8,202,759 followed by Delhi with 5,227,730 and Chennai 4,276,635.

Men outnumber women in all the 12 cities, where the population is above one million.

In all the four metropolitan cities, the literacy percentage was above 60 per cent with Greater Mumbai at the top with 68.16 per Cent. Sex-wise also Mumbai accounts for literates-males 74.43 per cent and females 60.58.

India's population, as on 1 March 1991 stood at 84630 million (439.23 million male and 407.07 million females). This includes the projected population of 7.72 million of Jammu Kashmir. The second largest populous country, India is the home of 16 per cent of world's population. The country, however, accounts for 2.42 per cent of the total world area.

The population of India as recorded at each decenial census from 1901 has grown steadily except for a decrease during 1911-21. In absolute terms the country's population has increased by 161.12 million during the decade 1981-91. This is ten times the population of Australia and is more than the population of Japan. An encouraging feature revealed by the provisional results is the decline in growth rate of the population in the last decade compared to 1971-81. It marginally decreased from 24.66 per cent recorded in 1971-81 to 23.85 per cent during 1981-91.

In most states the growth rate declared during the decade. However, Andhra Pradesh, Arunachal Pradesh, Madhya Pradesh, Maharashtra, Nagaland, Tripura, West Bengal, Domain and Diu, Lakshadweep and Pondicherry which account for one-third of the country's population, recorded increase in growth rate. Nagaland registered the highest growth rate of 56.86 per cent while Kerala the lowest 13.98 per cent.

On the Top

Uttar Pradesh continued to be the largest state, population-wise with 16.44 per cent people of the country living there (139,112,287) followed by Bihar with 1021 per cent

(86,374,465) and Maharashtra with 933 per cent (78,937,187), West Bengal occupied fourth place accounting for 8.04 per cent (68,077,965) of the country's population followed by Andhra Pradesh with 7.86 per cent (66,508,808).

Mumbai metropolis continued to be the most populated city of the country with urban population of 12.60 million, Kolkata taking the second place having 11.02 million. Delhi ranks third with population (urban) of 9.42 million followed by Chennai 5.42 million.

Density of Population

One of the important indices of population concentration is the density of population. It is defined as the number of persons per square kilometer. The population density has gone up from 216 in 1981 to 267 persons in 1991. In 1901 it was 77 persons. Among the union territory Delhi has the highest density of 6,352 persons per sq. km. followed by Chandigarh (5,632), Lakshadweep which has the smallest population size is the fourth most densely populated area with a density of 1,616 persons per sq. km. Pondicherry ranks third (1,642) followed by Daman and Diu (907). Arunachal Pradesh is the most sparsely populated area of the country with 10 persons per square kilometre.

The ten heavily populated districts of the country are Kolkata, Chennai, Greater Mumbai, Hyderabad, Delhi, Chandigarh, Mahe, Haora, Kanpur City and Bangalore. All of them have density of above 2,000 persons per square kilometer and 5.01 per cent of the country population lives in these districts. The average density of these ten districts is 6,888.

Male-female Ratio

In my study of the population, analysis of the sex composition plays a vital role. The sex composition of the population is affected by the differentials in the mortality conditions of males and females, sex selective migration and the sex ratio at birth.

Sex ratio is defined as the number of females per 1000 males. In India it has generally been adverse to men. The ratio has also declined over the years except in 1981 when it slightly improved to 934 from 927. In 1991, there has been a fall by seven points to 927 per thousand males. But Kerala represented a different spectrum. The state has higher number of females than males, 1,036 females for thousand males.

In the Indian context, a sex ratio of 950 and above be considered as favourable to females. The states and union territories coming under this category besides Kerala and Himachal Pradesh (976), Andhra Pradesh (972), Goa (967), Karnataka (960), Manipur (958), Orissa (971), Tamil Nadu (974), Dadra and Nagar Haveli (952), Daman and Diu (969) and Pondicherry (979). Chandigarh accounted for the lowest number of females per thousand male with 790.

Movement for Literacy

For the purpose of census, a person is deemed as literate if he or she can read and write any language with understanding. In the 1991 census, the question on literacy was canvassed only for population aged over years and above, unlike earlier censuses which took into account population of five years and above for this purpose.

The final results reveal that there has been an increase in literacy in the country. The literacy rate in the country (excluding Jammu and Kashmir) is 52.21 per cent (64.13 for males and 39.29 for females).

For the population aged over years and above the literacy rate has increased by 8.54 percentage points. The increase in male and female literacy rat are of the order of 7.63 and 9.44 points respectively.

Census—2001

The Census of India 2001, is historic and epoch making being the first census of the twenty-first century and the third millennium. It will reveal benchmark data on the state of abundant human resources habitating our country, their demography, culture and economic structure at a juncture, which marks a centennial and millenial transition.

Population–2001

India's population as on 1 March 2001 stood at 1,027 million (531.3 million males and 495.7 million females). India accounts for a meagre 2.4 per cent of the world surface area of 135.79 million sq km. Yet, it supports and sustains a whopping 16.7 per cent of the world population. The population of India, which at the turn of the twentieth century was around 238.4 million, increased to reach 1,027 million at the dawn of the twenty-first century.

Demographic Scenario in India

India is the seventh largest country in the world. It has an area of nearly 13 lakh square miles. It is one-third of USA and one-sixth of China but next to China, it has the largest population. India has 87 crore people. India is the biggest democracy in the world.

Population on Rise

The population of India was never so large before as it is today. In the days of Akbar, the total population was near about 7 crores only. Since then great changes have taken place. Vast jungles have been cleared. More and more land has been brought under cultivation. On account of advancement of science and technology during the last many years, life has become safer. Production of food grain has increased and the deaths from famines and epidemics practically eliminated. Education has expended. Living conditions have improved.

Our population has increased by about 94% during the period 1901-1961. The present rate of increase (2.1% per annum) is highest in the world. In the year 1999, our number will touch the figure 100 crores.

What happened in the past? Let us try to understand that.

Birth and Death Rates

Our birth rate of 40 per thousand has practically remained constant during the last 70 years, while the death rate has been reduced from 48.6 in 1911-21 to 18 per thousand in 1951-61. No Indian population increases at 2.2% per cent per annum compound interest.

High Mortality Before 1921 Due to Famines, Epidemics and Pestilences

Look at the records. We find that epidemics of plague, cholera, smallpox etc. were frequent. They affected large traits of the country and claimed a heavy toll of life. These abnormal events kept the death rate high. Monsoons failed. Food scarcity conditions affected India. And we should not forget First World War of 1914. People died like flies during 1911-20 or before 1921.

Declining Mortality after 1921

The situation changed radically after 1921. Except for the Bengal famine of 1943, which is estimated to have mused 15 to 30 lakh deaths, there has been no large-scale famine or outbreak of epidemics. We had Bihar earthquake in 1937 and partition of the country in 1947. Other than these, the muses of abnormal mortality after 1921 were progressively controlled.

There has been improvement in agriculture. Large arms have now been brought under cultivations by the newly constructed canals and wells. The better quality seeds are used. There is increased use of fertilizers. We do not allow scarcity conditions to exist. If they do, we are able to control these.

We have understood techniques of food scarcity relief. The measures are now more effectively implemented. Transport has developed. Relief can be rushed. There are no starvation deaths. On the other hand, the nation is better fed and is assured of at least minimum food supplies.

The medical services have improved. There is control of epidemics and important diseases. We have taken preventive steps. Vaccinations are there. D.D.T. spraying is there. Protected water supply is there. Large number of public health measures are also taken so that the epidemics do not break out during fairs and festivals.

We shall also like to sum up some modern factors affecting Mortality Control. Major factor responsible for this change is the modern discoveries in public health and medicine. New drugs in the form of sulphanimides and antibiotics, and new techniques of prophylaxis, i.e., prevention of infection have revolutionised the method of control of mortality in other countries also. And then we have international agencies like WHO, UNICEF which help by giving equipment, medicine, training and advice. All this has eliminated abnormal deaths.

Mortality Pattern

We begin with infant deaths.

Mortality in India is one of the highest in the world excluding Africa. Health conditions are far from satisfactory. Infant death rate is around 125 per 1000 births, i.e., one out of every eight babies born dies before completing the first year of life. Earlier it was one out of four. In Sweden, it is one out of fifty. Poor health of the mother leads to a large number of deaths of infants. Most of the babies do not start with a robust physique. They fall prey to many fatal diseases. In India, 40% of total deaths occur in ages below 5.

Important causes of deaths of population are: 1/6th of total death in population is due to infection and parasitic diseases in this group we have T.B., Typhoid and Tetanus. Another 1/6th is due to diseases affecting respiratory system. Another 1/6th is due to diseases of digestive system. Nutritional level of the people is very low. Protein deficiency and anaemia are quite common and so on. Low vitality-more deaths. It is another thing that with progress, death rate is declining. But the population is increasing which is not good for our future.

Male-Female Ratio

In some states in India, Kerala for example, the number females outnumber males. In other states, males exceed females Against 1000 males, the number of females is 923.

Density Distribution

There is high density of population in Kerala and West Bengal. Bihar, Tamil Nadu and Uttar Pradesh are fairly densely populated. Rajasthan, M.P. and Assam are at the lowest rung. As at present the density of population in India is 267 per square kilo metre.

Scheduled Caste Population

Twenty-five per cent of population in India can be described as scheduled castes. The maximum scheduled caste population is 36% in Jalandhar District of Punjab.

Average life of Indians is now 55 years as compared to 23 years in 1951. In some countries, the expected span of life is much higher. In USA it is 70 years.

Our level of literacy is very low. According to 1991 census, the all India average of literate persons is 52.11%. Females have a literacy percentage of 39. In Punjab it is 58.14% (average).

Urban and Rural

India is predominantly rural, About 80% of the people live in villages. This is a dominant factor. What is still more important is that there is a large number of small villages, which have less than 500 persons each. In 1961, there were 564,718 villages and 2,690 towns. More than 60% of villages, each with a population below 500, have only 1/5th of the rural population. There are only a few large villages, having a population of 5000 each. There are seven big cities in India and they hold 20% of the population.

Characteristics of Big Cities

On one side, we have a few highly congested cities. They have developed civic facilities like hospitals, doctors, good sanitation, convenient transport, telephones, schools and colleges, cinemas and other facilities for recreation. They are busy centre of industry, trade and commerce and have large employment opportunities. This attracts a good number of migrants in search of employment. Housing being inadequate, slums grow up and evils arising from overcrowding prevail. Hustle and bustle of life makes the people more impersonal in social life. The city life exposes them to new ideas and new things. They are more receptive to modernising influences. They are likely to be more willing to modify their outlook on matters connected with marriages and births. The compelling pressures of homing and cost of living may bring about conditions favouring a lower birth rate. Death rate should be lowered because of the medical and public health facilities, but the factor of overcrowding may well keep it up. On balance, death rate should be lower. There is a high mobility and considerable immigration.

Characteristics of Small Villages

Cities present one demographic picture. This is in strong contrast with that of the large number of small villages. They have few, if any, civic amenities. Medical, public health and educational facilities are very inadequate. Transport and communication are difficult. Literacy is low. Life is simple. People are, more or loss, isolated from the outside world. Villagers form a close community. Everybody is interested in everybody else's affairs. The hold of society is strong. People are bound by traditions and customs. Marriages and births must follow the time-honoured pattern. It is not easy to change what the forefathers thought or did. In the circumstances, birth rate is likely to remain high. Death rate may decline only slowly to the extent of medical and public health services touch village life. Migration is likely to be dishonoured, if the village can give the person some work, however trivial.

Characteristics of Other Towns and Villages

The remaining villages and towns between the two extremes of cities and small villages present a gradual transition from one demographic picture to the other. Development of civic amenities in the country is so inadequate that most of the towns are only poorly urbanised villages. Outlook of the town people is more akin to the rural setting. That is why the difference between the rural and urban birth rates and death rates is so small. The rural base is so big that in the final analysis what holds good for rural areas holds for India as a whole. In most of the States rural population forms about 80% of the total. In Assam, Orissa, and Bihar, the percentage is over 90. Only in Maharashtra, West Bengal, Tamil Nadu, Mysore and Gujarat it is around 75. These small differences are perhaps meaningful enough as potentials of change in a relative sense.

On account of five year plans, agricultural and industrial production has increased manifold but we still continue to be a nation of poor people. The reason is that the rate of our economic development is much less than the rate of our population. If we take the level of price into account, we shall find that despite remarkable increase in income per head, our standard of living is very low. Out of 100 people living in India only 40 get sufficient food and maintain themselves in good health, another 40 just enough, while the remaining 20 less than enough.

QUESTIONS

1. Describe the development of population in India.
2. Describe the trend of Indian population according to Census 2001.

9

Structure of Population

In Demography, the most important aspect is the study of the structure and characteristics of the population. This includes the personal, social and economic characteristics including age, sex, raw, nationality, religion, language, marital status, family composition, literacy and educational attainments, employment status, occupation and income, etc. Each population may be classified into different groups, according to the above mentioned characteristics. For example, Indian population may be classified into males and females; Indians and foreigners; literate and illiterate; employed and unemployed; children, youth and old; Hindu, Muslim, Christians, Sikhs, Jain, etc; married and unmarried; single or joint family-, and groups speaking more than a dozen languages recognized by the Constitution. Similar characteristics may be observed in any other population group. Again, these characteristics are not fixed once for all. They are constantly changing over the period of time. For example in 1961 the population of children in India was 41.08 per cent, whereas this rose to 42.10 in 1971. Thus, the number of young dependents increased over the period of time. Similarly, while in 1961 the percentage of literacy in India was 24.02%, in 1971 this increased to 29.46%, with further increase in 1981. These characteristics, again, do not show the same proportion throughout the country. For example, in India literacy has been always very high in Kerala as compared to other parts of the country. Similar comparisons can be made in the population structure of different countries.

For example, in 1970 the percentage of the age group 15 in India was 42.10% while in USA it was only 28.50%. This shows that the characteristics of population in USA are better than that in India. As a general rule the population characteristics of the developed countries are always better than those of the developing and undeveloped countries. In other words, the level of development of a country may be judged by the characteristics of population structure. For example, the percentage of females, children, illiterates, unhealthy, sick, old and disabled persons in a population shows the backwardness of society. It is not only a symptom of backwardness but also a cause which leads to further backwardness and hampers attempts to progress. This may be particularly studied in the case of the characteristics of Indian population which has the higher percentage of children, old, sick, disabled, other dependent, unemployed, illiterate people in the population. Any progress may be judged with the criteria of these characteristics. It is obvious that these characteristics hinder economic and social development.

Significant Features

The above discussion, incidentally, shows the uses of the study of population structure and characteristics. The following uses are more important :

1. It helps in judging the quality of the population.
2. It helps in making comparisons and identifying the level of development.
3. It is useful in the preparation of inventories of human resources necessary for all developmental planning.
4. It gives data concerning births and deaths, age and sex distribution, etc., useful for various purpose.
5. It provides material for the study of social changes.
6. It provides data for the study of present economic structure as well as the possibilities of future growth.
7. It provides data concerning health of people in the country so that planning may be made in this direction.
8. It presents an outline of the most glaring social and economic problem which may be given priority for solution.

Thus, it is clear that the study of structure and characteristics of population is a prelude to all successful planning for development.

Main Characteristics

It may be noted here that while some of the characteristics of a population cannot be changed such as nationality, other characteristics do change over different planes it periods of time such as education, marital status, etc. Of these two types of characteristics, the former are known as ascribed and the latter achieved. Thus, ascribed characteristics are biologically or culturally assigned. For example, Indians belong to Aryan race in the North and Dravid in the South. The racial characteristics is biologically inherited and cannot be changed. The Blacks do not become Whites over a period of time. The achieved characteristics, on the other hand, are those which are open to the choice of the individual such as marital status, educational attainments, occupation, etc. In India nationality, religion, caste, mother tongue, etc., may be included in the former category. Age, sex, race and mother tongue are ascribed characteristics everywhere. Sex and age are the basic biological characteristics. They influence social, economic and political structure. They particularly influence birth and death rate, migration (both emigration and immigration), marital status, compositions of family, manpower, national income and national production, educational add medical provisions and homing, etc. Planning for development in different fields such as education, housing employment, health, manpower, etc., is made on the basis of data concerning sex and age structure. For example, the number of male and female population in a particular period determine the number of educational institutions, teachers, text books, laboratory equipments, playgrounds, etc., needed for future planning. Similar examples may be given about the use of population characteristics in planning.

Sex and Age Relationship

The above discussion shown the importance of sex and age characteristics in a population. The following points may be noted in this connection :

1. They provide data on fertility, mortality, migration, marital status and economic characteristics.

2. According to Ralph Thomlinson, sex and age characteristics are, "visible, indisputable and convenient indicators of social status." Each individual is ascribed a status in society on the basis of sex and age.
3. These characteristics we determined by the role of a person in society and social institutions. These roles, of course, change according to culture and even in the same culture over a period of time. However, they are found in every culture in every period and accepted by the society everywhere. Thus, for example, in patriarchal societies the status of male is high and his roles are generally outside the home. The same may be said about females in a matriarchal society. In the modern industrial societies, however, the roles of males and females are not so much definite. The women are getting more and more employment outside the home. However, house-keeping is generally a feminine occupation though she may be helped by the male occasionally. Similar examples of roles according to age may be found in different societies. While the more traditional types of societies are age-oriented with elder men working as guides, the more modernised societies have what is known as youth-oriented culture.

Understanding Sex Issues

The most important characteristics of population is the sex structure. This is known by the percentage of males in the population, in other words, masculinity proportion. The sex ratio is expressed in the number of males per 100 females or the number of females per 100 males. For example in the year 1971 the urban sex ratio of males in some of the countries of the world was : India 116.6, Indonesia 110.0, Nepal 117.3, Sri Lanka 112.5, UK 93.6, Germany 84.1. The corresponding sex ratio in rural areas was almost everywhere lower as compared to the urban areas. This means that there is a higher number of males and females in urban areas and not so higher in number in rural areas. This is particularly due to the fact that migration from rural to urban is generally in terms of the male population. Again, the percentage of the ratio has been changing in different periods in the same country.

Sex ratio in urban areas is favourable to males. Quite a different picture is however projected by some urban area in Europe and USA. This is particularly due to female dominated internal migration in these countries as against the male dominated internal migration in India, Most of the males in India, while migrating from rural to urban areas, leave their families in the country due to the paucity of residences in cities. The migratory labour force is mainly constituted by the males. This migratory character also changes the sex ratio in urban population in India. It has been always higher than that of rural population. As is clear by the table given above some Indian cities like Kolkata, Mumbai, Delhi Kanpur, etc., shows unusually high sex ratios in favour of males.

In the country as a whole there were more males than females in Indian population. In 1961 the number of females per thousand males was 941 whereas in 1971 it was 930.

Due to certain reasons the sex ratio in India has been male dominated since the beginning of the 20th century. This trend has been increasing from 1901 to 1991.

- In the Himalayan region, a pair of bullocks toil annually for 1,064 hours, a man for 1,212 hours and a woman for 3,485 hours on a one-hectare farm.
- With men migrating first in search of livelihoods, the number of households headed by men has gone up from 20 per cent to 45 per cent.
- The alarming current sex-ratio of 927 females per 1000 males is even lower than the 1971 ratio of 930.

  Globally, men do two-thirds of the work, earn one-third of the income and own one-tenths of the total resources.
- The death rate for females has declined to 9.8 per 1000 and the sex differential in the infant mortality rate has been bridged with the decline in the rate for females from 129 per 1000 in 1978 to 79 in 1992.
- There is also a decline in the maternal mortality rate, which stood at 286 per 1000 in 1988.
- The 30 per cent reservation for men in seals to all local.

These were some of the gender issues highlighted by the draft of India's Country Paper to be presented at the fourth World Conference on Women at Beijing The draft, awaiting finalisation by the department of men and child development, was presented at the inter-ministerial meeting at Jakarta earlier.

Calling for a review of the development framework, the paper calls for the recognition of women as a part of the complexity called "development structures" through an equal allocation of resources and investment targets. Out of 96 countries recently surveyed by the international Research and Training Institute for the Advancement of Women, only in six countries including India, were men's issues accorded a place in the least of the development plan.

Analysing the structures and causes of poverty, the paper concludes that women are central to the success of poverty-alleviation efforts, and raising female earning power through efforts at the regional level could prove critical to demographic planning, child survival, increase in labour productivity and economic growth.

Approximately 35 per cent of the households below the poverty line are headed by females. The new economic liberalisation policy would have to be considered in the light of this gradual 'feminisation' of poverty, especially in a scenario where women have little access to productive resources, such as land or capital, the paper emphasises.

It calls for measures to ensure that the burden of unemployment generated by the structural adjustment programme does not fag disproportionately on the shoulders of men, particularly in the informal sector.

Nearly 84 per cent of all economically active Indian women are involved in agriculture or allied activities. The reallocation of forest resources away from the needs of local communities into the hands of urban and industrial India has increased the length of the working day for tribal and nomadic women in term of fuel fodder, water, and food gathering activities.

"Degradation of the environment with its negative impact on women call for reversal .... by re-establishing the symbiotic relation between nature and mankind and by capturing the perspectives of poor women in this regard," the paper observes. The paper attributes the improvement in women's health status despite inhibitory cultural norms, and draws attention to the increase in the life expectancy for females at birth to 58.1 during 1986-90 as compared to 31.6 in 1951. Gaps in health rate and the enlargement of men's reproductive choice have been identified as key issues to be addressed in the area of health.

Women continue to be marginalised on the employment front, though their participation increased from 19.7 per cent in 1981 to 22.3 per cent in 1991. Only few per cent of all employed women work in the organised sector, which provides social security. Within the organised sector, they were in the minority, accounting for a mere 14 per cent. At the other end, women account for 90 per cent of marginal workers in the economy.

Why Male Domination ?

The following factors have been identified as responsible for the amount pattern of a higher number of males than females in the total Indian population;

Differential Enumeration: The lower percentage of females in Indian population may be partially attributed to the unequal enumeration of males and females in census counting. Since in the rural areas census is not very much scientific and the enumerators are seldom allowed to directly meet the females, it is possible that a number of females may remain uncounted. However, most of the demographers agree that this cannot explain more than a very small part of the numerical imbalance.

Sex Ratio of Births: According to the study conducted by Ramachandran and Deshpande, the ratio of births in maternity homes was 106 in favour of males and there was not much regional variation. According to the Sample Registration Scheme, in 1961 the sex ratio of births in rural India was 107.8. According to the survey conducted by Vital Statistics Division of the Government of India, the sex ratio of the projected population for 1971 was 107.1 while it was assumed to be 108. Actually the ratio in 1971 was 107.5. This shows that the low percentage of females in Indian population is not due to more male births but other reasons.

Higher Female Morality: Demographic data for urban India in 1969 indicates higher death rates for males at all ages of infant life, with an exception of age of 29 days to 6 months for which the death rate for females is higher. Therefore, it cannot be said that there is a tendency of higher natural mortality of females in India. However, it has been found that female mortality is higher, if not due to natural reasons, then due to social reasons. Scholars have pointed out time and again that the status of the female in Indian society has been always considered lower than that of the males. The Khanna Study and the National Sample Survey reveal a higher female death rate pattern. Numerous KAP studies have said that in India parents show strong preference for male children. Studies have shown differential treatment to sick male and female children particularly in the rural areas. Maternal mortality has been shockingly high in rural areas due to the many reasons. Therefore, it may be concluded that the most important reason for lower female ratio in Indian population is the higher mortality of female children as well as mothers.

Male Dominated Emigration: it could be easily accepted that international migration in India is male dominated. This, however, cannot be said to be a very important point since not many people emigrate from India to outside countries.

From the discussion of the above mentioned probable causes of rude dominated sex ratio in India, it is clear that the most important factor is the lower social status of Indian women, resulting into insufficient medical aid and nutritive provisions.

Exercise of Determining Sex Ratio

The sex ratio of a country is determined by the following factors:

Sex Ratio at Birth: An examination of the sex ratios of registered births for a number of countries over a considerable period shows that the sex ratio of births generally remains in favour of male babies. The average ratio is 105 male babies per 100 female babies. This average varies between 101.2 to 106.6 in different countries. For example, it is 106./ in Ireland and Norway. It is more than 106.0 in Canada, Belgium, Poland, Romania and UK. On the other hand, South Africa shows 106.7 ratio, the lowest in the world. Sex ratio at birth is generally determined biologically, probably due to nature's balance in favour of males. Sex ratio at birth depends upon sex ratio at the time of conception and sex ratio due to deaths. It has been found that foetal deaths are generally higher in male babies. Sex ratio is also partly determined by demographic factors such as the age of mothers and the order of live births. There appears to be an inverse correlation between the age of the mother and the birth order of the child and sex ratio at birth. Comparatively more male babies are found among the first and second born children. Lower ages of mothers generally lead to the birth of female babies. Thus there is a negative correlation between the age of the mother and the sex ratio of the births.

Sex Ratio of Diseased Persons: Differential mortality is an important factor determining sex ratio. It has been found by some studies that in a number of countries more than one hundred males die per 100 females. The male foetus is biologically more delicate than the female foetus. Therefore, there is a higher proportion of male babies in still birth. Even after birth, the male baby continues to be at a disadvantages. In most of the countries, the crude death rates for males are higher than those for the females. Again, the expectation of life at birth for females is almost universally higher than that of the males.' India and Pakistan are exceptions to this rule. In developed countries the death rates are higher for males than the females, in every age group. The overall mortality for males is therefore generally higher. This results into imbalance in sex ratio. As the age advances, the sex ratio exhibits an increasing number of females. In all the regions of the world the sex ratio is favourable to females above the age group of 65. The same can be said about other age groups. Some causes for this tendency include male deaths during wars, reflected in sex ratios in most of the countries in post-war period.

Sex Ratio or Net Migrants: Yet another factor affecting sex ratio is the sex ratio of net migrants. Migration is generally sex selective. For example, in India it is male dominated. Internal migration is also sex selective. While it has been male dominated in India, it is female dominated in many European countries as well as in USA.

All the above mentioned three factors determine sex ratio in different countries. As has been already pointed out, the picture in the West, particularly about migration, is different from the East. Besides the biological factors, social and cultural factors have also been influential.

The Age Factor

According to the United Nations, age is, 'The estimated or calculated interval of time between the date of birth and the date of census, expressed in completed solar years!" It has been recommended that the information on age should be collected by asking the date of birth of the individual in terms; of day, month and year of the last birthday. This information obviously provides more accurate data. However, in countries like India, not many people keep a record of their birth, therefore information on age is collected by asking about the age completed on the last birthday." This is particularly true in the cases of illiterate and semi-literate people. Many of them do not know their age. If questioned, they tell it by guess which may be wrong even by a decade. Again due to absence of proper provision for registration of births in rural areas birth certificate cannot be used to know the age. Since most of the people do not need birth certificates at any time in their lives, therefore nobody cares to get it. It has been found that there is a general tendency among Indians to report their age in numbers ending with 0 or 5, resulting in concentration of population at a certain age in census data. Further mistakes might be committed due to carelessness on either part or deliberate mischief. In order to rectify these possibilities of errors, the demographers try to determine the nature and magnitude of errors and makes necessary adjustments. According to 1971 census age data in India it was found that the figures for the ages 9, 10 and 11 were respectively 5,976,600; 10,548,600 and 4,666,600 respectively. This clearly shows the tendency of preferring the 0 digit as mentioned show.

Age Data Analysed

For Demographic purpose age data is classified in five-year age groups such as 0-4, 5-9, 10-14, 15-20, 20-24 and so on. Thus classified, the age data are used for analysis of the age structure in any population. The age structure is generally studied with the help of per cent distribution or age pyramid. Other measures used for the purpose are the average age and a few other indices. The simplest measure of age structure is the percentage distribution. It indicates the number of persons in an age group, taking the total number of persons as one hundred. This helps in arriving at in idea about the age structure of any population. It may be also useful to compare the age structures of two or more populations at a point of time. This is particularly true in the case of Age-Sex histograms or Age-Sex pyramids.

An important measure in the analysis of age structure is known as the dependency ratio. This indicates the number of dependents per 100 workers. It may be computed on the basis of three broad age groups. Suppose these age groups are: 15-59, 15-64 and 15-60. In this data those having age below 15 are young dependents while those above 60 or 65 are old dependents.

Sweden has the lowest percentage of persons under the age of 15 while Kenya has the highest percentage. Again, Sweden has the highest percentage of person above 65 years, while this percentage is lowest for Fiji. Thus, the developing countries have high percentages of children below 15 and low percentages of persons above 65 years of age. The percentage of working population in the developing countries, ranges from 46.8% to 55.7%. On the other hand in developed countries the working population ranges from 61.6% to 69.0%. They have smaller population below the working age group ranging from 20.8% to 28.8%. The percentage of elderly persons however, is higher, ranging from 7.0% to 13.7%. The dependency ratio in the developed countries is much lower as compared to the developing countries. While the dependency ratio in developing countries is 90.5%, in the developed countries it is only 57.0%. The pyramids made of the population structure of developing and developed countries therefore exhibit very much different shape. While the pyramids of developing countries show broad basis and steeply sloping sides, the pyramids of the age structure of developed countries are almost rectangular in shape with a slide sloping the elder ages. It is ironical to observe that old countries have much more young population than the new countries and the new countries have much more old population. It has been observed that the age structure of the developed countries has considerably changed over the years, while it is not so in the case of developing countries. As has been pointed out, the age structure in the last three census reports in India is slower the same. On the other hand, in Sweden the proportion of children under 15 and the old persons above 64 was 33.25 and 5.2 in 1860, in the beginning of the 20 century it was 32.5 and 8.4 respectively. Similar changes may be observed in the age structure of population of other developed countries such as USA, France, England, Norway, Russia, Germany and other European countries. The age structures of the populations of the developing countries have changed very slightly. Thus, a substantial difference exists in the structures of the developing and the developed countries. Similar is the case about the dependency ratio.

The process of the decrease of children and increase of old person in a population is known as the aging of population. This is applicable in the case of developed countries. It should be noted that aging of a population is not a continuous process. It has also its downward curves. However, it has come to be established in the case of developed countries.

Age Structure Determined

The age structure of a population is determined by the following factors

Fertility. During the 1950's, researches of various demographers such as V.G. Valaorus (1950), Frank Lorimer (1951), Alfred Sauvey (1954), Ansley Coale (1956), and the United Nations (1958), demonstrated that the aging of the population in most of the Western countries is due to a decline in the fertility rates. The increase in the proportion of the old people and persons in the medium age was a product of falling birth rate. However, it was realised later on that mortality is an equally important factor. In the economically developed countries aging of population is particularly due to declining fertility. On the other hand, increased fertility has checked the aging of population in developing countries.

Mortality. It has been now realised that mortality is an equally important factor in the determination of age structure in a population. It effects the age distribution though to a much lesser extent than fertility. It has been demonstrated that reductions in mortality have resulted in a younger age distribution. The medium age of Indian population has dropped because of the decline in mortality. The same has been observed in Latin America during the period 1930-1960. The decline in mortality rate is particularly due to improvement in health and medical services and technology. While it has led to survival of children, it has also prolonged life in the older generation. This has led the French demographer Bourgeois Pichat to calculate that if fertility in France has remained unchanged from 1776 to 1951, while mortality declined according to the actual pattern, the population in 1951 would still have been a young population. The decline in mortality leads to younger age group in a country passing from high levels of mortality to low levels. On the other hand, if the mortality level is already low and the expectation of life is nearly 70 years there is not much scope for increase in Young Population. This leads to aging of the population as found in developed countries.

The above discussion shows that the fertility and mortality together effect the age structure of a population.

Migration. The effects of fertility and mortality are however changed considerably by the effects of migration, particularly the age distribution of the net migrant and volume of net migration. For example, if the proportion and number of young adults is large among the net migrants, the aging of the population is retarded. 0, the other the aging process tends to get accelerated if the net migrants include persons above 30 years of age. The influence on age structure of a population is effected both by international as well as internal migration. For example, internal net migration has influenced age-sex distribution in the population of Andaman and Nicobar islands in India.

War. As has been clearly shown by the last two great World Wars, the age-sex structure of a population is considerably affected by war. War casualties mainly include males in the younger age groups. War also adversely affects fertility since most of the males in the participating countries are separated from their wives for a long period. This also leads to "babyboom" in post-war period since it leads to more marriages and more sexual activity. The age-sex pyramid shows smaller sized whorls during the war and bigger sized cohorts after the war.

Marriage and After

Marital status, as is clear by the term, shows the status of a male or female with reference to matrimony. It shows whether a person is married or unmarried. The marital status is studied in demographic surveys. It is also obtained by periodic national census collecting information regarding marital status of each individual about a certain age. Each country collects data regarding marital status in the world which are compiled by the United Nations, in its yearly publications, The Demographic Year Book. According to the United Nations the marital status should be classified in the following 5 categories : Single (never married), married and not legally separated, widowed and not remarried, divorced and not remarried and married but legally separated.

The distribution population by marital status in the 1971 census is available on sample basis. It shows that almost 50% of the people in India have been returned, as never married. This may be due to the reason that all the persons below 10 years of age who have not married have been included under this category order instructions from the Census Commissioner. 44% of the people have been recorded as married. 6% have been recorded as widowed. The proportion of divorced or separated is very negligible since marriage in India is generally considered a sacrament. A higher percentage of males has been returned as never married. It is so since males marry later than the females. The high proportion of widows as compared to the widowers may be due to the fact that more widowers remarry.

The marital status distribution in other countries to judge the quality of Indian population. In India the universality of marriage custom and the child marriage influence marital status. On the other hand, in countries like Ireland persons marry at a very late age and so many persons never marry. Therefore, there is bound to be a difference between the marital status of persons in such countries. As a general role in War there is more prevalence of marrying late add also not marrying as compared to the countries in Asia and Africa.

In India maximum marriages, take place between 20 and 24 age group, in USA and Ireland it is in the 25-29 age group in which very few marriages take place in India. While most of the people are unmarried in more developed countries in 15-19 group. In India and Pakistan most of the people are married by this age. On the other hand, while the percentage of divorced and separated is almost negligible in India and Pakistan they show a sizeable number in more developed countries. These tendencies make a difference in the social and economic quality of the population. In India the data on marital status was collected from the Census 1881 onward. The universal pattern of marital status of Indian women even according to 1971 census show that by the age of 39 almost all the Indian women were married. The high percentage of married females in the age groups 10-14 and 15-19 are evidence of the prevalence of child marriages. As regards the marital status according to rural urban distinctions, it is particularly marked in the age group 10-14. In this age group while 14% of the rural females are married, this percentage for urban females is only 3.97. In the age group 15-49 the percentage of never married in urban areas is almost double of those in rural areas. It should not be presumed that the marital status of Indian women has been constant. Several changes have occurred over a period of 20 years, since the census 1951 to 1971. A decline in mortality rates had led to increased number of widowed, divorced and separated women. The percentage of never married women has increased over the years while child marriages are on the decline.

Marrital Age

It is difficult to find out actual data concerning age at marriage in India since marriages are not registered. However some demographers have calculated the mean age at first marriage in India. According to S.N. Agarwal, "The figures show that females marrying at the age of 12.5 years on the average in 1891, began marrying at the age of 17.1 years in 1971; similarly, the male who were marrying at the age of 19.6 began marrying at the age of 22.5 years. Thus, the female marriage age has increased by 4.6 years over the period of eighty years, that is, at an average rate of 0.58 years every ten years. The male age at marriage, on the other hand, has increased by 2.9 years only over the eighty-year period.

The increase in the female age at marriage is largely became of the reduction in child marriages. For example, while in the 1891-1901 decade, 46 per cent of the girls in the age group 10-15 were married, only 20 per cent of this age group got married in the 1951-61 decade. Again, while 11 per cent of the girls in the age group 5-10 were married in the 1891-1901 decade, the corresponding percentage was negligible in the 1961-71 decade."

Widowhood Age

According to the census 1911, the percentage of widows in female population was 1.7. It declined to 15.5 in 1931 and 8.8 in 1971. In spite of no legal restrictions to widow remarriage, it is not very much prevalent due to social stigmas. This stigma differs in different Hindu castes. In lower castes remarriage is more prevalent. It has been estimated that the marrige at widowhood in the age group 15-45 was 34 years in 1951-61 decade. In 1941-51 decade it was around 33 years. Still earlier, in 1911-21 decade it was around 30 years. The 1971 census works it out to 35.2 years. This is particularly due to improvement in mortality. According to some studies, almost 1/4th of widows get remarried. Of these most were below the age of 20. Very few widows, above 30 get remarried.

Educational Achievements

A significant characteristics of population is literacy and educational attainment. This characteristics shows the level of development in a country. According to the United Nations, literacy can be defined as the ability of a person to read and write with understanding a short simple statement on his every day life. Thus, literacy is the ability to read and write with understanding. No person without understanding can be called a literate. It has been recommended by the United Nations that the information on literacy should be collected from only those who are either 10 years of age or above. It is so since the ability to read and write is not achieved until one has had some schooling. The most important source of literacy data is the national census. It is collected during census operations-in all the countries of the world. The United Nations compiles information on literacy and educational attainment for all the countries of the world in the annual publication A Demographic Year Book.

The Crude Literacy Rate of 29.46, based on one per cent sample data of the 1971 Census, indicates that, in 1971, 29.46 per cent of the Indian population was literate, and that 70.54 per cent was illiterate.

Developed and Developing Countries Scenario

The ninth issue of One World' focuses on the crucial problem of education in developing countries, which make up the majority of the world population. The articles contributed to this issue stress three aspects of this problem :

Education is the basis of development. EXCELSIOR (Mexico) argues that education provides the indispensable foundations for scientific, technological and cultural progress.

Crisis. There is an acute crisis in education in most third world countries, and this crisis is according to *Le Soleil* (Dakar), a tragic reflection of the crisis of development which is presently more acute than ever in most developing countries.

Politika (Belgrade). Recalls the remarkable progress achieved at all levels of education in Yugoslavia since the Second World War, but nonetheless points to 'short-circuits' between the aspirations of the young and the needs of the country, and in particular to the lack of interest in manual trades. The same problem is vividly illustrated by the remarkable psychological study contributed by *Zycie Warszawy*, expressing the aspirations and frustrations of young peoles.

On the other hand, newspapers from developing countries *Dawn* (Karachi), *Indian Express* (New Delhi), *Le Soleil*, (Dakar), and even *Excelsior* (Mexico), express their consternation at the dramatically inadequate yield of the educational efforts which were made in their countries, even when these efforts were intensive.

Such inadequate results are not only due to lack of financial means, cultural, ideological and structural factors are in fact far more determining . Several papers stress in this connection the fact that their educational system were inherited from colonial powers more intent on perpetuating their empire than democratising education or respecting the indigenous cultures.

This inheritance is heavy. English and French, for example, remain the indispensable languages for communication and higher education, yet also perpetuate the elitist structure of the educational system. The elites vehicle models of thought, behaviour and consumption do not correspond at all to the needs of the majority of the population. *Excelsior* furthermore calls attention to the importance of cultural penetration in Mexico. This nation's economy and education are in a state of dependence which, although not complete, engenders submission and passivity.

To meet the needs and cost of education which were everywhere staggering, financial means are dramatically inadequate. The third world countries are literally beset by a host of necessities, and in particular that of defence, which is aggravated by the generalised (world) arms race. The aid which developing nations receive for education from the industrialised countries represents only 9 per cent of the amount they invest in this field. And 80 per cent of this aid goes to higher education.

The conclusions which may be drawn from these views are clear. Education runs against overwhelming obstacles in developing countries. These obstacles can be overcome only if there is an effective solidarity between rich and poor nations. This solidarity is indeed the fundamental aim of a new international economic order which implies, on the part of the rich and powerful nations, less egoism and the will to curb their natural tendencies to cultural and economic domination.

In order for education to become accessible to all, it must be realised that it constitutes the surest investment towards development. Education cannot remain the privilege of an elite. Every human being has inalienable right to education, as to health, freedom, or security. This right will become reality only when the means of defending and exercising it will be given to all, through a vast joint and generous effort of all the members of the world community.

Scene in India

The first information about literacy in India was provided by Indian Census 1871. Since then literacy is computed by each population census. During the period 1891-1931 literacy increased slowly from 5.4 to 9.5. Therefore, it increased faster after independence, showing 16.7 in 1951, 24.0 in 1961, 29.5% in 1971. In 1981 the total number of literates in country was computed as 23,19,91,932 which included 15,88,37,215 males and 7,91,54,717 females. This shows a literacy rate of almost 40%. While the proportion of literate females among the total literates was formerly less than half in 1971, in 1981 it is more than half. Among females the percentage of illiteracy in 1971 was 58% in urban areas and 97% in rural areas. The corresponding male percentages of illiterates were 39 and 66 respectively. Among literates females about 88 per cent were found educated upto the matriculation level. According to the 1971 Census data literacy in different age groups was: 10-14, 60%; 15-19, 63%; 20-24, 60% for males. The corresponding percentage for female literacy in these age groups was 38, 37 and 28% respectively. Literacy is very low in at men as compared to urban area, registering total number of illiterates in rural areas a 72.7% (61.2 male; 84.9 female) and 40.0% (30.5 male and 52.0 female) percentage in urban population. The percentage of educational attainments of matriculation and above was 2.2% in rural and 14.3% in urban men. In 1971 and 1981 Census among Indian states Kerala has shown the highest literacy rate followed by Tamil Nadu and Maharashtra. The lowest literacy rate was observed in Jammu and Kashmir. Among the Union Territories, Chandigarh retained the highest proportion of literates while the lowest literacy rate was observed in Arunachal Pradesh. These data concerning the state of literacy show wine improvement in the total condition. However, it is far from satisfactory.

Educational attainment of males and females is a still more important population characteristics since the progress of a country depends upon educational attainment of its population. It is a very important criteria of distinction between developed and developing countries. The educational attainment in the former were much higher than those in the latter. The of distribution of the educational attainment of males and females of age 15 and above in India shows that it is still classified in the lower rung of developing countries.

Composition on Religious Basis

A very important characteristic of a population is religion since it influences various types of demographic behaviour. This is particularly important in Asian countries and the countries of Indian sub-continent. The analysis of different census data has revealed the tendency of the growth of non-Hindu population faster than the Hindu population. In almost all the last census reports this has been confirmed. And yet the Hindus constitute almost 80% of the total population.

Composition on Ethnical Basis

Besides religion ethnic composition includes language. In India at the time of 1961 census it was found that the population spoke as many as 1,652 mother tongues. Of them the Indian Constitution has recognised 14 major languages with Hindi as the National Language. According to 1971 Census Hindi is spoken by 162.6 million people or by about 30% of the Indian population. Along with English, Hindi is an official language in most of the states. The percentage of Sanskrit speaking people was almost negligible. In Census 1981 the position of Hindi has not much improved particularly due to encouragement to regional languages in different states of the country and not much encouragement to propagation of Hindi. The status of Urdu has however somewhat improved with the increase in the Muslim population in the country.

QUESTIONS

1. Define population characteristics and describe their uses types and importance.
2. Discuss and describe age and sex characteristics of population in India. What are the causes of males dominated ratio ?
3. How will you analyse Age Data ? What factors determine age structure ? Discuss the importance of age structure in population
4. Describe mental status and its significance in Indian population.

10

Problems to Cope With

As per on the assumption of a round figure of 6,000 million as the world's population and an inhabited land area of 135.16 square kilometers, India accounts for about 2.4 per cent of the world's land area and 14.6 per cent of its population. In term of population, India occupies the second place among nations of the world, the People's Republic of China estimated to have 1,000 million Population, being the first. But if one were thinking of the Indian subcontinent comprising India and Pakistan, its population could be more than that of China, while in respect of persons per unit of area, this subcontinent would be quite as densely populated as any other comparable area in the world. Along with the Peoples Republic of China this may be regarded as holding the key to the world's demographic growth.

About 87 crores of world population do not have enough to eat while 3500 new mouths are added to world population every twenty minutes.

In his book India At the Time of Akbar, W.H. Moreland put the population of this subcontinent at 100 million at the time of Akbar's death. On the strength of this estimate, the population of India, in his openion constituted, would have been about 92 million around the year 1600. In the course of three centuries, these 92 million increased by a little over two and a half times to 238.4 million in 1901. This appears a very slow rate indeed compared to the fact of India's more than doubling her population in 50 years with a base as large as 252 million in 1921. Although this does no more than condom to the general world trend in the current century, the absolute magnitude of Indias population and the size of her annual population growth in the contest of her social and economic situation and her rate of economic growth, present a great multitude of problems.

Line of Division

The year 1921 has been aptly called the Great Divide which left behind the era of extensive famines and epidemics. The three decades beginning with 1921 registered slowly increasing growth rates, caused possibly more by assured food supplies than by any rapid improvement in public health and medical services, although the government, during this period developed, an efficient machinery for quickly containing and quenching epidemics. An extended network of communications facilitated accumulation of reserves of food at strategic points and assured their effective distribution at short notice. This and international collaboration reduced the threat of famines and minimised rigours of the Bengal and Chennai famines of 1943 and the Rayalaseema situation in 1946-47.

Recurrent famines, epidemics and pandemic malaria had carved up the country as it were between themselves in two distinct regions. A malaria map of India, reproduced in the All-India Census Report for 1941, came as a shock to those to whom the era of famines and malaria is already a fading memory. It described the whole of North and Central India together with the thick spine of the Deccan plateau down to the northern tip of Tiruchirapalli as subject to recurrent famines, while whatever was left east of this tract, from the eastern-most point to the extreme west and from the northern-most point to the extreme south, was shown in the grip of an endemic courage. What was more the tracts of recurrent malaria were almost contiguous to those of recurrent famines and epidemics like plague and smallpox and experienced reccurrent crisis in population growth between 1881 and 1931. It is no accident that it is roughly this tract, formerly ravaged by both epidemic and scarcity, with recurrent bursts of famine, that has shown the highest reaches of increase in 1951-1961 (21 to 30 per cent), for already in 1941-1961 it had shown a growth rate approaching 2 per cent per year. A much lower rate of growth (up to 20 per cent) is noticeable in the central and eastern tracts, the northern irrigation and the southern coastal belts, formerly in the endemic malaria and cholera zones of varying intensity and therefore subject to spates of recurrent crisiss, relative stagnation or variable increase between 1881 and 1931. It is possible that this latter area will attain still higher rates of growth before showing a decline. It will be recalled that the census want in 1961 surpassed even the most generous of expectations, having exceeded by more than 8 million the highest estimate ever made before the census.

International migration being negligible and natural fertility still having its way, the birth rate has remained fairly constant over the decades subject only to second order effects of mortality changes on the sex-age; composition of the population. The growth of India's population has thus been determined almost solely by variations in mortality, while fertility has remained uncontrolled. While the birth rate had always been a little over 40 the death rate declined from 47 to 21 per thousand between 1921 and 1961. Infant death rate declined very considerably during recent years, although the level is still high. According to the 14th Round of the National Sample Survey, infant death rate was 153 per 1,000 live births for males; and 138 for females, giving an average of 146 for both sexes. Deaths during the first month of life form about 45 per cent of the total infant deaths, of which 25 per cent occur under one week. The remaining infant deaths are divided about equally between the periods 1-6 months and 6-12 months. Deaths in infancy are mostly accountable to exposure (broncho-pnemonia), malnutrition and weaning diarrhoea, infections and parasitic disease as well as such congenital causes as immaturity, birth injuries and malformation.

Rate of Bereavement

Arthur Geddes held everybody under a debt by looking at infant deaths and mortality at higher ages in supremely human terms as bereavement rate. He was closer to the secret of India's unchanging and high fertility than any other demographer when he observed that 'a map of regional types thus constitutes a map of essentially differing or contrasted impact upon the heart and mind, upon the social and personal 'Psychology' of given population groups. To map the areas of differing human impact thus form a first and vital stop in exploring the changing, fluctuating social psychology of a people. The next step is to discover the actual response the psychological reaction to the impact of experience."

It is possible that this high bereavement rate is responsible, on the social and psychological as well as on the personal and human level, for an average of more then 6 children still being born alive per "man of unbroken marriage during the reproductive age. This fear of loss may be responsible for a psychological recklessness to which the compulsions of ensuring a minimal supply of family about during the peaks of agricultural operations lead a special edge. When, to this are added the starkness of the rural scene and the attendant apathy and fatalism that has prevailed for so long, the natural desire to look up to sons for support in old age, the scarcity of wage employment for women and the lack of old age pensions and social security or insurance benefits, one appreciates why the one specific fertility rates for currently married men should rule a high plateau between 230 and 260 in the age span of 20-30, or the fertility rate should still be as high a 173.6 for all ages.

Effects Analysed

An accelerating expectation of life at birth in a situation of uncontrolled fertility leads to two opposite sets of social and economic effects. To take the darker side first, it has made for large accretions in the younger dependency age group of 0-14 became one of the important results of an increase in life expectancy is a decrease in the infant death rates and deaths at young ages. It has also made for greater savings of life at old ages beyond 60. Either way, it has resulted in increasing the dependency load on working adults in the age group of 15-59. The first effect of a rising expectation of life therefore has been not only an increase in the dependency load on the adult working male or female in the family but increased national allocations over a whole men which achieve no immediate gain in economic growth, viz., child and maternity care, public health, hospital and maternity amenities, primary and secondary education and therefore on educational housing, teachers and teachers training, over food and other consumer goods, often necessitating imports and frittering away of valuable credit or foreign exchange. This could be done in India only by diverting scarce resources from sectors of savings and economic growth to sectors of consumption. To this extent the nation is certainly deprived and called upon to make greater sacrifices of future goals to the immediate problem of living. On the other hand, a rising expectation of life has brought in lasting economic and social gains. A longer life has introduced stability in economic climate, favoured augmentation of human skills, productivity per worker, technical know-how, longer "it larger returns from educational investments, particularly scientific and technological, and greater savings and continuity of economic effort in national life. It has made for greater real assets, both human and material, and has been responsible for far-reaching schemes of social and health security, old age, accident and premature death pensions, rapid expansion of individual life insurance and other safeguards—all in the space of the last decade. The reduction of maternal and general mortality has made for greater employment of women in the wage sector, and extension and continuity of individual economic enterprise.

Planned Family

All this might have brought in much richer harvests, had it been attended by a rapidly declining fertility thereby reducing dependency and much avoidable "infructuous" expenditure both on the national and the individual plane. Indeed such a realisation, however instinctive or inchoate, has given family limitation, to judge by the results of recent surveys, universal currency in recent years as a desirable personal and national goal. Regardless of whether the State accepts family limitation as being at the wry centre of an national planning, which indeed is what our Government had done, it is the millions of individual decisions taken in the context of millions of individual family plans and aspirations that will determine the success of the movement and yet preserve human dignity and the supremacy of flexible individual choice, so valuable in a working democracy.

The introduction of insurance, securities, old-age pensions, annuities and medical amenities among the salaried, business and professional classes has paved the way, in recent decades, for small families in these social groups. The widening of the organised industrial base and the increasing employment of women in the manual and white-collar wage sectors have served to moderate the desire for more children not only became pregnancy interferes with earnings and community of service but because an improving survival rate affords greater satisfaction in parenthood by reducing the bereavement rate. Nothing stimulates the desire for family limitation more than the prospect of a fuller and richer life in which the individual more and more comes two his own.

Ever since Japan entered the modern industrial age in a big way, her birth rate has responded fairly closely to the ups and downs of business cycles. Deliberate family limitation became part of Japan's life as early as 1920. It is not a product, as is often wrongly imagined, of post-World War II. The McArthur regime introduced unprecedented measures of democracy in Japan ; the demolition of the cult of the Emperor, the land reforms, the breaking of trusts, reforms of inheritance and personal laws, franchise and elections, equality of the sexes, economic emancipation of women. These instruments of change, apart from the baby boom which may be expected after any war in which a nation has been deeply involved, were an invitation to rapid population growth. Japan's answer to this threat was a change in the eugenics law which legalised abortion. But what is significant is that abortions are on the wane since 1956. There was growing awareness that drastic methods may boomerang, that, however attractive on the short run, they make for unstable internal class relationships, may even generate psychosis and jeopardise a nation's strength in the event of a war. The usual humane methods consistent with human dignity and individual preference now prevail.

Distribution of Population

Even as there were areas of high density where a greater proportion of the population is concentrated in a comparatively small proportion of area, the distribution of population generally conforms to natural features. It is usual to divide India into seven natural regions : the Himalayan, the Northern plains, the Central Indian Hills and Plateaus, the Peninsular Hills and Plateaus, the West Coast, the East Coast and the Islands.

The region of lowest density is the Himalayan. The Northern Plains region has always been the most populous. The region of highest density, excepting for Kerala, is still the Indus-Jamna-Ganga Doabs and the West Bengal basin. Stemming from the narrow strip of Gurdaspur, Amaritsar, Jullundur and Ludhiana in the north-west, the broad belt of Uttar Pradesh merges with North Bihar and finally with West Bengal, the density in the entire region being seldom below 500 per square mile and often above 1,000 in spacious bands astride the river.

The Central and Deccan Hills and Plateaus, delineated by Mohindergarh (Punjab) in the north to the Nilgiris (Chennai) in the south, Santal parganas in the cat and the Arabian sea in the west, we fall under a density of 500 in the entire territory, except for the districts of Ahmedabad, Kaira, Baroda, and Surat in Gujarat, Greater Mumbai and Kolhapur in Maharashtra, Hyderabad Guntur, Krishna, West Godavari and Srikakulam in Andhra Pradesh and Bangalore in Mysore. Within this territory again, see we three large continuous areas with still lower density (all below 200 per square mile), that may be described as the western desert and lowlands, the Madhya Pradesh teak and scrub forests and south-eastern hills and upland forests. The first consists of the desert district of Rajasthan bounded by Ganganagar in the north, Sirohi in the south,. Nagapur in the is an east and Jaisalmer in the west and the lowland districts of Kutch and Surendranagar of Gujarat. The second and central area starts with Tonk of Rajasthan in the north-west and embracing Chittorgarh, Bundi and Kota of Rajasthan stretches across the northern, central and eastern districts of Madhya Pradesh. The third area straddles four States and covers Adilabad (Andhra Pradesh), Chanda (Maharashtra), Bastar (Madhya Pradesh) and Koraput, Kalahandi and Baudh-khondmals (Orissa).

The West and East coasts again are tracts of high density, the peaks being reached around Mumbai-Thana, in Kerala, along Thanjavur, Chingleput and Chennai and again in Krishna it the East and West Godavari districts.

The Himalayan region contains a little over 3 per cent of India's population in less than 14 per cent of India's area, the Northern Plain region just under 37 per cent of population in just over 22 per cent of India's area, the Central and Peninsular Hills and Plateaus-the great heartland of India-contain a little over 19 per cent of population in a little over 27 per cent of India's area, the Deman Hills and Plateaus a little under one-fifth of Indias population in just under 22 per cent of India's area, the West and East Coast hold 11.2 per cent an and 9.7 per cent of population respectively in a little under 13.5 per cent of India's area each.

Growth of Towns

To one who follows the above account, it will not come as surprise that the greatest absolute concentrations of urban population occur in the Gujarat (Cambay plain surrounded by Kathiawar and Gujarat uplands); a long and broad band surrounded by another wide band of lower concentration encasing the Tapti from Nagpur in the east to the Gujarat coast; in the triangle formed by Nasik, Mumbai and Gujarat; the Krishna valley of Maharashtra continued into the entire stretch of Mysore's Malnad, extending in lesser concentrations to the Maid" and the Hyderabad core, and except for brief gaps in the West Coast to the whole of the West and East Coastal belts, including the whole of Chennai joining up with Bangalore through the Hosur Gap; and the southern half of West Bengal which proceeds in a diagonal band up the club handle of Burdwan district to Dhanbad and Hazaribagh of Bihar. There is again the solid quadrangular tract embracing north-western Uttar Pradesh and almost the whole of Punjab. There are tracts of secondary but often heavy concentration as in the desert and uplands of Rajasthan; the Malwa, traditionally the great passage-way between the capital and the western seaboard in Cambay, the Narmada-Tapti Doab, traditionally the great internal frontier of India, the homeland of cotton and important exchange tract between the north and the south; and the great Deccan tract which has grown rich on kingdoms and cotton. Finally, there are the isolated tracts of modern urban growth like Singhbhum, Sundargarh, Durg, Bhopal, Gwalior or Jabalpur.

This again provides the clue to the historic aspect of India's urban growth. As may well be guessed, a large number of towns would still be exalted villages in which the landed gentry would build up their own life, seek their own company and urban amenities, consolidate their leadership and ensure the advancement of their progeny. A second and large group of towns would be large agricultural and contact marts engaged in recent years in proliferating into small and medium organised industrial activity. These two groups would very naturally dominate the heartland of India, even encroaching on the large, navigable, conti-nental riven. A third group would consist of trade and commerce and mercantile towns which would again very naturally concentrate on the West and East Coasts and the prosperous valleys and estuaries of the large rivers. With this group will naturally go a section of the service and administrative towns on account of the opportunities of cultural contact that the mercantile and trading centres afford and the thickening of administrative activity that these tracts demand, but it will be readily conceded that this category of service and administrative towns will have the best distribution throughout the country. A fourth group would consist of the great metropolitan arms, some of which bound to be at strategic points conveniently making communications such as Delhi, Hyderabad and Bangalore. The fifth group would be centres of industrial activity, either resource located or conditioned by the economies of power, transport and communication, or allocated on considerations of national, regional or local importance and proximity either to raw material, power, communication or markets.

Although the urban population has been growing rather rapidly but in view of its small proportion to the total population, 'it makes no effective impression on the demographic or socio-economic situation of the country as a whole. The functional classification of India's towns also suggests why the rate of urban growth should still be modest and why the urban poll of migration from the rural areas should still be weak. According to European "if American experience and even that of Japan it is manufacturing that exercises the strorngest, most Persistent urban pull. Besides, manufacturing alone is capable of a rapid multiplying universe. In India the number of manufacturing cities and towns is still small compared to urban arms with other predominant functions which cannot fail to weaken the urban pull. An analysis of growth rates over the decades shows that the growth rate of manufacturing towns is slightly higher as a whole than that of any other category, but only slightly, and no functional category of town can claim regional prominence in the matter of growth rates. In other wards, no matter what predominant function they fulfil, towns which are on power, road and railways arteries appear to show a higher rate of growth than those which are not, suggesting thereby that manufacturing activity may be making itself felt, however weakly, through the incrustation of other functions.

The main trend of the increase seems to be that cities are becoming bigger owing to immigration thus disputing, while making more than the capacity of it the opportunities of maximisation of investment and resiources offered by large cities. This concentration and congestion of urban population in a few cities brings about a peculiar type of closed circuit migration from urban to urban and certain other kinds of turnover migration between rural and urban areas, apart from impeding flow of rural to urban migration to lower cities and towns, which ought to expand at a much more rapid rate. The performance of twelve cities, Greater Mumbai, kolkata, Delhi, Chennai, Ahmedabad, Hyderabad, Bangalore, Kanpur, Nagpur, Pane, Lucknow and Howrah, clearly brings out the greater attraction of migrants to this class of towns probably on account of better amenities and scope for business, trade and service.

The Urbanisation

But although a little more than 57 per cent of India's urban population fives in towns of more than 50,000 each, the fact remains that many of the small towns are not much more than urbanised villages particularly in social and economic organisation and outlook, which affect the demographic trends. The characteristic urban outlook and mode of living, which is associated with the word urban in Western countries may obtain in some measure in the cities with a population of 1 million but not to say great degree in other towns. Even in respect of literacy, the cities stand out far apart from the non-city urban and rural area.

It may be worthwhile to run over briefly the broad areas 'in which rural-urban differences in social and economic organisation and outlook exist and those in which they are less evident. Difference exist in the field of literacy and the differences widen in higher levels of education. In marital status, the proportion of never married is distinctly higher in urban than rural areas, the complementry rate of married is distinctly higher in urban than total area. The complementary rate of married being lower in urban than rural area, but the numerical smallness of the differences between rural and urban proportions still suggest an essential homogeneity on the social outlook of the population in the matter of marriage although the age distribution of married persons in rural and urban areas shows that the practice of marrying late is gaining ground in towns.

A Great Difference

A major rural-urban difference is still to be found in the low urban proportions of females per 1,000 males and difference in age distribution between the sexes. The low ratio implies an unstable, migratory population, a substantial amount of single household, congestion in housing and concentration of male population of working age. An analysis of household composition data in advanced industrial districts revealed that while married sons are, as a rule, appreciably fewer in urban than in rural areas as a reflection of the urban mentality, it is curious that other married male relations which may mean fathers, uncles, brothers and so on are often proportionately more numerous in urban than rural areas. This indeed is evidence of how little living together or the joint family has weakened even in the cities of advanced industrial districts. It is also evidence of the load of dependency in urban areas which weakens the motivation for advancement and status- seeking.

Pattern of Fertility

In the matter of birth and death rates in urban areas, several conclusions seem to emerge. First, that neonatal death rates are still very high own in such cities as Mumbai, Kolkata, Chennai and even Delhi suggesting thereby that although these cities have about the best provision in the country for sanitation, care and treatment of infants. They also have slum areas with conditions favourable for a high infant rate. Secondly, there was still no evidence of any reduction in the fertility level in towns each with population of 1 lakh and over, if at all there was a slightly upward change. Even the million-plus cities showed average characteristic of high fertility levels. Mumbai alone presented a picture appreciably below the level of the high fertility group, but it was still higher than the level of Western countries of low fertility. Even the New Delhi levels were well above those of Mumbai. In short, the averages for this is million plus cities showed that excepting for Mumbai the fertility pattern of fecund women was not much different from these of other towns having less population. Essentially family growth conformed to a high-fertility pattern.

Problems of Migration

An analysis of migration statistics even for avowedly industrial districts confirmed that migration from outside the State is still negligible except in Assam, West Bengal Delhi and the industrial areas of Mumbai, Thana and Ahmedabad. Except for technically qualified personnel in industrial locations, inter-State migration still plays no major role in the greater part of India. Secondly, migration into most of these urban areas tends to be evenly distributed between short and long term.

Further analysis of migration data by duration of residence is also upset many notions based on the experiences of urbararisation in the Western world, where nothing like the Indian volume of floating or rapid turnover migration in towns has been in evidence. By floating or rapid turnover migration is meant a situation where the volume of population composed of art Inam ation and natural increase. Such a situation obviously obtains in such high industrialised areas as Greater Mumbai, Kolkata, Chennai, Hyderabad, Thana, Poona, Hooghly and Rampur. Places like Delhi, Kanpur and Ahmedabad are not very far behind. The top industrial layer of urban India is, therefore, very much in this process, thereby exposing the precariousness, vulnerability and instability of industrial skill, experience, knowledge and human worth in the principal metropolitan centres of the country. The statistics also underline the lack of a true industrial proletariat who have staked their lives in the city and severed their room in the village. It is only in the urban areas of districts like Bangalore, Ludhiana, Vadodra, Coimbatore, Chingleput, Singhbhum, Burdwan, Howrah, 24-Parganas, Schore and others where we seem to have a stable and numerous resident population whose progeny also continue to live in the self-same town and where the rate of natural increase could be distinguished from and is comparable to the proportion of decadal marragration.

Problems of Immigration

The differential rates of immigration by rural and urban origin at once suggest that area which import more raw hands than white callar workers have more or rapid turnover of immigrants of rural origin, notably Greater Mumbai, Kolkata, Chennai, Kanpur, Ahmedabad, Hyderabad, Singliblima, Dhanbad, Bradwan, Howrah, Hooghly, 24-Pargarras, Gorakhpur, Lakhimpur, Karnali or Ranchi. The high proportion of immigrants of urban origin in places like Delhi, Chennai, Hyderabad, Bangalore, Vadodara, Chingleput, etc. seems to accord with the general experience of expansion of non-factory, trade, transport, communication and service establishments and also of manufacturing concerns requiring high technical skill like factories turning out precision products and chemicals. The districts like Bangalore, Thana, Points, Chingleput, Sehore and Gwalior are illustrations of the proportion of immigrants of urban exceeding that of rural origin.

The circulating migration of urban population from town to town leads to several crinclusiom. The absolute volume of this type of circulating temporary migration of urban population and its proportion to rural born immigrams being quite hight. It is obvious that this population will offer substantial resistance to the stream of migration from twat to urban areas, reducing eventually both its volume and velocity. The natural increase among the resident and migrating urban-born population will reap obvious advantages over rural born immigrants in point of education outlook, aptitude, technical skill and even urban homing and will tend to push back incursions into urban livelihoods by rural migrants. Thirdly, the extent of circulating urban migration suggests that a fair proportion of the total pool of urban population has to keep cointinuously on the move in search of opportunity and better employment. This means that the home towns themselves offer only limited openings for advancement, and what is available elsewhere must be disputed by those who we already in other towns and, therefore, comparatively out of reach of rural-born competitors. All this my have the effect of telling back still more resolutely the stream of rural migrants into urban areas.

Competence in Technical Matters

It is not often realised that in urban areas, of even reputedly highly industrialised districts, the proportion of persons with any kind of certified vocational or technical training is often much lower than for urban India as a whole. The bulk of the factory operations here are without any approved technical training or academic competence, which means that the old established industrial areas rely more on practical job experience of a mechanical nature than on intellectual and technological competence so vital for higher levels of growth. In the matter of non-technical diplomas, non-technical university degrees, the all-India average is often higher than what one finds in the so-called highly industrialised districts suggesting the possibility in the current decade of a greater flow, from other urban areas to industrial districts of trained operatives and white collar workers in managerial and executive jobs. Even in the matter of technical diplomas and degrees in specialised fields it is surprising how few districts are anywhere near double the value of the all-India averages, that important industrial areas like Kolkata, Chennai, Bangalore, Poona and Dhanbad should be so close to the Indian average, or that districts like Kanpur Ajmer, Coimbatore, Chinglelput, Howrah, 24-Parganas, etc. should be around half or less than the all-India average. Again, except for the metropolitan city districts, the urban areas of even highly industrial districts enjoy no more than tenuous superiority over non-industrial districts in offering educational facilities to students. At the same time the high proportion of unemployment among persons holding technical degrees in districts like Mumbai, Delhi, Hydrabad, Bangalore, Ludhiana, Thana, Pune, Vadodra, or Ernakulam is also a sign of the constraints prevailing in the employment market of even those districts and cities which we usually associate with industrial progress.

In working for rural-urban differences one cannot fail to be struck by the weak and in some cases tenuous differences that even highly industrialised districts possess from what is shared in the State or even all-India level. It would hardly be an exaggeration to say that none of them, except for Gareater Mumbai and Kolkata and in, odd cases, Delhi, betray any significant departure from the pattern obtaining for the State as a whole. Even the rural urban differentials are weak in the majority of cases, except for sex-ratio and age-sex composition.

Urbanisation, Practice and Level

This brings us to the question of the nature of urbanisation in India. The census data may come as a shock to those who would like to believe in wide rural-urban differences or who would imagine that the ordering of life in urban India was very different from that in the rural areas. Common labels or names have a way of hiding genuine differences and nothing can be more misleading than to think that urban in India is the same as in Europe or Asia. It is important to appreciate the widely different historic contexts of the growth of urban area in the West and India. There is little correspondence even between the India of today and the Europe of the pre-Industrial Revolution era for even in the latter the towns were in chronic short supply of labour, while the population base was much too small to present a threat of surplus or difficulty of transfer from agriculture to non-agriculture. Any analogy with the USA has to be ruled out at the start. What happened in Europe in the second-half of the eighteenth century and throughout the nineteenth has no parallel to the Indian situation. Firstly, no country in Europe started with more than a mere fraction of India's population. Secondly, their urban population base was, again, a mere fraction of that fraction and nothing comparable to the 26 millions of urban population with which India started in 1901. The pull that the city or town exercised on the rural areas of Europe in the era of the Industrial Revolution was due not only to countryside and the low rate of natural growth. The low population base in the countryside led to many early improvements in agriculture and farming and to the scraping off of savings for industrialisation. To this was added the benefits derived from the colonies by way of raw materials and the competition for utilisation of manpower at home and the colonies. The low rate of natural growth in the towns constantly demanded and inflow of labour from the rural areas to man the growing industries. Improvement in agricultural practices and mechanisation of farming also rendered a large rural population surplus which now formed the hard core of an urban proletariat which had no means of getting back to the countryside. But the pith of the matter was the low urban population base which cried out for expansion all the time. The natural rate of growth of this population was wholly inadequate to meet the growing demand for labour.

Rural Migration Repelled

There is foreseeable demands of industrial expansion in the current decade, particularly when we remember that the gross capital investment per capita in the industrial sector is apt to be quite high. While this is by no means intended as a suggestion that the rural-urban flow will slow down in the pounded back, the absolute volume of natural increase in the urban population itself may well have been at the back of the slow rate of urban growth, despite the fact that the investment on industrial growth and on cities and townships has been of an unprecedently high order. It seems that from now on the natural growth of urban population will work as a repellant as well as a pull to migration from rural areas. The amenities available in the town by way of educational and other facilities will contribute towards a higher level of technological efficiency in the younger generation which my tend to push back the stream of rural migration. On the other hand the lack of pronounced rural-urban differentials may tend to reduce the force of outward push from the village. Even now, as we have seen, urban life in most districts is largely an extension of the essential pattern of rural life. There will be a steadily widening and deepening reserve pool of labour of all grades available in the city or town itself to respond to new opportunity.

Economic Development, Facing Odds

Twentieth century was characterised by planned economic development; each nation adopting its own strategy depending upon its socio-economic and political structure. India, however, after independence, adopted planning as an instrument for achieving rapid economic development.

Under the Five Year Plans, concerted efforts have been made to better the quality of life both individually and collectively. The achievements have not been commensurate with the aspirations and expectations of the people, mainly due to the constant race between the population growth and economic development. The demographic monster has been swallowing the fruits of planned economic development thereby adversely affecting the economic life of a country.

Aims and Objectives

(i) To develop an understanding of the concept of economic life of the country;

(ii) To develop an understanding that economic life of a country depends as much upon human resources as upon natural resources;

(iii) To enable the pupils to understand that the two resources are interconnected one affecting the other;

(iv) To help them to understand that population as a means of economic development, supplies, labour-skilled and unskilled and entrepreneurs:

(v) To enable them to understand that there has been and there is a rapid growth of population in India;

(vi) To develop an understanding that natural resources, such as land, soil, forest, water, etc. available in a country are limited;

(vii) To enable them to appreciate that the disequilibrium between the human resources and natural resources results in serious repercussions on the economic life of a country;

(viii) To enable the pupils to realise that a planned family is essential for a better economic life;

(ix) To develop the ability to use and interpret the data on human and natural resources rationally; and

(x) To develop in the pupils the ability to make correct decisions in matters relating to their economic life.

Country's Economic Life

The economic life of the people in a country is determined by the standard of living. The real income of the people is a resultant factor of various variables. Some of the important variables are the raw of economic development, the level of consumption, size of the population, capacity of food in-take, health and medical services, education of the people, housing, etc. All these variables have a direct impact on the level of living. It is the primary responsibility of the government to secure these facilities for the welfare of its people. How these factors are secured, depends upon the system of production and distribution followed in a country.

There has to be a reasonable balance of various factors for the steady growth in the economy. The rapid growth in population without corresponding economic growth upsets the entire economic life. The economic life of the family depends upon the size of the family income accrued to it, the level consumption of various agricultural and industrial products, clothing, housing, etc. Therefore, planned family at the micro level secures better standard of living to the members of the family. At the macro level, the politics adopted by the government in the areas of population growth and economic development decide the economic life of the country.

Development Planning

The grave crisis through which our country is passing, calls for immediate and effective action; but before this can be done, a re-appraisal of policies and the evaluation of results are obviously necessary. The achievements in the field of agriculture, industry, trade, transport, etc. in India since independence have been tremendous. India has chosen planned economic development as a machinery for rapid economic growth. Though planning has been adopted for economic development yet India has avoided using totalitarian for this purpose. We are following mixed economy to achieve socialistic pattern of society. The private sector and public sector contribute their resources in respective economic spheres and cooperate with each other to achieve economic goal set forth by the country.

Depending upon the social, cultural, historical, economic and political backgrounds, we have chosen democratic socialism as a goal. Various countries have adopted their own strategies of economic development. In capitalistic countries, private enterprise what is known as laissez-faire economy, is the key factor. The entire economic activity is undertaken and organised by free enterprise without much of governmental restrictions and controls. The intervention of the 'State' that is the government is very much limited. This has resulted in the gulf between haves and have-nots. The conflict between the labour and management is a constant irritant in the process of economic development. In Communist Countries there are various forms of socialism. The main emphasis is laid on the nationalisation of means of production and distribution. There are collective farms, and state-controlled industries. The economic activities are controlled by the government where individuals have very little freedom. This has resulted in regimentation.

Therefore, in India an attempt has been made to promote both public and private sectors in the field of economic development. The Planning Commission is charged with the responsibility of assessing the existing human and natural resources on the one hand and the demands, expectations and aspirations of the people on the other. The main objective of the planning is to initiate a process of development which will raise standards of living and open out to the people new opportunities for richer and mom varied life. The Planning Commission formulates derailed plans for the most effective and balanced utilisation of the country's resources in the fields of agriculture, irrigation, industry, trade, transport, health, education, housing and other activities. Investment during the first two five year plans to totalled Rs. 10,100 crores including Rs. 4900 crores in the private sector. During the Third Five Year Plan the outlay in public sector was Rs. 7500 crore and Rs. 4100 crores in private sectors. The Fourth Five Year Plan envisaged a total outlay of Rs. 24,398 crores, comprising Rs. 14,398 crores outlay in the public sector and Rs. 10,000 crores in private sector.

Economic Development : Factors

The economic development depends upon the maximum utilisation of existing resources. These resources are mainly human resources and natural resources. The judicious combination of various resources leads to economic development. The prosperity of a nation is judged by the per capita income and levels of living of its people. When people are poor, their incomes are less, their savings are less, the mobilisation of capital is less, the investment is less and in turn the income is less. Thus, the vicious circle continues. This has to be broken, and it is possible only when planned effort is made. The increase in the productivity is an essential factor. The land, labour, capital and organisation which are generally considered as four factors of production have to be properly utilised. The productivity in agriculture, in industry, in mining, in manufacturing have to be increased. To achieve democratic socialism, distribution of the dividends among its various constituents is an important factor. The concentration of wealth with limited few, monopolistic trends, exploitation of the weaker sections are the bottlenecks in the process of democratic socialism. The exchange mechanism, banking policy and the price control are some other factors on which economic development depends.

Unfortunately, in our country the fruits of economic development have not reached the masses to the extent desired. An appraisal of various factors is necessary. Have we failed in our planning? This is a controversial subject. If we have failed, is it due to bad planning or bad execution or both? If we have not failed, are there any basic and inherent questions can be found only if we can critically analyse the nature and limitations of human and natural resources.

Human Resources : Scope and Nature

A nation's wealth lies not in its lands and waters, not in its forests and mines, not in its flocks and herds but in its healthy and happy men, women and children. It lies in the energy, initiative and moral fitness of its people. The population of a country is both an asset and a liability depending upon its resources. The population as a means to economic development, supplies tabour. This is in the form of either physical or mental labour. Labour is both skilled and unskilled. It helps to provide workers in the farms, fields, mines, hunting, forestry, etc. The skilled labour is necessary for exploitation of the resources available in a country. It supplies entrepreneurs, technicians, scientists, educationists, industrialists, traders, etc. The human resources in collaboration with natural resources help in the process of economic development. The population is the supply side of the labour. Its demand depends on the demand for goods and services which are required for human well-being. Like other goods, value of labour too is governed by its demand and supply. As a natural consequence, if the supply of labour increases than what it could profitably be utilised, its value diminishes, its productivity diminishes and in turn the per capita income of the labourer diminishes. The supply of labour mainly depends on the growth of the population.

Growth Factors

India is one of the greatest populated countries, which contains one-seventh of the world's population but has only 1/45 of the land areas. The population is increasing a the rate of 2 45% per annum, which means an addition of 12 millions to the population, per year. The 1971 Census recorded Indian population as 547 millions, which is equal to the population of U.S.S.R., America, Australia, New Zealand and Japan put together.

The growth in population is governed by three important components: its birth rate, death rate and migration. But the net migration in the country is very small. Population is primarily determined by the excess of births over deaths. Over the last 80 years, while birth rate fluctuated only slightly and kept about 40 per thousand or a little over, there is a sharp decline in death rate which stands at 218 per thousand during the census period 1951-60. According to the estimates made by the Expert Committee on Population set up by the Planning Commission, the death rate had further fallen to 14 per thousand during the period 1966-70.

This is mainly due to extensive health and medical facilities, both preventive and curative, provided by the Government. This gap between the birth rate and death rate is the major factor responsible for rapid growth in population. The rapid growth in population adds to the supply of labour on one hand and the number of dependents on the other. The dependents in a family may be either children or old-age persons. Whatever may be the category, they do not add to the gross national product of the country but they require essential social services like schooling, health, medicine, housing, law and order, etc. This is essentially an expenditure but not investment in the sense that they do not add to the capital formation. According to the 1961 census 40.2% of the total population was in the 0-14 age group, 47.9 per cent in 15-49 and 11.9 per cent in the 50 and over age groups. This means that a relatively large burden rests on the productive and active population.

Resources of Nature

India is endowed with plenty of natural resources. The proper exploitation of these resources in a planned way leads to economic development. But these natural resources are essentially limited in nature. The land is limited by territorial boundaries. Total geographical area is 32.68 crores hectares. The cultivable land is to be exploited and the barren land has to be convened into cultivable land. According to 1965-66 estimates, the total cropped area is only 15.49 crore hectares. The minerals are available in plenty. The iron ores, coal, manganese, mica, forests, which are available in our country have to be harnessed for the betterment of the people. Forests occupy 6.03 crore hectares land according to the estimates of 1965-66. These resources were exploited during the British rule, to serve the interests of colonial powers but not to serve the Indian masses. After independence, a clear-cut strategy of planning became inevitable not only to exploit them properly but also to conserve them for future generations. The excessive exploitations of resources results in their exhaustion. A day may come when we may not be left with adequate resources. There is no justification for over exploitation.

Forced by the pressures of explosion in population, the intensive and extensive exploitation is going on. Excessive dependence of our people on agriculture and the breakdown of joint family system are leading to sub-division and fragmentation of land resulting in uneconomic land holdings. The uneconomic holdings are not suitable to agrarian revolution.

Economic Development Hampered

In our country the race between the population growth and economic development is going on resulting in serious disequilibrium in human and natural resources. The fruits of economic development are being swallowed by the rapid growth of population. The situation has come when we are running fast to remain where we are. While the levels of living have not improved substantially, the growing unemployment among the educated and uneducated youth is creating serious economic, social and political problems. There is a serious anti-thesis in all walks of life-floods and draughts, strikes and lockouts, growing urban sky-scrapers and slum, luxurious dinners and starvation deaths, scenic beauty and unhealthy environments, affluence and misery, important to material and spiritual values and several others only reflect poverty amidst plenty.

If the Socialism has to be ushered in content and spirit, determined and well-coordinated actions are necessary. The gap between pronouncements and practices, should be bridged. A multipronged attack in all fields is necessary. This requires faith, conviction, confidence, willing participation and cooperation of all. The efforts must be made to promote economic growth and check rapid population growth. For all these efforts, education and education alone is the key-factor. Any amount of coercion or legislation would not bring the desired results. Through education we have to create an awareness and consciousness in the younger generation to bring in necessary attitudinal changes, to enable them to take correct decisions to improve the economic life.

QUESTIONS

1. Describe Population Problems in India.
2 Which, according to you in the most important Population problem in India ? Give reasons.

11

State Policies

The Ad hoc Consultative Group of Experts on population policy, act up by the Population Commission of the United Nations Economics and Social Council Population policy means, "Measures and Programmes designed to contribute to the achievement of economic, social demographic political and other collective goals, through affecting critical demographic variables, rarely, the size and growth of population, its geographic distribution (national and international) and its demographic characteristics."' Further, it has been pointed out that population policy should include measures End programmes likely to affect critical demographic variables as well as those specifically designed to do so? In defining population policy Berelson has outlined the following three principal characteristics :

1. It includes the action taken by government in the form of a statement of position, laws, decrees or administrative programmes.
2. It covers population events.
3. It refers to both the intentions and consequence designed to alter population events.

New Population Policy

1. Couples below poverty line following two-children principle will have free health Insurance.

2. The minimum age of marriage for girls will be raised to 20 years from 18 years.
3. States with better population management will get more central aid.
4. Registration of both, death, marriage and pregnancy will be compulsory.
5. The boundaries for Lok Sabha seats will not be redrawn till 2026.

Thus population policy is characterised by the three components of population change, viz., fertility, mortality and migration. Thus, population policy of a country refers to the governmental measures with reference to population change. It decides the goals to be achieved in the fields of fertility, mortality and emigration. This my be understood in more details as follows:

Policies Influencing Mortality: Mortality is an undesirable characteristic of population. Therefore, population policies aim at reduction of mortality. This has been done particularly through the concept of public health and the national programmes of eradication of 'mass killers', the epidemics small pox; malaria, cholera, etc. The World Health Organisation has defined health as, 'A state of complete physical, mental and social well-being and not merely the absence of disease or infirmity!" This definition of health has decided the goal of public health in different countries. The public health campaigns have led to unprecedented decline in mortality. It has been pointed out by a United Nations Public Health report that not a single pandemic has created since 1918 when influenza caused 25 million deaths in the world. According to the United Nations Secretariat, 'As might be expected, all governments have formulated policies designed to reduce morbidity and mortality, and none has considered acceptable as policy of permiting survival rates to remain low in older to prevent further increase in rates of National Population Growth."' In 1974 the United National World Population Conference in Bucharest adopted checking of mortality level as the goal of World Population Plan of Action. It was resolved that, "Countries with the highest mortality levels should aim, by 1985, to have expectation of life at birth of at least 50 years and an infant mortality rate of less than 120 per thousand live births."

Policies Influencing Migration: These we concerned both at internal and international migration. Internal migration is a constitutional privilege in most of the countries. The policy towards internal migration seeks to relieve population pressures. In most of the countries today metropolitan reasons have very high population growth rates. Therefore the Governments aim at reducing this pressure. However, it has been reported by the United Nations that most of the developed countries do not have any policy to discourage migration to urban centres. The less developed countries also generally do not depict such policies. Therefore, it has been pointed out that such population policy must be adopted.

Most of the countries today have well-defined policies concerning international migration. Rules for entry and exist from the countries use becoming more and more elaborate. Governments are imposing increasing restrictions on international migration. An example of such restriction may be seen in Great Britain at present, particularly reiterating immigration of Asians. An Immigration Act adopted in 1971 was enforced in January 1973 to introduce a uniform system of immigration control for all the countries. This Act aimed at discouraging immigration, Similar population policy concerning immigration may be observed in Australia. Again, sometimes restriction on emigration are imposed to control 'brain drain, such as found in India these days.

Population Policies Influencing Fertility: These may be classified as anti-natalist.

Pro-natalist policies: Thomlinson has described three approaches to an affective pro-natalist policy :

(A) To accept existing values and attitudes and eliminate or diminish the economic liability of having children.

(B) To modify the norms by glorifying values concerning reproduction. This includes such legal measure as lowering the minimum age for marriage and reinstating the old custom of divorce on the basis of infertility.

(C) To relax the taboos on illegitimacy.

All the above mentioned three approaches were adopted by Hitler in Nazi Germany. Pro-natalist policies have existed since ancient times in one form or the other. They could be seen in Germany, Itlay and Japan between the two World Wars period. Sweden had a highly developed population policy maintaining lowest birth rate in the world. In France, various measures were adopted in persuance of the pro-natalist policy in the Code de law Famille of 1939. In 1962 a natality, committee was appointed in Israel, which in its report in 1966, recommended the Grant of Financial Aid to large families and restriction on induced abortions. Japan reversed her anti-natalist policy by implementing several programmes having demographic implications such as the Eugenics Protection Law of 1949 which made abortion easily available.

Anti-Natalist Policies. Anti-Natalist Policies aim at limiting the growth of population. This aim is as old as the ancient Greek State. Both Plato and Aristotle emphasised the value of the quality of population and sanctioned anti-natalist policy. This was again emphasised by the famous Eassay of Malthus published in 1798. It was further accepted by John Smut Mill when he declared in 1821 that, "The great problem is that to find out how to limit the number of births." Margaret Sanger championed the cause of birth control in more recent years. Anti-natalist policies may be both direct and indirect, short-term and long-term. The direct anti-natalist policies include provision of contraceptive services liberalisation of abortion laws and raising age at marriage.

Provision of Contraceptive Services: One finds both optimistic and pessimistic approaches towards the population check by provision of contraceptive services. Arguments are available on both the sides. Therefore, it has been concluded by Davis, "The need is not to abandon the family planning programmes but to par equal or greater resources into other approaches" However, it is undeniable that today family planning programms are getting whole-hearted support everywhere. It has been accepted as a basic human right that persons can decide the number and spacing of their children. On December 10, 1967, the Human Rights Day, it was affirmed by Heads of States or Prime Ministers of twelve countries, "We believe that the objective of family planning is the enrichment of human life, not its restrictions, that family planning by assuring greater opportunity to each person, frees man to attain his individual dignity and reach high live potential." The Population Council of New York has recently pointed out that in 1974-754 countries have family planning supportive policies covering 94% of the population of the developing countries. India was the first to adopt a family planning programme in 1952 followed by China and Hong Kong in 1956.

Liberalisation of Abortion: This has been the measure adopted by Japan during the period 1948-1958 in which her birth rate was reduced to 50% of the normal birth rate. "Today, 60 per cent of the world's population live in countries where abortion during the first trimester is legal either for social and economic reasons or on request without any specific indication. Another 16 per cent live in countries where abortion is permitted on extended medical grounds, for eugenic indications, and/or for humanitarian reasons, such as those associated with rape or incest!" In 1975, several developing countries were found to have liberal abortion laws, including China, India, Singapore, Hong Kong in Asia, Uruguay in Latin America and Tunisia and Zambia in Africa. Liberal abortion laws however can be effective only with the provision of medical infrastructure, as found in most of the European countries.

Raising Age at Marriage: Raising age at marriage cuts down reproductive spun. Thus, it reduces fertility. For example, it has been calculated that the increase of three years in marriage age has resulted in three to four per cent cut in the birth rate in India. The birth rate may be reduced by 25 to 30 per cent by raising the female age at marriage in India to 19 years or more. However, this measure will be effective only when the law relative to it is uniformly enforced through a country.

Indirect Age-natalist Policies: Besides the above mentioned direct anti-natalist policies, there are some indirect anti-natalist policies such as incentives to check population growth, dis-incentives to child birth, improving the status of women, social and economic development, urbanisation, nutrition and health services, social security and population education. These may now be discussed in details as follows.

Incentives: Incentives have been defined by Rogers as, "Direct of indirect payments in cash or in kind that are given to an individual couple, or group in order to encourage some overt behavioral change." Incentives are offered to the individuals, couples or groups, they may be in cash or in kind. They may be immediate or deferred. As a general rule incentives have been valuable indirect anti-natalist measures. However it has been pointed out that they are unithical and seem to be an exploitation of poverty. There is ample scope for cheating and fraud. The motivational aspect is neglected. However, these defects may be overcome.

Disincentives: While incentives are positive rewards, disincentives are negative rewards. While incentives impel, disincentives restrict. The variety of disincentives may be visualised by the following disincentives provided in Singapore in 1968. (i) Couples with a large number of children would not have priority over newly-wed couples in the allocation of subsidised public housing, (ii) Under the Employment Act; no paid maternity leave would be given after the third child, (iii) The subsidised accouchement fees in Government Maternity Hospitals were modified so that higher fees were charged for higher parity confinements. Other disincentives, which came into effect on August 1, 1973, were announced by the Singapore Government in order to discourage large families. Accouchment fees, maternity leave, priority points for public housing and income-tax relief were all adjusted to, encourage each family to have no more than two children. Disincentives have been criticised on the ground that they penalise innocent children. The population also resents them. Therefore, generally they are used in exceptional cases and certainly not as much as incentives.

Improvement of the Status of Women: Several studies have pointed out a close relation between high fertility and low status of women. On the other hand, improvement of the status of women has everywhere led to decrease in fertility. Improvement of the status of women requires higher standards of education, higher socio-economic status, exposure to urban environment and greater interest outside the home. All these factors have led to fall in fertility rates. Improvement in the status of women is also linked to higher age of man, affecting fertility adversely. It also gives women an opportunity to exercise their discretion in number and spacing of children.

Social and Economic Development: As may be clearly seen in the developing countries, lower social and economic status leads to higher fertility rates. It also results in high death rates. On the other hand, as is clear in the example of developed countries, social and economic development leads to reduction in birth rates. Thus, it is effective indirect anti-natalist measure.

Urbanisation: As a general rule fertility is low in urban area as compared to the rural areas. Therefore, an indirect anti-natalist policy includes the urbanisation of rural communities. This does not necessarily require rural emigration to cities. Urban mentality may be created even in rural areas with good results.

Nutrition and Health Services for Children: An important cause of more childbirth is the high infant and children mortality rate. Provision of Nutrition and Health Services for Children leads to reduction in the infant and child mortality. Thus, the need of high rate of fertility is considerably reduced.

Social Security: An important reason of large number of births is the desire for a son for reasons for social security as may be found in India. The provision of social security measures against sickness, unemployment, invalidity, old age and death may be useful in restricting birth rates. This has been observed in Tea Gardens of South India where social security measures were known as restricting birth rates.

Population Education: Population education at school to the children and out of school to adults has been found to inculcate an appreciation of population problems and awareness to the need of population control. This facilitates the adoption of family planning measures. Therefore, it has been adopted on a large scale in developed countries. However, the impact has not been very clear in the developing countries as yet. In India the National Council of Educational Research and Training has recently incorporated population education in the syllabi of school education. Voluntary agencies like Family Planning Association of India have also undertaken population education programmes for school children and the out of school youth.

United Nations' Role

United Nations has played a significant part in determining the population policies of developed and developing countries. In 1946 the Population Commission was set up by the Economic and Social Council and a Population Division was established in the Department of Economics and Social Affairs. Since then different organisations have tried to influence population control in different countries. These include the Asian Population Conference 1963, Second World Population Conference 1965, World Health Organisation Programmes since 1965, UNICEF schemes in 1967, FAD 14th session in 1967, UNESCO programmes since 1966, ILO programmes since 1967, World Bank soft loans for population activities, United Nations Fund for Population Activities (UNFPA) in 1969. The above mentioned organsations and their programmes have resulted in the effective role of the United Nation in the fields of Population Statistics and Projections, Population Studies and Research, Population Policies, Family Planning Training and other educational activities in the field of population.

In 1974 United Nations celebrated World Population year (WPY). A World Population Plan of Action was announced by members states. The original plan was revised several times and finally adopted by most of the developed and developing countries who are members of the United Nations. It highlighted the need for rapid social and economic development more necessary than population control. It represents the agreement of the 136 member nations. A summary of its most important features will give an idea about the rule of the United Nations and the World Population Plan of Action.

1. The need for economic and social development as well as a more equitable distribution of wealth was emphasised;
2. Though all nations recognised that the population growth is high, most nations did not regard this as a music for alarm;
3. While the critical name of population growth was questioned, the interrelationship of population growth to socio-economic development was emphasised;

4. The sovereignty of each nation to determine its own population policy without external interference was accepted;
5. Countries which considered their birth rate detrimental to their national progress were invited to consider the advisability of setting up quantitative goals and implementing policies which might lead to the attainment of these goals by 1985;
6. There was resentment that population was considered to be a problem of the poor nations and the need to view it from the global point of view was emphasised;
7. Surprisingly, family planning was not considered a an agent of change to speed up the development process. The provision of family planning services was supported more on grounds of basic human rights than on demographic grounds;
8. It was recognised that the resources of the world were getting depleted and the issue of differential resume utilisation was raised;
9. The need to consider the role and status of women in the contest of development was highlighted. The question of the relationship between fertility and the status of women was considered secondary to its importance in the scheme of human rights;
10. Because of the magnitude of the population problem, the need for international assistance to carry out population activities highlighted.

Indian Policies

India's population policy may be studied in the following four periods, demarcating different approaches to the population problem. There have been shifts in the approach and the emphasis. There have been gaps in the policy and programmes. A brief review of these different periods is as follows:

Before Independence

The British reluctance in framing a population policy for India has been pointed out by Chandrasekhar in the following words, "Till the early twenties the British measured the prosperity of their rule, to some extent by the magnitude of the net addition to India's population. The degree of satisfaction over and the justification of the British rule in India was directly in proportion to the substantial increase in the population that the Census; revealed every decade."[1] This reluctance on the part of the British rulers was partly due to controversy over birth control in Britain and partly due to the policy of not interfering in local matters. During the two World Wars, Indian elite showed concern about the population growth. This was mostly concerning the density of the population. The 1931 Census revealed population growth but it was controversial whether India was over-populated. The Neo-Malthusians were of the opinion that India was over-populated. In 1916 RK Wattal supported family planning movement in his book. The population Problem in India, the first birth control centre in Mumbai was opened by R.D. Karve in 1925. Ravindra Nath Tagore strongly supported the family planning movement. The following were the main landmarks towards progress in this direction during pre-Independence period:

1. In June 11, 1930, the Government of Mysore opened the first Government Birth Control Clinic in the World.
2. In 1931 Chennai University started instructions in methods of birth control.
3. In 1932 the Government of Chennai agreed to open birth control clinics.
4. In 1932 the All India Women Conference in Lucknow recommended instructions in methods of birth control in recognised clinics to all men and women.
5. In 1935 the Indian National Congress set up a National Planning Committee under the chairmanship of Jawaharlal Nehru. This committee emphasised the need of birth control measures. It suggested raising of the marriage age, sterilisation of insane and diseased persons, maintenance of vital statistics and periodic demographic surveys.
6. On December, 1995, the Society for the Study and Promotion of Family Hygiene was founded.

7. In 1939 the Birth Control Worldwide in Uttar Pradesh and the Matri Seva Sangh in Madhya Pradesh established birth control clinics.
8. In 1940 R.N. Sapru successfully moved a resolution in the Council of States for the establishment of birth control clinics.
9. In 1940 the Society for the Study and Promotion of Family Hygiene changed its name to the Family Planning Society.
10. In 1943 Famine Enquiry Commission called the Woodhead Commission; gave an adverse report to the practice of birth control.
11. In 1945 the Government of India set up the Health Survey and Development Committee under the chairmanship of Sir Joseph Bhore. This Committee recommended birth control services for the promotion of the health of the mothers.

Besides the above development, an important influence in population control during this period was the support of M.K. Gandhi to this movement. He declared, "There can be no two opinions about the necessity of birth control. But the only method handed down from ages passed is self-control or Brahmacharya. It is an infallible sovereign remedy doing good to those who practise it. The union is meant for pleasure but for bringing forth progeny." M.K. Gandhi, however, did not support other birth control measure along with so many national leaders. Secondly, they thought that independence and not population control is the main problem. However, the elite pressed the government to propagate and encourage information on birth control and its practice.

First Phase

The period was the period of five year plan. A brief resume of population policy developments during this period is as follows:

First Five Year Plan (1951-1956): The Draft Outline of the First Five Year Plan, published in July 1951, had a section on population pressure : its bearing on development, recognising that there is pressure of population in India which requires a population policy as essential to planning.

Second Five Year Plan (1956-1961): It was maintained that the rate of population growth was a key factor in development and planning. The need for cubing the birth rates is accepted though population control programme was not considered as an alternative to socio-economic development.

Third Five Year Plan (1%1.1966): It accepted the objective of stabilising the growth of population over a reasonable period as the centre of plan development.

Fourth Five Year plan (1969-1974): It viewed population also from the point of view of social change. It insisted upon family planning as an essential and inescapable ingradient of development.

Fifth Five Year Plan (1974-1979): It included family planning in the context of the National Minimum Needs Programme. It incorporated the National Population Policy announced in April 1976. It laid down target for a birth rate of 25 per thousand, and a population growth rate of 1.4 per cent, by the end of the sixth plan period. Outlay and expenditure of family planning programme in different plan periods are as given below.

Emergency Period

During this period the Government of India, under the four-point programme of Mr. Sanjay Gandhi and the twenty-point programme of Mrs. Indira Gandhi made concerted and firm efforts towards mass sterilisation, in a bid to check population growth. The entire State Machinery was utilised for this purpose. Incentives were given for sterilisations. Camps were organised and even cases of forcible sterilisation were not rare since most of the government servants were asked to bring cases for sterilisation under the fear of losing yearly salary increments and even the job. Riots were witnessed at several places in the country in protest against the use forcible sterilisation. Information about other methods of birth control was widely disseminated and a successful movement was launched to check population growth. However, in the absence of sufficient propaganda in favour of family planning movement and due to the widespread illiteracy, superstition and religious conservatism, the movement could not succeed but rather resulted in the fall of the goverment in the following elections.

It was for the first time in the History of Independent India that some thought was given to the politicies of the Family Planning Programme. It was decided that eight per cent of the central assistance to State Plans would be earmarked against the performance of the family planning programme. The Policy Statements included long-term measures such as raising the age at marriage to 18 for girls and 21 for boys, and improving the levels of female education. A legislation was proposed with the provision that any violation of the age of marriage law would be treated as a cognisable offence. The measures for family planning included a system of graded monetary compensation based on the number of living children at the time of sterilisation with Rs. 150 offered when the couple had two living children and Rs. 100 and Rs. 70 when the couple had three and four or more children respectively. Group incentives were introduced in order to bring about greater involvement. A multimedia motivational strategy was outlined. Family planning was recognised as a multifaceted problem requiring the contribution of all the ministries to the implementation of the programme. A long-term programme for population education of the younger generation was accepted as a supportive measure. Legislation was proposed for compulsory sterilisation of a couple after they had a certain number of children. Each State was given the option to frame its own legislation in this direction. They were advised to enact such legislation for those who had three or more children. The Union Government announced modification of the service/conduct rules of Central Government Employees for family planning purposes. The principle of compulsion was accepted in spite of the fact that the Indian delegation strongly contested the propriety of coercion at the World Population Conference at Bucharest in 1974.

Due to the above stringent measures, spectacular results were achieved. An increase of 95.9% in sterilisation was noted in 1975-76 over the year 1974-75. A further increase of 216.2% was noted in the succeeding year 1976-77. Of these the percentage of males sterilisation was as much as 75%. The achievements of targets was spectacular. 106.4% target was achieved in 19511961

90.9 in 1976-77. It was estimated that 29.12 million births were averted by March 1977. The performance of different States in 1976-77 was : Bihar 229.0, Madhya Pradesh 374.3, Uttar Pradesh 209.4, West Bengal 2243, Gujrat 158.5, Haryana 425.3, Maharashtra 153.5, Punjab 299.8%. Delhi surpasses all other areas with target achievement of 477.6% sterilisation in 1976-77. All these States had achieved spectacular improvement upon their performance in former years. This spectacular success was appreciated all over the world. The role of incentives as well as disincentives was equally important in this process. For example, under the Uttar Pradesh Essential Articles and Things (Restriction on Grant or Supply to Unplanned Families) Order, 1976, the following items were linked with acceptance of sterilisation : the issue and supply of rationed articles; licences and permits under any order issued under any section of the Essential Commidities Act or Under Rule 114 of the Defense and Internal Security Rules, Licence or permit for the allotment of a scooter or motor car from the discriminatory quota of the State Government, and permits for public carriers, autorickshaws, taxis; a permit for a building under the Uttar Pradesh Buildings Act, 1972, or issued by any Development Authority', allotment on rental basis of a house owned by the State Government or by any Development Authority, free medical aid, concession in educational fees, stipends; reservation of seats in medical colleges or other technical institutions; facilities regarding payment of dues of electricity charges in installments.

The stringent coercive measure adopted resulted in a lot of torture upon the public. This wall not reported during the period of emergency due to strict censor over the press. However, soon after the lifting of emergency, *The Times of India*, April 1, 1977, reported, "Then suddenly the now-butchery began. The handling of the programme went form one extreme-apathy, niggardliness, bad planning, poor organisation and general maladministration to the other coercion, quotas, bureaucratic over-zealousness, fear and brutality. The national population policy (NPP) promulgated a year ago seemed (and seems still to many people), despite the many fine sentiments it expressed to have been framed only to legitimise the assault on human dignity that was euphemistically called sterilisation campaign." The ruling Congress was defeated in March 1977 particularly on the issue of the excesses of the family planning programme particularly in the Northern states.

After Emergency

The Janata Government, after coming into power, announced that coercion would not be used to implement the family planning, programme which was now renamed as the Family Welfare Programme. Therefore, all the rules and regulations with element of compulsion were dropped. However, the importance of family planning movement was equally emphasised. Sterilisation was now reffered to as 'voluntary sterilisations and the word 'expectations' was substituted for the earlier word—targets. The Government accepted many of the measures included in the National Population Policy announced by the Previous Government, such as raising of the age of marriage, integration of services for maternal and child health with the Family Planning Programme, popularisation of Family Welfare Programme, etc. Some of the measures taken by the Government include emphasis on the voluntary nature of the programme, securing the cooperation of rural cooperative institution system of graded compensation for sterilisation, etc. This lukewarm policy resulted in considerable decline in the performance level of different states towards family planning expectations. A general decline was noted everywhere. It was clear that the programme received a serious Setback due to political reason and the prospects of its success were rather bleak.

However, the Indira Congress staged a quick comeback, in the year 1977. This change of government has again set the ball rolling though the government is very cautious not to use coercion anywhere. New incentives are being introduced. For example, recently the Uttar Pradesh Goverment announced an additional yearly increment to the salary of teachers having two or lesser number of children and undergone sterilisation. Similar steps have been also offered incentives for family planning purposes. More advertisement is being given to the methods of birth control. Abortion has been legalised and service for it is now available in most of the urban areas at cheaper rates. Steps are being taken to increase the supplies of other means of birth control.

Family Planning

India's population rose from 36.11 crore in 1951 to 84.63 crore as per the 1991 Census. On 2.4 per cent of the world's land area, India accomodates more than 16 per cent of the world's population. The population is increasing by about 1.7 crore every year. The average annual exponential growth rate has fallen for the first time after independence to 2.14 per cent in 1981-91 from 2.22 per cent in 1971-81. As per the Sample Registration System (SRS), the annual natural growth rate of population has come down to 1.94 per cent in 1993 from 1.91 per cent in 1991, the birth rate has come down from 29.2 in 1992 to 28.7 in 1993 and the infant Mortality Rate (IMR) has come down to 74 per thousand live births in 1993 from 79 in 1992. The Family Welfare Programme in India aims to provide family planning services within the broader context of maternal and child health care. It disseminates information and education to enable couples to make voluntary and informed choices regarding the size of the family and spacing through contraception.

The National Health Policy (1983) had set a goal of Net Reproduction Rate (NRR) of Unity, corresponding to CDR of 21, CDR of nine and natural growth rate of 1.2 per cent for 2000 AD. It was stated in the Eighth Five Year Plan Document that NRR-I would now be achievable only in the period 2011-16 AD. The population of India crossed the one billion mark by 2001 as true to the projections made by the Standing Committee of Experts on Population Projections. As per the UN Population Projections (Medium Variant), the India's population could overtake that of China by 2035 AD, when India's population will be 1.545 billion as against China's population of 1.516 billion.

The Success Story

The National Family Welfare Programme was launched in India in 1951 with 'the objective of reducing the birth rate to the extent necessary to stabilise the population at a level consistent with the requirements of the National Economy' (First Five Year Plan Document). The achievements of the Family Welfare Programme since its inception are summarised below.

It is estimated that if the averted births had taken place, the average annual exponential growth rate of population during the 1981-91 decade would have been of the order of 2.71 per cent as against 2.14 per cent actually registered in 1991 Cemus. The Eighth Five Year Plan had laid down following goals to be achieved by 1997.

Among the states, there is considerable variation in reducing the growth of population e.g. States like Kerala and Tamil Nadu with crude birth rates of 17.4 and 19.5 respectively have performed very well. On the other hand, the crude birth rates in Bihar (32-0), Madhya Pradesh (34.9), Rajasthan (34.0) and Uttar Pradesh (36-2), which constitutes about 40 per cent of India's population are higher than the national average of 28.7 per thousand population in 1993. Similar variations are seen in respect of the infant mortality rates. At one end of the spectrum, Kerala has an IMR of only 13 per thousand live births whereas it is as high as 106 in Madhya Pradesh and 110 in Orissa. Total fertility rates in Bihar (4.6), Madhya Pradesh (4.4), Rajasthan (4.5) and Uttar Pradesh (5.2) are significantly higher than the all India average of 3.6 (SRS : 1992).

In keeping with democratic traditions of the country, Family Welfare Programme seeks to promote on a voluntary basis responsible and planned parenthood with two-child norm, male and female, or both, through independent choice of family welfare methods best stated to the acceptors. Family welfare services are offered through total health care delivery system. People's participation is sought through voluntary agencies, opinion leaders, peoples representatives, government functionaries and various other structures and influential groups. Imaginative use of mass media and inter-personal communication is resorted to for explaining various methods of contraception and removing socio-cultural barriers. As a result the number of acceptors of various family planning methods have started increasing over the years.

Machinery for Implementation

Family Welfare programme implemented through the state governments with cent per cent Central assistance. In rural areas, services are provided through the network of subcentres, primary health centres, and community health centres. Establishment of subcentres programmes has been made hundred per cent Centrally-sponsored scheme (except the salary of male health worker and construction of subcentre building) from April 1981. Against the requirement of 134 folds subcentres there are 1.31 lakh subcentres functioning as, on 30 September, 1993. It is proposed to establish 17,030 subcentres during Eighth Plan.

Methods of Birth Control

During 1994-95, 42.90 lakh sterilsations were performed in the country. The number of IUD insertion during the same period was 62.40 lakh. Besides, there were 171.13 lakh CC users and 47.46 lakh OP users. *Nirodh*, besides being provided free, is also sold under the social marketing programme which is being operated through a network of over three lakh retail outlets of 11 leading consumer goods, Pharmaceutical and oil companies. With a view to make condoms available in rural and far-flung areas at reasonable prices, scheme of distribution of condoms through Public Distribution System has already been implemented in many states. It is estimated that 45.4 per cent of 15.5 came eligible couples, whose wives are in reproductive age group of 15-44 years, were protected by one or the other approved family planning methods as on 31 March, 1994 averting 16.88 crore births since inception of the programme.

Termination of Pregnancy by Doctor

It is estimated that about one-fourth of the maternal morbidity and mortality are due to illegal abortion in order to prevent these health hazards to women, the Medical Termination of Pregnancy Act, 1971 was promulgated. Under this Act, medical termination pregnancy can be done in pregnant women upto 20 weeks, if pregnancy is likely to result in birth of a congenitally malformed child or continuation of pregnancy is likely to harm the mother in the existing circumstances and in cases of contraceptive failure.

Research studies in India have shown that vaccum aspiration is a safe and effective method for terminating first trimester (three months) pregnancy. During the last few years studies on first trimester NTP using antiprogestin compounds like RU 486, alone or along with prostaglandins are being carried out to see whether these could provide a safe, effective non-surgical method for termination of early pregnancy. It has been observed that about 10-15 per cent of abortion seekers came during second trimester of pregnancy. A wide variety of methods have been investigated for second trimester NTP. Whatever is the method used, second trimester of pregnancy termination is not as safe as first trimester pregnancy termination. All available data indicate that in order to minimise period, to avoid the recurrence of an unwanted pregnancy, women should be provided with concurrent contraception : IUDs, OCs, Condoms, etc., or sterilisation. Since inception of the programme in April 1972, 97.5 lakh terminations upto December 1994 were conducted under NTP Act.

Health Care Programmes

The National Health Policy (1983) in context of the global objective of 'Health for All by 2000 AD' has inter alia set the following normative goals relative to maternal and child health care : a reduction in infant mortality to less than 60 per thousand live births; (b) reduction in maternal mortality to below 200 per one lakh live births; (c) reduction in child mortality (0-4) to less than 10 per thousand population. As a part of the overall strategy to achieve these goals, the following specific programmes have been under implementation as cent per cent Centrally-sponsored schemes: (i) Universal Immunisation Programme (wider implementation since 1985-86), for reducing mortality and morbidity due to six vaccine preventable diseases, namely, diphtheria, pertussis, tetanus, poliomyelitis, measles and childhood tuberculosis. The primary target group for this programme is infants and pregnant women. When the immunisation programme was launched in 1985, IMR for the country as a whole was 97 per every thousand live births. The intensification of immunisation programme has contributed to a significant decline in IMR in the last few years. The decline has been particularly pronounced in 1990 as compared to earlier years. During that year the IMR declined (by 11 points) to 80 per thousand live births from 91 in 1989; and (ii) Oral Rehydration Therapy (ORT) Programme (under implementation since 1986-87) for reducing mortality and morbidity due to dehydration caused by diarrhoea. The primary target of this programme is children under five years of age. Diarrhoea diseases are a major health problem in the country especially among children below five years of age. On an average, a child suffers three episodes of diarrhoea per year. The National Diarrhoea Diseases Control Programme, initiated in the Sixth Plan, was, therefore, intensified in the Seventh Plan with a conscious decision to promote Oral Rehydration Therapy, and (iii) Prophylaxis Schemes (under implementation since Fourth Plan Period), against nutritional anaemia among pregnant women as well as children and against blindness due to Vitamin 'A' deficiency among children under three years of age. Nutritional anaemia is one of the major public health problems especially affecting pregnant women and pre-school children. Anaemia affecting the mothers also affects inter-uterine growth of the foetus. Similarly, nutritional anaemia among pre-school children makes them susceptible to disease and death. Vitamin 'A deficiency is widely prevalent in the country among the pre-school children.

Survival of Children

The package of services under Child Survival and Safe Motherhood Project are to be expanded under two major components: (a) child survival component under which the ARI control programme will be expanded along with provision of the kit based supply of drugs. In addition, essential newborn care for ensuring survival of newborns is being introduced. Exclusive breastfeeding is being promoted as an intervention for child survival; and (b) safe motherhood component under which first referral units will be set up in the six states of Assam, Bihar, Madhya Pradesh, Orissa, Rajasthan and Uttar Pradesh.

Schemes in Vogue

All India Hospital Post-Partum Programme. All India Hospital Post-Partum Programme (AIHPP) was introduced in 1969. It is a hospital-based, maternity-centered approach to family planning. The primary objective of the post-partum programme is to improve the health of the mother and children through MCH and Family welfare Programme which included ante-natal, neo-natal and post-natal services; immunisation services to children and mothers; and prophylaxis against anaemia and blindness. The programme is based on the following rationale : (a) that women who have recently delivered are of proven fertility, and are at risk to become pregnant again rapidly, and (b) at the time of delivery and during the lying-in-period, they are generally more receptive to adopt one or the other family planning method. The post-partum programme offers necessary facilities to such women. It has proved to be an efficient way of delivering family planning services. The Programme now covers 550 medical colleges and two-post graduate institutions. With a view to provide MCH and family welfare services in rural and semi-urban areas, as well as to improve the health of mothers and children, the post-partum programme has been extended to 1,012 sub-district hospitals.

Facility for Test

In order to detect cervical cancer among women acceptors and non-acceptors of various family welfare methods, the PAP Smear Test Facility Programme has been introduced in all the medical colleges of the country. Under the scheme, a post of a cyto-technician as per state government's scale of pay and financial assistance and contigencies provided. The cytotechnician is required to work under the overall guidance and supervision of the professor of pathology of the medical college. The programme has been extended in a phased manner in 105 medical colleges all over the country. The state governments have sanctioned the programme in 80 medical colleges only.

Sterilisation Beds Scheme

Under the scheme, beds are provided to voluntary organisations/local bodies/institutions on the basis of their performance of previous years and on the recommendations of the state government and regional director of health and family welfare of the respective state. Maintenance grant under this scheme at the rate of Rs. 3,000 per bed per annum is provided to each institution subject to a minimum performance of 75/60 tubectomies per bed per annum for government institutions and local bodies/voluntary organisations respectively. A total of 3,610 sterilisation beds have been reserved under the scheme.

Assessment Made

Population explosion in developing countries is a matter of international concern. For India with 16% of the world's population and 2.4% of the global and area, it is a problem of serious magnitude. Its current population growth rate of 2.03% (SRS, 1989) with an annual addition of 1.6 crore presents a formidable scenario. India's population size has increased from 34.2 crore at the time of independence to 84.4 crore as per the 1991 Census. Already, there is tremendous pressure on our resources for providing even the basic needs, such as fund, homing, education, health, to the country's large population. If the present growth of population is unchecked, the demand for even basic facilities and services would far outstrip their supply and there would be a serious impact on our socio-economic development, the quality of the lives of the people and the environment. Indeed, population control has to be the foremost national priority.

Although India was the first country in the world to launch the National Family Planning Programme in 1951, over the years many other developing countries like Thailand, Indonesia, China, Sri Lanka, etc. have achieved a much greater degree of success in controlling population. China has an annual growth rate of 1.44% (1989) and Indonesia 1.59% (1989). The National Health Policy adopted by the Parliament in 1983 envisages that by the year 2000 AD, the Net Reproduction Rate would be Unity, with the population growth rate at 1.2% birth rate of 21 per thousand, death rate of 9 per thousand, infant mortality rate a below 60 per thousand live births and couple protection rate of 60%. The largest figures available indicate that while due to the efforts made in providing better and more extensive health care, the death rate came down to 10.2 per thousand, the birth rate is still very high at 2.03%. The infant mortality-rate has come down, but was still high at the rate of 91 per thousand. The couple protection rate at 44.1% was also much below the target. A sustained national efforts was therefore, called for to achieve the goal of balanced population profile by the turn of the century.

The family planning programme in India is being promoted on voluntary basis, as a people's movement in keeping with the democratic traditions of the country. The two-child norm is being promoted through independent choice of the family planning method best suited to the acceptor. The programme in the field is implemented by the State Governments and Union Territories Administrations and there is very wide disparity in the success rate. While it has had considerable success in the southern states, specially Kerala and Goa where the birth rate has come down to about 19 per thousand, its impact on the large northern states like U.P., Bihar, Madhya Pradesh and Rajasthan, has been limited and the birth rates in these States are still in the range of 33 to 37 per thousand.

It is realised that the people respond to the family planning programmes more readily, if they are assured of the survival of their children. Therefore, for many years Family Planning is being paused as a part of the Integrated Programme of Family Welfare with special attention to the health and well-being of the family, specially mothers and children. A vast rural and urban infrastructure has been established to implement the Family Welfare Programme in the country. Immunisation Programme has been universalised to ensure better prospects of child survival which in turn would create the right psychological ambience for the small-family norm. The desire for large families, specially male children in the prevailing socio-cultural and economic milleu, characteristically low status of women, low female literacy, early marriage of girls and high infant mortality rate are stumbling blocks in the progress of the Family Welfare Programme. The lack of popular commitment and will inhibit its faster tempo. The Programme is perceived as a Governmental programme, devoid of popular participation. Quality and out-reach of its service-delivery network are deficient in many parts of the country. Over-emphasis on terminal methods lead to inadequate coverage of younger couples with high-fertility potential. Communication system are not effective enough to dispel the prevailing apathy, ignorance, and misconception about the programme among the masses.

Confronted with the grim prospects of population explosion and the inadequacies of the present strategies, radical and innovative strategies are called for to revamp the programme and bring about a more rapid decline in fertility. Population Control and Family Welfare Programme need to have a national consensus, cutting across political, religious and cultural differences. It needs to be based on active community participation and has to be transformed from a governmental programme into a people's movement. A differential need based strategy needs to be developed in the 206 low-performing districts in the country which are mostly in the few North Indian States, viz U.P., Bihar, Madhya Pradesh and Rajasthan to create an immediate impact. The status of "men and female literacy are key factors for fertility decline, as seen in the State of Kerala and elsewhere. Age of marriage of girls is yet another crucial factor. In the few large North Indian States mentioned show, the average age of marriage for girls is well below the national average of 18.3 (1981) and the statutory minimum age of 18 yens. Studies indicate that if the average age of marriage of girls in India is pushed up by two years, it my result in lowering the birth rate by about 25%. Besides, a comparatively higher age of marriage "old bring down maternal and infant mortality.

Information, Education and Communication (IEC) effort is vital to the Population Control Programme. Fortunately, there has been a quantum jump in female literacy (24.8% in 1981 to 39.42% in 1991) during the last decade, thanks to specific measures undertaken by the Government. Population education should be a part of school and college education. It should also form an important ingredient of adult education and non-formal education. Communication strategies should be so devised as to be effective enough to bring about attitudinal changes and dispel apathy, ignorance and misgivings about family planning and small family norm. All non-governmental organisations—private sector, voluntary agencies, private medical practitioners and practitioners of Indian System of Medicines, Local bodies and Panchayati Raj Institutions should be fully involved in a massive effort of community participation. The service delivery system and its out-reach should be expanded with emphasis on quality of service. A package of effective incentives and disincentives should be formulated specially for younger couples in high-reproductive range who require spacing methods of contraception. New generation contraceptive should be introduced in the country to make an impact on younger couples.

Thus, there is an imperative need to develop an integrated multi-sectoral strategy to handle the population problem in all its demensions. Given strong political will, commitment of the people and vigorous implementation of revamped strategies, there is no reason why India should not be able to contain its population within manageable limits and open the way for utilisation of its resources for improving the quality of life of its people.

Population Policy 2000

The Union cabinet on Tuesday date 15th Feb; 2000 announced the much-awaited population policy though without clarifying the sensitive issue of delimitation of Lok Sabha constituencies.

The policy, which has a special terms on health and education to achieve a stable population by 2045, includes freezing of the number of seats in the Lok Sabha at the current level of 543—which is based on the 1971 census till 2026. As per the original schedule, the number would have changed in 2001.

Government sources, however, did not clarify whether the decision meant that the number of seats allocated to different states can be changed (taking into consideration the population increase or decrease in individual states), while keeping the overall number a the present level.

They also refused to say whether the government plans to bring a delimitation Bill after getting the population policy passed in the coming session of Parliament.

The issue is a sensitive one as southern States such as Kerala and Tamil Nadu, which have taken a lead in population control, feel that if the delimitation is carried out next year as per the original schedule, northern States will gain at least 40 seats.

"The government should consult other parties before taking a final view on delimitation," said Prithviraj Chauhan of the Congress.

It is learnt that controversy delayed the approval of the policy, formulated as far back as 1994 by a committee order M.S. Swaminathan. After discussing it threadbare in three separate meetings, the present cabinet, in keeping with the suggestion of noted demographers, decided to freeze the number of seats till 2026.

The policy, while continuing with the two-child norm, takes a comprehensive look at issues determining population growth. Health care of mother and child, health and sanitation as well as compulsory education figure high on its agenda. It aims to achieve a reduced population growth through decentralised decision-making.

Its immediate, medium and long-term objectives will be reviewed regularly by a National Commission of Population chaired by the Prime Minister. Chief ministers, NGOs and public health professionals will be among the other members of this commission.

Union family welfare secretary A. R. Nanda told *The Times of India* that a detailed action plan has been worked out which will be followed virtually for the next 45 years but more intensively for the next 10 "crucial" years.

The action plan will have the following main features.

Self-help groups at village, panchayat levels comprising mostly housewives who will interact with health care workers and gram panchayats.

- Elementary education to be made free and compulsory.
- Registration of marriage, pregnancy to be made compulsory along with births and deaths.

A National Commission on Population chaired by the Prime Minister has been announced to monitor and guide the implementation of the policy. The commission will have chief ministers and the Central Minister in charge of the Department of Family Welfare and other concerned Ministers as members.

Health and Family Welfare Minister N. T Shanmugham told newspersons after the Cabinet meeting that reputed demographers, public health professionals and representatives of NGOs will also join the commission to review the policy implementation.

The current freeze of Lok Sabha seats was imposed as per the 42nd Constitutional Amendment with the 1971 census as the basis. The freeze is valid till 2001. This enables state governments to fearlessly pursue the agenda for population stabilisation, the freeze is being extended till 2026.

It was explained that if the freeze was lifted after 2001, unchecked population growth in a state like Uttar Pradesh could raise the number of its seats substantially, while another state like Tamil Nadu pursuing small family norm vigorously, could end up losing some of its Lok Sabha seats. The situation could thus reward a state ignoring population control and punish one doing its utmost to keep population increase order check.

On May 11 this year, India is projected to have one billion (100 crone) population. Through various measures the population figure could be controlled at 110 crores in 2010, otherwise it could reach 116 crores in that year.

The immediate objective of the policy is to address the urgent needs of contraception, health infrastructure, health personnel and to provide integrated service delivery for basic reproductive and child health care.

There are 14 national socio-domographic goals to be achieved by 2010.

Among them are promoting delayed marriages for girls not earlier than age 18 and preferably after age 20; and achieving 80 per cent institutional deliveries and 100 per cent deliveries by trained persons.

Policy Highlights

Prime Minister heads national pannel to monitor policy implementation.

Freeze on current Lok Sabha strength to be extended from 2001 to 2026.

Strict enforcement of Child Marriage Restraint Act and Pre-Natal Diagnostic Techniques Act.

Incentives to adopt two-child norm.

- Facilities for safe abortions to be increased.
- Integration of Indian System of Medicine in provision of reproductive and child health services.

Population policy lacks teeth. At last the Union Cabinet has cleared the population policy today after many hiccups. A decision on the controversial policy has been deferred at least thrice. The policy, which was to have incentives and disincentives to contain population, ultimately turned out to be a watered down policy and purely voluntary.

The National Population Policy 2000, appears to be only carrots and no sticks to contain the population. A Cabinet Minister, who was quite upset about the controversial policy today remarked "It is only carrots an7d no sticks." In fact, some of the recommen-dations made by the Group of Ministers, like limiting the number for legislators and parliamentarians to two was also not accepted.

While the Prime Minister is said to be keen on the two-child norm for legislators, the cleared policy does not reflect his will. Home Minister L.K. Advand has also favoured a two-child norm. The BJP's Chennai Decimation is in favour of small family norm. However, a majority in the Cabinet is said to be opposed to any hint in the policy that implies compulsion. In fact, the government is even shying away from using the term "population control" and prefers to call it "population stabilisation".

Interestingly, political parties have rejected a suggestion on a bill limiting the family to two children for MPs in December last. Ultimately, the Cabinet obviously has decided to keep aside all contentious issues aside and simply voted for a passive policy.

Right from the beginning consensus seems to be eluding the Cabinet. Also political parties are shy of using any coercion fearing adverse public sentiment.

The population policy was to be placed before Parliament during the last session, but it could not be done due to some reservations expressed by some ministers, especially from the South and even by Deputy Chairman of Planning Commission K.C. Pant.

The Southern Ministers are said to have argued that because the South has done well in containing population they should not be punished.

The one important sop to the South is that the Cabinet has decided that the size of the Lok Sabha will remain the same until 2026. If the delimitation takes place next year, then the size would have changed.

The South, which has done well on population control, would be affected by delimitation now as the parliamentary constituencies would be decided on the size of population. Kerala or Tamil Nadu have less number of constituencies than U.P. or Bihar, which have not controlled their population.

The new policy aims to achieve a stable population by 2045. The policy has identified 14 national socio-demographic goals.

They include compulsory school education up to 14 years of age, reduction of infant mortality rate below 30 per live births, reduction of maternal mortality rate to below 100 per 100,000 live births, universal immunisation, achieve 80 per cent institutional deliveries, access to information, containing AIDS, prevention and control of communicable diseases, promotion of small family norms and a people-centered family welfare programme.

A Positive Step

Population policy scheme requires Rs. 300 cr. more. The "management paradigm shift" focussing on the voluntary sector and utilisation of village self help groups is the high point of the National Population Policy 2000. While steps to constitute the National Commission will have to wait till after the policy is placed before Parliament, an additional budget of Rs. 3000 crore is required for major portions of the policy to be implemented. This was stated by Union Minister for Health and Family Welfare N.T. Shanmugham at a Press conference here today.

Stating that a major chunk of the funding will come from the private sector, there are plans to tap the corporate sector and NGOs to provide a resource share for the policy to effectively take-off on the ground, the Minister said.

With nothing new to add to the already released population policy, the Minister reiterated that the immediate objective is to address the unmet needs of contraception. The long-term objective is to achieve a stable population by the year 2045. Strategic themes included child health among others.

The BID to have the FM as Chairman of the National Commission on Population and the move to push the target year to achieve stable population by 35 years have drawn flak from some quarters even while there is an agreement on the Cabinet clearance on the National Population Policy being a "Positive step".

Fears were also expressed on the implementation aspects of the policy with experts being apprehensive on whether this document is "implementable". While there was criticism on the "hush-hash" manner in which the policy was adopted. Concern was also expressed on where the money for providing incentives will come from ?

While Michael Vlassoff, UNFPA Representative for India was guarded about his reaction to the policy, Dr. P.R. Talwar, demographer, came out strongly on the Government pushing the stability target from 2016 to 2046. He was also critical of the Population Commission being chaired by the Prime Minister on the grounds that he would never have sufficient time to devote to such a crucial issue. Dr. Talwar advocated that the high-profile Commission under the Prime Minister should be substituted by smaller working groups "outside the government" to monitor coordination and implementation of the policy.

Mr. Valssoff, on the other hand spelt out the "positives" of the policy, which were the absence of a "coercive element" and "Draconian measures". Stating the policy to be "on the right track", Mr Vlassoff said it was a "clear statement" of what the notion wanted to do and the direction its people were taking. 'It clearly demonstrates the growing commitment of the Government to population concerns," Mr. Vlassoff said.

As against this, Dr. Nina Puri, President, Family Planning Association of India felt that the policy was "soft" on the male participation. "The message the new policy sends across is that the women will bear the burden of population control with the men being let off easily," Dr. Puri said. The new policy, she felt, diluted the one-pronged issue of sterilisation while couching so many things like education, gender concerns, immunisation, AIDS, etc.

"Is the Government serious about the overall development, and will it be able to weave these issues as a coherent whole ? Where will the money for incentives come from?" asked Dr. Puri.

Dr. Saroj Pachauri, Regional Director, Population Council, was, among those who "liked" the policy on the grounds that it was gender-sensitive, addressed the needs of adolescents and strengthened the capacity at the village level. He was, however, wary of incentives, as "they never work".

Background

The British Period. The British rulers of India were not interested in formulating any population policy for India. They were not interested in making birth control movement a success in India. There were two masons for this: (a) The birth control movement was a controversial issue in their home land; (b) They never wanted to interfere with the traditions, customs, values and beliefs of Indians—sex being a very private affair.

World Wars I and II. The intervening period during these Wars saw some concern towards population in India but not much could be achieved as Indian were occupied with freedom movement. And the cause of concern was density of population and not the rate of growth because the rate of mortality was equally high. We were also not very sure whether or not India was over-populated. But some economists were advocating that lesser population meant better standards of living.

Period Between 1916-1947. Several important developments took place between 1916 and 1947. In 1916, Pyare Kishen Waltal published 'The Population Problem in India' in which he advocated family planning. In 1925, Raghunath Dhondo Karve, a professor of mathematics opened the first birth control centre in Mumbai. In the same year, Rabindranath Tagore advocated family planning in his letters. In June 1930, Mysore Government opened the first Government Birth Control Clinic in the world. In 1931, the Chennai University accepted the proposal to impart instructions in methods of birth control. In 1932, the All India Women's Conference at Lucknow recommended that men and women should be instructed in methods of birth control in recognised clinics. In 1935, the Indian National Congress set up

National Planning Committee under the chairmanship of Jawaharlal Nehru. As the recommendations of this committee are of historic importance, they are quoted here in full: (1) We agree with the view that the size of the Indian population is a basic issue in national economic planning, in so far as its unrestricted increase of proportion to means of subsistence, affects adversely the standard of living, and tends to defeat many social and ameliorative measures. The problem has been fundamentally caused by the lack of all-found co-ordinated economic development. While measures for the improvement of the quality of the population and limiting excessive population pressure are necessary, the basic solution of the present disparity between population and standard of living lies in the economic progress of the country on a comprehensive and planned basis. (2) In the interest of social economy, family happiness and national planning, family planning and limitation of children are essential; and the state should adopt a policy to encourage these. It is desirable to lay stress on self-control as well as to spread knowledge of cheap and safe methods of birth control. Birth control clinics should be established and other necessary measures taken in this behalf to prevent the use or advertisement of harmful methods. (3) We consider that a gradual raising of the marriage age and discouragement of polygamy are desirable in the interests of the limitation of the size of the family. (4) An eugenic programme should include the sterilisation of persons suffering from transmissible diseases of a serious nature, such as insanity or epilepsy. (5) The maintenance of vital statistics and the carrying out of periodic demographic surveys on comprehensive lines are necessary; and appropriate machinery should be devised for the purpose.

In December 1935, the Society for the Study and Promotion of Family/Hygiene was founded with Lady C. Jehangir as its President. By 1940, the Society for the Study and Promotion of Family Hygiene charged its name to Family Planning Society, incorporating Birth Control Clinic of the Bhagini Samaj in Mumbai.

Birth control remained a controversial issue.

The views of Gandhiji may also be considered on it. Gandhi was a man of versatile genius. His views affected all aspects of life of Indians. He accepted the need of birth control. He advocated it on ethical and moral grounds for he maintained that would improve the moral fibre and physical health of the individual. His method was that of abstinence. Gandhi further said, "It is our duty at the present moment to suspend bringing forth heirs to our slavery."

Interestingly, a group worked against birth control movement was national leaders. They said that foreign domination was responsible for creating tention in the minds of the Indians and hence their prolific childbearing.

Upto 1947, only ground work for birth control movement had been done. The movement was limited to few cities alone.

First Phase (1951-85)

The era of planned development dawned in India with the launching of five year plans in 1951. We have to have a look at Family Planning efforts during these plans.

The First Five Year Plan (1951-56) recognised that India had it population problem. It stated, "The pressure of population in India is already so high that a reduction in the raw of growth must be regarded as a major desideratum."

The Second Five Year Plan (1956-61) accepted the need for curbing the birth rates, "This highlights the need for a large and active programme aimed at restraining population growth, even as it reinforces the cue for a massive development effort"

The Third Five Year Plan (1961-66) stated, "The objective of stabilising the growth of population over a reasonable period must therefore be at the very centre of planned development."

The Fourth and Fifth Five Year Plans echoed similar sentiments. Family Planning is our national minimum need.

In 1977, there was a political revolution, Mrs. Gandhi was voted out of power. Then came Morarji Desai Government. This government changed the name of Family Planning to Family Welfare. It was committed to the programme of population control but ruled out any compulsion in it. .

The Sixth Five Year Plan (1980-85) kept Rs. 10,000 million for the family planning programme. The long-term demographic goal recommended by the working group on Population Policy appointed by the Planning Commission was approved by National Development Council.

It involves reducing the net reproduction rate (NRR) to one by 1996 for the country as a whole and by 2001 in the states. The implications of this long-term demographic goal are as follows:

(i) The average size of the family would be reduced from 4.2 children to 2.3 children.

(ii) The birth rate per thousand population would be reduced from the level of 33 in 1978 in 21.

(iii) The death rate per thousand population would be reduced from about 14 in 1978 to 9 and the infant mortality rate would he reduced from 129 to 60 or less.

(iv) As against 22 per cent of the eligible couples protected with family planning, 60 per cent would be protected.

(v) The population of India will be around 900 million by the turn of the century and will stabilise at 1,200 million by the year 2050 A.D.

In the Seventh Five-Year Plan (1985-90), the outlay for the family welfare programme is Rs. 3,256 crore. It had been pointed out that in view of the progress made in the Sixth Plan, the goal of reaching a net reproduction rate of unity could be reached only by 2006-2011, instead of reaching it by the year 2000 A.D. as envisaged in the Sixth Five-Yew Plan. The following goals for the year 1990 had been set:

(i)	Effective couple protection rate:	42 per cent
(ii)	Crude birth rate:	29.1
(iii)	Crude death rate:	10.4
(iv)	Infant mortality rate:	90.0

In order to reach an effective couple protection rate of 42 per cent, 31 million sterilisations, 21.25 million IUD insertions would have to be performed by 1990 and during the terminal year of the Seventh Plan 14.5 million users of conventional contraceptives/ oral contraceptives were to be enlisted.

Family Planning Programme. Many authors have tried to write in detail on the family planning programme in India. A brief summary of it can be given. The following are the points:

1. Organisational Structure
2. Approaches to Implementation
3. Family Planning Methods
4. Achievements

Organisational Structure. The family planning programme was started in 1952. It is the responsibility of Central Ministry of Health. It is a centrally sponsored and financed programme implemented by the states. Not talking of officers and their designations, it should suffice here to state that in 1966, a full-fledged department of Family Planning was established within the Ministry which was redesignated as the Ministry of Health and Family Planning and a Minister of Cabinet rank was placed in its charge. There is a Cabinet Committee of Family Planning. Then there is a Family Planning Council with the Minister of Health and Family Planning. The Council has a standing committee. Similar councils were set up in the States as well. These councils are mainly meant to review the progress of the family planning programmes and to make policy decisions. At the District level, we have Family Planning Bureaus. All cities having a population of 10 lakhs are allowed the pattern of District Family Planning Bureaus. In 1977, we had change of nomenclature-from Family Planning to Family Welfare. The programme is of utmost importance. It is primarily the responsibility of Ministry of Health and that is why some critics say that it has shown poor performance. The Health Ministry is a weak ministry and it is politically unimportant ministry. They want a Commission on Population.

Implementation Approaches

Many approaches have been followed:

The Clinical Approach or the Planned Parenthood Model. It leaned heavily in favour of services for women rather than for couples. It also leaned heavily on medical personnel, which is scarce in India. It reached only a fraction of population and did not make much impact on birth rates. This clinic approach was the approach of 1960s.

The Extension Approach. The credit for this goes to Lt. Col. B.L. Raina. Extension approach was invented in 1963. It is an educational approach. It tries to bring a change in the knowledge, attitudes and behaviour of people in regard to family planning. Here the leaders of the people are to be identified and their help is to be taken to make people accept family planning among their own groups. Leaders work with people. The help of Panchayats is also to be taken. There are three conditions which have to be satisfied if extension approach is to work:

(i) Group acceptance;

(ii) Knowledge about family planning; and

(iii) Easy availability of supplies and services.

The Integrated Approach. It is not a new approach. It was classified in Second Five Year Plan, "Family Planning Service is likely to succeed if the clinics are associated with maternity and child health work or with centres which provide medical aid and welfare services." In the Fifth Five Year Plan, the Family Planning Programme will form an integral part of Maternal and Child Health (M.C.H.) and Nutrition Services. With this change in strategy, it is expected that programme will find wider acceptance among the people. The principle of integration of family planning services with maternity and child health services has thus been accepted since long. The basis of integration is that infant will be well protected. He will not be allowed to die. Full care will be given to the mother and child. Hence, please limit your family. One step towards this is immunisation of the infant and the mother against many diseases. Vitamins are also to be given.

Multipurpose Workers

Multipurpose workers are also to be appointed. They were appointed because many primary health centres and sub-centres were not able to adequately meet the health and family planning needs of the population. Under this scheme of appointment of multipurpose workers, comprehensive health care is to be provided through a team of two workers, one male and the other female. One sub-centre will cover a population of 5000 people. "It is envisaged that under this scheme, integration and health and family planning services and nutrition, education will take place from the subcentre through the PHC (Primary Health Centre) and District levels to the states."

One more facet of integrated approach is the post-partum programme, which is restricted to hospitals, where women are admitted/enrolled for delivery and abortion. The all India Post-Partum Programme was initiated in January 1970. Sub-District Hospitals were also covered by it by 1980. Medical colleges do also have such centres. Sub-divisional level centres were also to be established.

The rationale behind this programme is that when women go to hospitals for maternity care, they are in a positive frame of mind to receive family planning education.

(d) The Cafeteria Approach. Like in a cafeteria, all sons of snacks are available, you have to pick your choice-similarly applied to family planning. It means that all sorts of family planning devices are available, you have to pick the one that suits you. The cafeteria approach was very popular during 1970s. It still is. All methods of family planning are available.

(e) The Camp Approach. It means mass vasectomy camps. Large number of operations are performed in a single day. Vasectomy is a permanent method of limiting one's family. These camps can succeed and also can fail. These fail when people do not cooperate. In these camps, festival-like spirit prevails and people are kept in a cheerful mood. Incentives also lead to a great success of these camps. People accept the idea.

Family Planning Methods. We are only listing the method and its effectiveness. We are not discussing the practice of it.

(a) The Rhythm Method : Orthodox people practice it. Not very effective for large scale application. It is difficult to keep track of infertile days.

(b) Diaphragm and Jelly Method : Its correct use is difficult, useful in West but a failure in India.

(c) Foam Tablets : Equally failure in India. Their use is aesthetically unacceptable to many couples.

(d) Sterilisation : Female sterilisation is most acceptable. It is acceptable in urban areas. Male sterilisation is resisted. It is resisted still. Many myths are associated with vasectomy.

(e) The IUD or Loop or Copper T: Suits many women. It is also cheap and simple. You can reverse it whenever you like and that is its plus point.

(f) The Condom : Nirodh is distributed all over India. It is still very cheap. It is effective also. Villagers are to be taught the proper use of it.

(g) The Pill : It is most popular family planning method. It has got to be used carefully because of its side effects.

(h) MTP: Medical Termination of Pregnancy is very common now. Abortion has been legalised. The disadvantage is that it has led to many immoral practices.

The achievements. The achievements have been great. Millions of births have been prevented.

Family Planning Blocked

The main difficulties in this programme are as follows.

Traditional Beliefs of Our People. India is primarily a rural country. Urbanization has been slowed down. The rural masses are resistant to new ideas. They continue to be tradition bound. They still believe that the child is a gift of the God. The force of tradition has not been weakened. In order to weaken this tradition, it is very important that the health workers should come from the rural background so that they are able to convince the villagers about the need of family planning. We cannot wait till all villagers are educated. There should be pressures on workers so that they understand the meaning of small family norm.

Social and Demographic Characteristics. The family planning programme has created an attitude for it and there is no doubt that the message has gone home but it is felt that there is no strong motivation on the part of the masses to accept it as a way of life. The result is that family size continues to be large. People still feel insecure. They are afraid of infant mortality still. Infant mortality is still high in India. It was 98 per thousand births in 1956-60 compared with other countries like England, it is very high. In England, it is 23 only per thousand live births. The figure 98 is not reliable either. It can be as high as 120 or even 130. This is as per demographer's Aggarwala. Moreover, with increased cost of living and rise in agricultural wages, a large family is looked upon as more earning members and contributors to the family's income pool. Children earn for the family. The notion still prevails as such, there is no motivation on the part of the rural people to limit the family size. It matters little if infants continue to die.

Effectiveness of Family Planning Devices. We have yet to make Indian people contraceptive-minded. They may be aware of these but they do not know how to use these and use these effectively. To quote Gunnar Myrdal, "Both sexes must be motivated, and in the intensive stage of educations campaign, husbands and wives must be approached separately." We are so far following 'Cafeteria' approach that is, the availability of large number of contraceptives free or at very cheap rates to people. This approach has not worked either because people do not know the use of these contraceptives. The 'Clinic' Approach has already failed. So there are problems. Many jokes have been invented as a result of the massive distribution and use of contraceptives. What is to be prevented is the birth of the fourth child or fourth order birth. This is the intention of the Government of India behind enunciating the policy of a small family of two or three children.

Suggested Measures

There are two conflicting views on it.

(a) That economic hardship of parents will make the idea of family planning strong in their minds. Thompson and Lewis state, "Perhaps the most hopeful sign that conception control will spread fairly rapidly in the future in many underdeveloped countries is that more and more parents are beginning to complain of growing economic difficulties in raising their families. It would appear that this better understanding of family economic difficulties would supply a new and increasing powerful motive for keeping families relatively small."

(b) The second view regarding acceptance of family planning is that cultural setting in many developing countries and communities is such that the modern techniques of contraception would be difficult to introduce without a certain amount of socio-economic development, This was true of Western countries. But we in India cannot wait that long. And general education alone cannot change attitude of people in favour of small families.

Population education and Family Planning programmes are to be pursued in India with more vigour.

There was a Regional Workshop on Population and Family Planning. The experts, have suggested three types of measures, to check rapid growth of population:

Individual Measures. These include late marriage, self control, use of contraceptives and longer breastfeeding period.

National Measures. Family Planning programme, provision of clinical facilities, population education programmes in schools, rise in the legal age of marriage, withdrawal of certain Government facilities to a family beyond a particular size and reward for promoters of family planning.

International Measures. This means international organizations in birth control; financial aid for the national programme of population control facilities for training personnel for population control and dissemination of information about population control in different countries. India has obtained necessary assistance from international agencies.

The success of individual measures depends upon the level of general education attained and the sense of social responsibility a individual has-which in turn is the result of sound education.

Family Planning is applied to limited number of people. The war has to be fought on a bigger front also. It means give education—give population education right from school stage onwards—the only the numbers will be contained.

National Population Policy in Brief

Finally the main points of National Population Policy are as follows:

(1) Raising the age of marriage to 18 years for girls and 21 years for boys;

(2) Freezing the representation in the Parliament and State Legislatures upto 2001 on the basis of 1971 census;

(3) Reservation of 8% of central assistance/resources specifically for States showing better performance in family planning;

(4) Annual review of progress of family planning by the Union Cabinet;

(5) Increased incentives for adoption to family planning methods;

(6) Groups incentives to make family planning a mass movement;

(7) Introduction of model schemes for voluntary organisations for family planning;

(8) Promotion of research in reproductive biology and contraception;

(9) Inducements and fringe benefits to those who have accepted family planning;

(10) Development of a new multi-media motivational strategy, with a rural-oriented approach;

(11) Launching sterilisation programmes based on facilities and conditions in various states;

(12) Adequate outlay for education of girls; and

(13) Introduction of population education in the educational system.

QUESTIONS

1. Discuss Population Policy in Indian context.
2. Describe Population Policy 2000. What are its characteristics ? What are the criticism against it ?
3. What are the highlights of National Population Policy ?
4. Discuss Population Policy in Indian context.
5. Describe Population Policy 2000. What are its characteristics? What are the criticism against it?

12

Environmental Education

Population and Environment are two sides of the same coin. Man is a product of the environment and environment acts on man or if we say that environment makes a man, it would not be wrong. Man is to adjust to environment. And when men go on multiplying, the environment stands threatened. B,S. Parakh thinks that there has to be an integrated approach to both population and environment. These are twin problems and are to be tackled accordingly.

This is a book primarily on population education. We have discussed population enough. But what is environment? What is environmental studies? These need an exploration. Here we shall lay more stress on environmental education.

Aims and Objectives

Environment Education

(i) To help the students gradually unfold, explore and understand environment and appreciate its secrets.

(ii) To assist the students to understand and appreciate the laws of nature and then implications to the man.

(iii) To lead the students develop appreciation and deeper insights into inter-relationships, interplay, interaction and interdependence between man and environment.

(iv) To encourage the students to observe nature, appreciate its beauty, understand its laws and adjust with it, in order to live in harmony with nature.

(v) To impress upon the student that the nature and the environment around him is man's inheritance which the present generation has to pass on to the innumerable generations that are yet to follow.

(vi) To make the students think about man's destiny, the future of mankind and the duty of every generation to leave this planet a befitting place for mankind to live infinitely, to enjoy life and prosper peacefully by respecting laws of nature.

(vii) To develop an attitude among the students that would promote conversation of nature, environment and natural resources avoiding wastage and promoting the increasing use of renewable resources in place of exhaustible ones.

Main Motive

(i) To help the student to understand the population phenomenon in all its dynamics and dimensions.

(ii) To assist the students to understand and appreciate the current population explosion, its determinants and consequences.

(iii) To lead the students to understand the phenomenon to demographic transition where modern societies have been able to establish a rational balance between death rates and birth rates through planned and determined efforts.

(iv) To assist the students explore different alternatives open to them in handling the problem of population explosion and the socio-economic, political, psychological and physiological implications of each one of them.

(v) To help students to appreciate the need for a small family norm in the interest of an individual, family, country and the world at large.

(vi) To help the students realise that a small family norm is not only desirable but is also now attainable because of the advances in science and technology.

(vii) To impress upon the younger generation that man through the use of science and technology has been able to bring down the death rate and through the same rational approach and the use of the same science and technology he is capable of bringing down the birth rate as well.

Basic Issues

Environment Education

1. Environment means surroundings or conditions under which a person or a thing exists and develops his or her character.
2. Environment as a whole consists of two basic elements: physical or natural and man-made or Cultural. While river is an example of the former, a canal is an example of the latter.
3. The physical environment consists of both biotic and abiotic elements. Plants and animals are examples of the former, whereas land, water, air, climate phenomena are examples of the latter.
4. The entire life on the planet is confined to a very narrow area of a few kilometres among the earth surface both below and above it. It is particularly confined close to the interfaces of land, water and air. This narrow belt containing all the living organisms is known as biosphere.
5. Eco-system comprises the physical environment and all the organisms which live therein.
6. In a given territory a large number of plant and animal species grow together developing a chain of interaction and interdependence. Any change in any of the species disturbs the life of other species and is called disturbance in ecological balance.

7. Man is a unique and dominant species because of his ability to think, to communicate, to handle tools, to cooperate and to plan for future.
8. Except man, no other species on earth has ever succeeded in changing, modifying or manipulating environment to his own liking or advantage.
9. Man has been interfering with his environment in various ways, such as clearing forests, breaking grasslands, bringing more and more land under the plough, and digging, drilling and mining minerals.
10. Many of the changes man has brought about in his environment have been for his food, but not all the changes are necessarily in his own interests.
11. Some of the changes not really in his favour are: large-scale deforestation, over-grazing of grasslands, shifting cultivation, unscientific cultivation of uneven lands leading to erosion of soil and water and impoverishment of the soil and overhunting of wildlife, disturbing ecological balance in nature.
12. Of late, man has been exploiting some of the valuable natural resources extremely recklessly, for instance, mineral oil, natural gas, coal, copper and tin.
13. Man's interference with environment has often led, unknowingly though, to extinction of certain animal species, disturbing inevitably the ecological balance in nature.
14. Some of the large-scale changes brought about by man have changed local climates with serious repercussions.
15. Man is a mere consumer of food. He is not a manufacturer of food. In fact, manufacture of food is an exclusive prerogative of the vegetable world or the plant kingdom. Plants manufacture food through the process of photosynthesis with sun's energy.
16. Man has to clearly distinguish between renewable and exhaustible resources and their relevance for continuance of human civilization.

17. Man has to learn more earnestly how best he can use natural resources that are renewable, for instance, solar energy running water, wind, tidal energy, various forest products and agricultural produce, including animal products.
18. Man has to learn new economics based on recycling of resources like scrap, rags, used paper and the like.
19. Ever-increasing population with a premium on high standards of living has been responsible for rapid depletion of natural resources, pollution of air, water and soil and deterioration of environment.
20. Highly industrialized and affluent countries suffer from pollution of air and water on a big scale. They are also guilty of consuming raw materials and energy resources in a disproportionately high measure to the size of the population.
21. Widespread use of insecticides, pesticides and chemical fertilizers also lead to pollution of water and high concentration of these harmful chemicals not only in water but also in fish, birds, and their eggs. Their repercussions on man are also clear.
22. The poor countries also have to face the problem of pollution which arise mainly out of poverty.
23. Ignorance and apathy lead to following blindly unhygienic habits such as polluting the sources of potable water.
24. Man has to learn the laws of nature, its secrets and mysteries for making their optimum use to his advantage.
25. Man can benefit more by respecting laws of nature than by ignoring them.
26. Man cannot live and prosper by being constantly at war with or indifferent to nature. On the other hand, he must learn to live in peace and harmony with nature.

Population Education

1. With the present trend for population growth, the population of our country is likely to double in about 28 years. In other words, we would be adding another India to be fed, clothed, housed, and properly looked after in terms of health, education and jobs after every 28 years.
2. Rapid population growth in our country is due to the widening gap between steady birth rate and falling death rate over the past fifty years. The final solution lies only in establishing balance between the birth and death rates.
3. The use of science and modern technology is the only way to bring down the birth rate as it has already helped us in bringing down the death rate.
4. The reliance on science and technology in one case (combating death) and depending upon fate of God for the other (unplanned birth) is a pure and simple contradiction.
5. Since there were more deaths in every family in the past, the average size of the family was relatively small. Now that there are fewer deaths in each family the average size of the family has considerably increased.
6. In India the proportion of young population is very large. It also means that the bulk of the population is economically dependent and unproductive. It further follows that the per capita income would inevitably be very low. Further more, young population calls for greater expenditure on food, clothing, shelter, health, education, leaving very little capacity to save for providing them jobs when they grow.
7. With bigger and bigger proportions of our young population entering into reproductive age-group, the population of India is bound to increase faster in years to come.
8. In our country per capita income has not risen in proportion to the national income as there was tremendous rise in the population of our country.

9. Rapid population growth is at once both the cause and effect of our poverty. The vicious circle of poverty and population growth needs to be broken somewhere (in fact only here and now) with concerted efforts.
10. In spite of our achievement in doubling the food and the agricultural production, our masses are still unable to have a balanced and nutritious diet and a healthy and satisfying living owing partly to rapid growth of our population.
11. Although the per centage of the literates in our country has risen from nearly 15 to 30 since independence, the absolute number of the literates has also increased considerably from 300 million to 386 million as per 1971 census.
12. The number of doctors in our country has also been doubled (from 56,000 to 1,12,000) during the period but our ratio between doctor and the population is miserably low as compared to other countries.
13. Women should be given greater say in deciding the optimum size of the family and the welfare of its members. With a small family size mothers would enjoy better health have more time to look after the welfare of family members, more leisure to participate in social and economic life of the family, community and the country. To the extent our GNP (Gross National Product) and per capita income would also rise.
14. Women engaged in economically productive jobs outside the home may be the most dependable determinant of small family norm.
15. Unfavourable sex-ratio and steadily falling proportion of women to men (from 972 to 930 females pet thousand males since the beginning of the century) should be an eye-opener to the existing status of women in our country.
16. A healthy mother is the secret of a happy family. This can be ensured through a fewer and well-spaced births.
17. A small family alone can be in a better position to provide all the needs of all the members—food, clothing, shelter and, above all, health and education.

18. The battle of population control is to be fought and won in every family. Only small families can ensure restraint or control in the rising population of a country and that of the world at large.

Environment Classified

Environment is of the following five types:

(1) Natural

(2) Social

(3) Economic

(4) Political

(5) Moral

Psychologists say that environment is of three types:

(1) ***Physical or geographical*** which is same for a large number of people.

(2) ***Psychological which is different for everyone.*** Here it consists of the forces which affect the mind and behaviour. We give an example. In a house there are two brothers. Now for them, the physical environment is the same but psychological environment is different; one is elder brother and the other is younger brother. One is leader. The other (younger) is darling of the family. One (elder) will enjoy the maximum love of the parents for maximum years—being first born, the younger will have lesser years of love and affection of parents. So these things are there. That is why we talk of psychological environment.

3. ***Self—as Environment.*** This is the third type. One's own self is split into two parts 'I' and 'Me'. 'Me' part begins to criticise 'I'. If that happens, things become difficult. That is why we say that if such a thing happens, things become dangerous.

But at this stage, we are concerned with the following two types of environment.

1. Natural Environment.
2. Social Environment.

Natural Environment. It is further divided into two parts on types:

(a) Renewable, and

(b) Non-Renewable.

(a) Renewable environment is natural which includes soils, forests, vegetation and wild life.

(b) Non-renewable includes minerals, petroleum and its products, coal, etc.

In broader term natural environment is related with nature which includes air, water, forests, minerals, animals, birds, etc. or organic and inorganic substances. All the components of the environment keep themselves in balance but man has polluted the environment by his ignorance and carelessness.

Social Environment. The social environment is expressed in the action and reaction of social relationships. All the aspects of man's life are included in the scope of social environment, e.g., political, economic, religion, spiritual, physical, intellectual, etc. Man is a social creature from the very birth. He cannot live without social conditions. His development is possible only in society. Therefore, man's social, economic, political, religious, intellectual and spiritual relations come in racial relationships, community relationships, religious relationships, group relationships, domestic relationships, school relationships. The matrimonial, national and international relations also become examples of social environment.

These days we are exploiting our national resources, such as water, earth, light, forests, animals, etc. In return for it if efforts are not made consciously to make up the deficiency, they will come to an end. Man had cut off forests to satisfy his endless hunger and adopted artificial means of irrigation. He took to dairy farming. He raised crops on mountains. The fertility of the soil decreased and it is becoming sterile. As a result of increasing pressure of population, land is becoming limited. Industrialisation also affected the land.

A report given by the United Nations gave us an alarming situation about land, forests, animals and birds. This tendency continues in all areas. If attention is not paid to this side, the future of man will become dark.

Environmental Pollution

Pollution is the noun form of the word "pollute". To pollute means—to make dirty, unholy or to render unfit. In this way, pollution means 'to make unfit for human use', for example:

(1) The dirty water of the sewers pollutes the pure water of the rivers and many diseases spread.

(2) The smoke of the factories is inhaled and impairs the health. Thus air is polluted.

(3) The gas from the refinery at Mathura spreads in the air and causes cancer of the stone of which the Taj is built.

(4) The dust of sand pollutes the fresh air and creates lot of problems for public health.

The latest example is that of Union Carbide Gas Company whose poisonous gas caused untimely death of about 2000 persons and incapacitated about 10,000 persons. This is the greatest tragedy of air pollution in the history of mankind. The substance which pollutes is called pollutant. Thus, this substance enters the environment by human carelessness, ignorance or lack or knowledge and pollutes it. Thus smoke, dust, sulphur dioxide, carbon monoxide, mercury, hydrocarbon, etc. are pollutants of air and water, etc.

Natural Pollution of Several Types

Natural pollution is of the following types;

(1) Water Pollution.

(2) Air Pollution.

(3) Land Pollution.

(4) Thermal Pollution.

(5) Nuclear Pollution.

(6) Noise Pollution.

The main cause of pollution is ignorance. Actually, we people don't know what we are doing and in this state of affairs public must fully realise the consequences of this.

In 1988, people died of cholera in New Delhi-Why? Simply because of pollution primarily water pollution.

Green Wealth

Forests cover only about 30 per cent of the land surface of the world at present. They were much more extensive in the past. But man has been clearing them to provide land for cultivation and for other uses.

The Advantages

There are several advantages of forests, we shall list only major ones of these:

(1) ***Provide Products.*** Forests provide valuable products, such as timber, wood pulp, gums, rubber, etc.

(2) ***Prevent Soil-Erosion.*** Besides providing these products forests play an important role in preventing soil erosion. They permit more water to seep through the soil and reduce the quantity of run off water on the surface.

(3) ***Environment for Birds.*** Forests also provide suitable environment and necessary seclusion for the survival of wild animals and birds.

(4) ***Soil fertility*** is increased.

(5) ***Fall in temperature/rain.*** Forests are responsible for bringing rain. This keeps the temperature low and keeps the region cool.

(6) ***Dust storms*** are checked.

(7) ***Source of Income.*** Forests are a source of income in the form of forest products like timber and wood for fuel and furniture.

(8) ***Deserts*** are checked when we grow forests.

Classification of Forests. Forests are classified into several categories according to type of trees and other vegetation. In the equatorial region there are evergreen forests. They consist of tall trees with dense undergrowth. These forests are not commercially exploited except in a few scattered accessible tracts. The main reasons for the lack of the development of these forests are the unfavourable hot wet climate, inaccessibility and high cost of clearing the undergrowth and construction of roads. The presence of a very large number of species of trees in a small area hinders commercial exploitation of these forests. Primitive people in these forests live by hunting and gathering food and other forest products.

Equatorial forest in Malaysia and Indonesia have been cleared in some places and rubber and other plantations have been established.

Forests in monsoon regions of India are less dense than the equatorial forests. These forests are accessible and are exploited for commercial timber like teak and sal and for firewood and charcc l as fuel resources. Rubber, coffee and tea plantations have replaced forests in some areas. Paper is also manufactured by using bamboo as primary raw material.

In mid-latitudes, broad leaved forests are found in the regions receiving heavy rainfall. Such forests in West Europe and parts of Eastern United States have been almost cleared for cultivation and other needs. The existing forests are commercially exploited for timber and wood pulp as there is great demand for them in these developed nations.

Coniferous forests of high latitudes in Europe, Asia, and North America are the most valuable in terms of utilisation. These forests yield soft wood from pine, fur and spruce trees. The Scandinavian countries, Russia and Canada utilise the forests systematically and export forest products like timber, wood pulp, paper and newsprint.

Destruction of Forests

Large scale exploitation of forests since the Industrial Revolution has led to the depletion of forest wealth over large areas. This has caused:

(1) Soil erosion.

(2) Increased run off and repeated floods.

(3) In many parts of India indiscriminate clearing of forests for firewood and charcoal has resulted in permanent loss of the forest cover.

(4) Low-scrub vegetation.

(5) Increased pollution of air. There are no forests to purify the air.

(6) More floods are bound to be there as there is none to check.

(7) Shortage of land water is bound to be them.

Revival of Forests

As demand for forest products has been increasing there is an urgent need for conserving of existing forests. There is also an urgent need to increase the area under forests by:

(1) Planting trees at least in areas front where trees have been cut in the recent past. Such reforestation will not only help in increasing the forest wealth but also in reducing soil erosion and run off and increasing supplies of ground water.

(2) ***Planning.*** Forests are capable of regeneration, provided a systematic plan is adopted for replanting trees in areas cleared by cutting. This type of planned renewal and controlled utilisation is practised in many countries which have a large demand for various forest products. Such regeneration of forests is, however, a recent phenomenon and it takes into account the need for preserving the forest wealth for future.

(3) ***Political Role.*** Politicians are playing a dirty role in destroying the forest wealth. This has been noticed in Himachal Pradesh and other states in India. Contractors are destroying forests for personal gains. This has got to be checked.

(4) ***New attitude*** towards forests has got to be adopted.

(5) ***Van-Mahotsavas*** should be seriously taken up and celebrated.

(6) People should be alert about this.

Ecological Balance

Ecology is defined as study of plants or animals or of people and institutions in relation to environment in which they live. It is only towards the end of nineteen seventies that ecology has caught the imagination of people of planners and educationists alike. Earlier we did not bother about our environment and took it for granted. We are now worried when we see that ecological and environmental (air, water and noise) imbalances have started to occur in our life and have started to take their toll. We are alarmed. To cope with this, many universities in the world offer scholarships to help prevent environmental pollution.

It is imperative that we carefully preserve our renewable resources of soil, water, plant and animal life to sustain our economic development. Overexploitation of these is reflected in soil erosion, floods, rapid destruction of our forests, floral and wildlife resources. The depletion of these resources is irreversible; and since the bulk of our population depends upon these natural resources to meet their basic needs, particularly of fuel, fodder and housing material, it has meant a deterioration in their quality of life.

Environment not Valued

The summary of the Sixth Five Year Plan (A Government of India publication) lists many causes for this state of affairs:

Lack of Consideration. There is no consideration of costs of environmental degradation at the policy planning level, e.g., construction of roads, mining activities and placement of pylons or high power lines cause large-scale landslides, destroying fertile fields in the valleys. Similar is the situation with regard to several hydel projects.

Lack of Long-term Perspective. There is lack of long-term perspective in our development planning, e.g., soils are tending to get saline or alkaline due to improper use of irrigation and soil organic matter and fertility are tending to get depleted due to use of organic wastes as fuel rather than as manure.'

Profit Motive. All agencies tend to maximise their own profit and ignore the costs they impose on the society at large, including costs of environmental degradation. For example, studies by the Central Board for the Prevention and Control of Water Pollution have shown that the discharge of community wastes and industrial effluents is the major cause of water pollution. At present, 56% of Class I cities and 87% of Class II towns do not possess sewerage facilities.

Quick Profits. While a community depending on a resource for its subsistence generation after generation has a stake in its conservation, an entrepreneur with the option of shifting his investment is only interested in quick profits even if it leads to destruction of the resource base. The inshore prawn fisheries of Goa, sustainably exploited for centuries by local fishermen, are now being overfished and depleted through the exploitation by trawlers largely owned by entrepreneurs from non-fishing communities. Similarly with the development fruit industry in J & K and Himachal the felling of trees for making packing cases is proceeding in an indiscriminate manner.

Poverty. A large fraction of our population is today being forced to take out a subsistence by cultivating marginal land, overgrazing depleted pastures, cutting wood from dwindling forests and destroying the base of our natural resources in many other ways. Poverty drives them to do this.

Mining. brick-making and similar activities create scars on earth and do considerable damage both to soil productivity and scenic beauty. It is important that rehabilitation measures should be strictly enforced in areas subjected to mining, brick-making and similar activities.

Improvement Practices

That there is a dire need to educate for ecology and environmental balances cannot be denied. Time is to wake up or face tragedy or catastrophe of unimaginable dimensions. We shall fall victims to chronic and fatal diseases. Some suggestions to educate in this direction are as follows:

Give publicity. Our general public and policy makers should be effectively exposed to environmental issues. We must broadcast talks over radio, TV. on this issue. Films can also be shown to make people aware of the need to maintain ecological balances. Publicise the problem. Posters should also be displayed. Hoardings at crossings should make people conscious of their duty in this regard.

Lectures on the topic should be arranged in schools and colleges. We cannot ignore citizens of tomorrow. It is they who will have to face ecological imbalances. Warm them of the impending disaster soon.

Legislate. Major lacunae in our environmental legislation includes measures to prevent air and noise pollution, overexploitation of fisheries, control of impact of mining on environment, a provision its taking over the treatment of industrial effluents by the Government and preservation of landscapes of special significance. The legislations should be suitably amended and enforced. We should rise above petty corrupt practices.

Regardless of any local outcry that might arise if the hills are brought under protection, management and development, steps to revive their national ecology must be ruthlessly taken.

To quote from *The Hindustan Times*, "in the context of the vast amount of scientific data now available on deadly toxins it is important to change factory laws ensuring that newly set up factories safeguard the health of then workers and introduce measures to dispose of the affluents rarely. And old factories should be given government loans to introduce modern protective devices against pollution."

Teacher Education and Ecology. Make ecology a part and parcel of teacher education programmes. Why cannot it be a part and parcel of the paper on Indian education and its problems? It is it healthy sign to note that some steps have been taken in this direction by some universities in the country.

Similarly from class VIII onwards, environmental studies should be made a compulsory subject. As at present, in the CBSE affiliated schools, it is there in the primary classes but the children cannot appreciate its significance.

Movements like CHIPKO start from time to time in different parts of the country against indiscriminate felling of trees. In a way, these movements draw our attention to the tragedy that is going to come to us. We should not ridicule these movements. They have a value of their own. Something must be done in this direction.

Create More Jobs. Ecological imbalances occur rapidly. It is a search for livelihood which thaws people to encroach upon the hills. Why do we riot engage them permanently in afforestation, soil conservation, lumbering and downstream employment created by timber processing, etc., that would flow from the restoration of mountain forests and pastures. Other hill people in other hilly countries, according to an article published in *The Hindustan Times*, like Switzerland, the Austrian Tirol, the Italian Alps—have done it. Why not then the Indians in the Himalayas?

Treat Sullage. If increasing denundation of the hills is giving rise to problems of siltation, urban pollution is contaminating river waters. What is needed is the development of simple system to intercept and collect town sewage and subject it to primary treatment. The cost will be heavy but something has to be done. Similarly, rivers of northern India need cleaning up. A "Save the Rivers", project should be launched.

Research in Ecology. It has to be encouraged. It is time that we did that. We want thinkers in this field.

Positive Attitude Towards Environment. One of the prime objectives of any ecological or environmental programme is the development of attitudes which are positively oriented towards the total environment. This implies more than simply the knowledge of factual material; rather it implies the development of personality imbued with motivation, which can take factual information and apply it to solution of problems. Environmental education must, therefore, provide a body of information, this will lead to the understanding of the total bio-physical environment, develops an emotional commitment for environmental quality that will motivate the citizens to work towards solutions to biophysical environmental problems and serve to inform citizens as to how they can play an effective role in achieving the goals they have established.

Limit Population. If you want to survive and not die of pollution or if you want to preserve the world, then start adopting birth control measures. Large population has resulted in environmental imbalances. But the problem is that some religious group do not support birth control measures. How can one's brothers and sisters add to destruction of the world? The child may wonder! This is a problem that has to overcome.

Guiding Points

Borrowing from 'Critical Issues it' Education' by James J. Lewis and others (Prentice flail Inc.): here are tips which may offer assistance in implementation of environmental education.

In the elementary grades, especially when the students are hyperactive, project work may be useful. For example, student groups have recently made use of aluminium can drive as a means of cleaning up the environment. This technique can be expanded to include vacant plots, streams and other physically polluted areas of one's environment. In schools, activities might center on Art campaigns to produce posters which would make local citizenry aware of pollution conditions. Local shopkeepers might be approached to place these in their windows, thereby providing relevance for the children between school and community. The local science fair might also be used if given a proper orientation such its, "Ideas to end pollution". In addition, guest speakers may speak at assembly programmes and other functions in connection with keeping our environment neat and clean.

At lower grade levels, perhaps exposure to plants and animals may be arranged in the classroom as well as pet fairs, where children are encouraged to bring their house pets to school. This would increase the sensitivity of other children towards the diversity of living things. At all grade levels, experiences with gardening and tree planting could be provided. It is well known that the in school experiences are brought home to his parents. This will ensure school and community involvement with these school projects.

At high school levels, students, being older and hopefully more mature, might enjoy becoming involved in actual community renewal. Clean up campaigns, anti-litter drives, anti-rat campaigns and perhaps 'paintings' might both involve and educate students about their own environment.

An extremely inexpensive and memorable experience might be obtained if student were encouraged to film the entire school ecology programme, developing a narrative record of the progress, people and projects. Besides being all invaluable experience it would provide the togetherness of a multi-faceted student body and community, working on projects beneficial to all.

However to make any anti-pollution programme successful, the active involvement of people is essential. That is one purpose of publicity. Even in the more developed countries of the world, governments have been found wanting. It was only after people raised their voice and launched mass movements refer to CHIPKO movement against growing industrial health hazards that official agencies decided to do something about it.

As at present, the levels of pollution and environmental imbalances are fortunately low but increasing. The situation calls for a bold new approach to development which will be based on techno-environmental and socio-economic evaluation of each developmental project.

Teacher's Role

(1) ***Awareness.*** The teacher should be aware of the fact that there is a need to educate about environment. It is a new topic and society is to be educated about it and that would be possible if he is aware of it.

(2) His own Efforts to improve the environment should be visible to one and all. He should play positive rate in it.

(3) ***Curriculum.*** The topic of education for environment should be included in curriculum and teacher should seize every opportunity to teach this.

(4) Co-curricular activities to improve upon the environment should be introduced. This has been touched upon in detail towards the conclusion of the question previous to it.

(5) Articles on environment and it partly can be written by a teacher.

(6) A public lecture can also be delivered by the teacher.

(7) Exhibition can also be arranged by him.

Action Plan to Reduce Environment Pollution. A six-point programme of action to reduce burden cast at the environment due to use of fossil fuels like coal for energy purposes to save the world from the excessive levels of carbon dioxide, has been envisaged at the recent international conference of the International Association for Energy Economics (IAEE).

IAEE president Dr. R.K. Pachauri had told a press conference that the conference held in Luxembourg suggested greater investment in increasing energy efficiency than in energy expansion and a global dialogue between the North and South to reduce the carbon dioxide levels. Dr. T.N. Khoshoo, distinguished scientist and former Secretary, Environment, was also present at the press conference.

It was suggested that in such a dialogue it should be proposed that the North waive its debt claims on the South in return for energy efficient strategies being adopted by the South. The rising carbon dioxide levels raise surface temperatures all over the globe, disturb climate on a global scale and threaten to choke the world into mass scale death of all living organisms, the so-called Green House effect.

The six-point programme also includes a much more positive approach for development of renewable energy technologies to reduce the burden of energy on the environment. This would also make energy supplies available on a decentralised basis, Dr. Pachauri said.

Asked whether it was wise to have energy strategies that need long lines of transmission to bring energy to villages, Dr. Pachauri, who is also Director of the Tata Energy Research Institute, agreed that the renewable sources of energy could take over considerable part of the work for which electricity was being used in villages at present. Dr. Khoshoo declared that such energy technology packages using renewable sources were already available.

Dr. Pachauri and Dr. Khoshoo said that both in urban and rural areas much more efforts were needed to popularise and utilise solar systems so that the demand on the conventional fuels for energy could be reduced.

Dr. Pachauri claimed that the conventional belief in the linkage between commercial energy use and growth had been shattered. While developed countries have proved that growth was possible even without further increase in energy consumption, developing countries, which needed more commercial energy, should concentrate on energy conservation. So far, conservation in this country was getting only lip sympathy, he said,

"Capacity utilisation is more important than capacity expansion."

Dr. Pachauri claimed pointing out that along with better control over transmission and distribution losses, more energy could be utilised per every rupee spent on conservation than on expansion.

The developed countries should be compelled to provide more technology transfer for energy conservation policies to help the carbon dioxide levels on the globe as a whole to be kept within manageable limits. The next global conference of energy economists would be held in this country in 1990.

More Tips

(1) The contents of environmental and population education should be identified with the help of specialists and we should be very sure about these.

(2) Where to incorporate these ideas on environmental and population education (popularly known as Plug Points) should also he identified.

(3) The textbooks should be revised and school curriculum should be enriched.

(4) The textbook writers should be made familiar with these ideas and also the need to incorporate these ideas into the books.

(5) If possible prepare additional instructional material. This additional instructional material should be in various forms—a curriculum guide, a handbook, lesson plans, etc. It can also be in visual forms—graphs, charts, pictograms, etc.

(6) Large number of co-curricular activities can be introduced—there can be panel discussions, one-act plays, songs, etc. on these two related topics.

(7) Teachers have got to be oriented in these topics. Then only the message will go home.

(8) Teacher Training Curriculum has to be reshaped. These topics, i.e., environmental and population education must form content of Teacher Training Curriculum.

When the teachers of tomorrow remain indifferent towards these two topics, how can they teach these topics'?

(9) Sex Education should be introduced in elementary classes even!

(10) Tap local resources. If a qualified teacher is not available, let local doctor talk on family planning.

Basic Facts

Steps taken by the Government of India to Prevent Environmental Pollution

Increasing population means depletion of sources-material and non-material. Increasing population means environmental pollution-Pollution of earth, air, water, space, noise. Nothing will be spared. The Government of India is conscious of this. It has taken some steps to create awareness amongst people and to prevent environmental pollution. Some to these steps stand summed up as under:

Celebration of Environment Day. It is June 5th every year.

Passing of Laws. There are 200 laws related to preservation of environment in India. Notable amongst these are;

(i) Shore Law or Shore Act passed in 1853.

(ii) Constitution was amended in 1976. It is the 42nd amendment that we are talking about. Under this some matters related to environment were brought under the consideration.

(iii) In the Directive Principles of state policy, Article 48A was added. It stated, "State will make efforts to protect and develop environment, forests and other living beings."

(iv) Under Article 51 'A' (g) in the chapter of Fundamental Duties, it has been said, "It will be duty of every citizen to have sympathetic attitude towards every living being and to protect and develop forests, ponds, rivers and wildlife. The subjects related to forests and wildlife were shifted from State list to concurrent list.

Central Board of Pollution Control. A Central Board of Pollution Control was set up in 1974. Primarily it checked water pollution which occurred due to industrialisation and population rise.

Some State Pollution Boards have also been set up. Punjab has one such Board with Headquarter at Patiala.

Environment Protection Act, 1986. Earlier there were solid laws for environment protection. But under Environment Protection Law of 1986, there is a provision of giving severe punishment to those who do not protect it. With the enforcement of Air Pollution Control Law, 1981 and Environmental Protection Act 1986, there has been an increase in the activities of Board and they have also been given the power to punish those who do no work or implement the law. Some jail term and fine have also bee suggested.

Environmental Courts to be Established as per Suggestions of the Supreme Court. Interestingly, it is being done with a view to expedite cases. The Supreme Court sometimes order some industries to be shifted outside the residential areas so far so good. And then some Judge grants stay for the reasons best known to him. But environmental Court is a good thing.

Administration plants and trees.

Check the use of DDT and other insecticides.

Environmental Pollution is increasing both on land and sea. This has got to be checked.

A regulation exists that before you set up an industry, take government approval regarding pollution, e.g., the cement industry.

Environment Regulation Scheme has been started in 18 districts of India to create awareness among young people. What happens when forests disappear and water is polluted? "This scheme is about all this. "Eco-clubs" stand started in many schools,

India has done its best in international field also. It participate in Earth Summit held at Rio in Brazil in 1992.

Rising population and world environment go together. This fact should never be lost sight of.

Social Sciences : Application

Social sciences are widely read subjects at the school level. It includes history, civics, economics and geography. Population education can be easily given through these subjects in an integrated way. These subjects will help the students understand the population phenomenon in its wider perspective highlighting its historical, political, economic, cultural, moral etc. effects in a very comprehensive way. The phenomenon can be studied in its totality. How can it be done? B.S. Parakh has tried to show in a very interesting manner. His article/paper appeared in NCERT publication "Population Education for Teachers". The publication appeared in 1974. In a summary form, we present it in these pages.

Impact of Social Studies

Social Studies can easily do this whenever he is teaching social studies. He can integrate population education in it.

A Unit on Population Problem lays stress on the following key concepts:

1. There is close interaction of population growth and development process with regard to developmental programmes for raising standard of living of people.
2. Population size and quality of life are related.
3. Family size can be chosen. It can be controlled. It is not beyond human control.

This Unit in NCERT books (CBSE syllabus) has three major components.

(a) Demography or population dynamics,

(b) Population growth and economic development, and

(c) Population growth and social development.

Under the first part, it brings home to the student that population has been growing rapidly as a result of widening gap between death rate and birth rate.

The second component states it clearly that standards of living depends upon people and how they assume responsibility to meet the challenge.

In the third, our attention is drawn to various social ills, such as poverty, indebtedness, illiteracy, delinquency, etc.

Population Problem : Historical View

In history, we can tell stories about prehistoric man-migrations, advent of agriculture leading to a settled or a sedentary life, decline of well-developed civilization at the hands of hordes, etc. We can talk about famines and industrial revolution.

When was life then? What is life now? What is the scope of further expansion? This is to be told in time perspective. History teacher should be able to highlight the following concepts:

1. Homosapiens as a species have to undergo the longest period of mining in order in prepare for life and to stand on its own.
2. The institutions of marriage and family were unique to homosapiens.
3. Early man has to pay great prices to survive and gradually adapt himself to his highly exacting environment.
4. Calamities took a great toll in the first as compared to today.
5. Man organised himself in clans and made great progress.
6. Modern nation state coupled with technological advancement and through international cooperation has made a man capable of meeting many challenges and well in time.
7. Invention of agriculture led to first ever population explosion. Later on we had industrial revolution.
8. Disease continue to dominate. Hence some sort of balance remains.
9. The current population growth is, however, mainly due to a silent revolution brought about by advances in public health, nutrition and medicinal facilities.
10. We do not have any more virgin lands. It is time to reduce population.

Geographic Knowledge Applied

Geography develops a national and global perspective of population problem. Geography also tells people that as a result of increasing population, the sources are dwindling. Land and people ratio is also decreasing. Population develops in favourable spots and is unevenly distributed. A geography teacher can bring home the message that man should learn to respect the laws of nature, balance in nature and ultimately learn to live in harmony with nature.

A Few Examples

(i) Absolute population figures use found meaningless as compared to figures of average or nutritional density. (The nutritional density is the ratio between population and cultivable land).

(ii) Our own country has large population out of proportion as compared to other countries.

(iii) Classification of population in terms of rural/urban, males/females and productive and dependent leads to comparisons which use more meaningful.

(iv) Population is exploding in India.

(v) GNP is declining. It should make us aware of the need of checking population. Only then the standard of living will rise.

(vi) Resources are being depleted due to continuous and unprecedented growth of population in the country.

Population Explosion : the Economic Angle

A few of the concepts that could be fruitfully developed are:

1. Full development of human resources calls for big national income and GNP and a high standard of living and vice versa.
2. A high rate of economic growth, higher standard of living and greater economic productivity have generally a positive correlation.
3. High standard of living and a high rate of economic growth and higher productivity implies better health, a nutritious and balanced diet, better education and

greater degree of technological skills, a very high consumption of energy, raw materials and above all full and fair job opportunities. All this calls for a very high rate of savings.

4. The most important characteristics of a developed economy is the low birth rate of its people. Conversely a developing or under-developed economy is one in which its people show a very high birth rate. It is this difference in birth rate and not the death rate that distinguishes the developed economy from the developing one.
5. The more the population, the less the growth of economy.

All this does not mean that population education is a negative concept. It is a positive concept because it aims at better management of natural resource base, the fuller development of human resources, rise in productivity, higher standard of living and above all a better quality of life.

Relationship with Civics

In Civics, the students study the population problem and its political elements, determinants and consequences. Let them study how provincial autonomy since 1937 and then independence since 1947 have contributed towards a gradual fall in death rate resulting into present population explosion. And one should also know that population explosion has a potential to erode several cherished values such as liberty, freedom and dignity of individual.

Some of the important understandings that can be developed through civics are:

(i) Rapid population growth creates several social and political problems in addition to financial and economic.

(ii) Great influx of unskilled labour into cities in search of job takes place when rate of population growth is higher than rate of economic growth in general and in rural areas in particular.

(iii) There will be shortfall in civic amenities like schooling and health services.

(iv) More population means more tensions.

(v) Social customs, traditions, taboos, superstition stand in the way of rational population policies and individual decisions with regard to family size.

(vi) Ethics of population education forbids increase of family size or the population of a country that cannot be properly looked after, housed, clothed, fed, educated and provided with adequate job opportunities. Such forced cultural and moral deprivations for men are against the tenets of all ethics and morality, not to speak of real spirit of religion.

Thus, we have seen what can be taught in Population education through social sciences. How can it be taught is the next question. It can be introduced in various ways.

QUESTIONS

1. What are the objectives of Environmental Science ?
2. What are the objectives of Population Education ?
3. Describe the types of environment.
4. What pollutes the environment ?

13

Teacher's Role

An important contribution of any population education programme will be the involvement of teachers and parents drawing on their personal behaviour. Unless teachers themselves have a strong conviction about the need and urgency of limiting the population, they can hardly influence the attitudes and behaviour of students in the classroom.

Accordingly, population education has to receive high priority in teacher education colleges and teacher education courses. These teachers will then take the course in schools and colleges. The message will go home. The role of the teacher in spreading the message of population education among the masses is very great. In the words of former Minister of Health & Family Planning, the role of teachers on be described as follows.

"Here I must emphasize the fact that the training of teachers for population education should be given the utmost attention. The teachers are the backbone of this educational movement and the success of this innovation will depend largely on the ability of these pioneers to put across the concept of the small family norm to young, intelligently and effectively. This means that teachers themselves must learn a great deal about the dynamics of the population problem and, what is equally important, should muster techniques of imparting such information in an attractive and compelling manner".

The teachers of their own very little understand their role. They are not clear about the concept. They say that it is not their goal. They fear that parents might object. The importance of population education for teachers is thus great. In this contest, there are four situations which need consideration.

(1) Ignorance of teachers.

(2) Apathy of teachers.

(3) Resistance of teachers.

(4) Lack of incentive.

We shall explain these in some detail.

The ignorance of teachers. The teachers will have to be given new orientation and we have to hope that they will pass it on to students. The focus should be on intellectual and internal change. Teachers have to be convinced that something is to be done to control population and they have a part to play in it. They are to create a nation-wide concern on the problem. What should our children know and how should it be taught in our schools?

Apathy. They are just unconcerned. Teachers are just indifferent. We have to bring an attitudinal change in him. Bringing an attitudinal change is not an easy task. This can be brought about by an interactive communication.

Resistance. Our teachers resist any change. Rather they do not want to change. They would like to stay the way they are. How on their resistance be broken? We need to change the administration and organizational structure of the school system. Social pressure can help us achieve this.

Lack of incentive. Here we are concerned with incentives in the form of rewards. If a teacher comes out with a creative idea for implementation of the scheme, he should be suitably rewarded. And what rewards people want? Some want money, power and status within the system. There are many ways in which the status of creative and competent teachers can be improved.

The problem is to make teachers aware of Population Education and to see to it that they pass on these ideas to their students.

The Indian Education Commission (1964-66) popularly known as the Kothari Commission has suggested curriculum for teacher education both at the primary level and at the secondary level. Without going into the details, it can be safely suggested that there is a considerable scope for incorporating some concepts of population education at both these levels. Some universities have done it. The point is that teachers at primary and secondary levels should be well acquainted with the consequences of population growth and its implications to the standards of living and quality of life.

Fundamental Efforts

There have been many seminars and workshops on this issue.

- In 1969, the M. S. University of Baroda organised a workshop on it.
- In December, the Pathfinder Fund (New Delhi) organized a teachers' workshop on population education in New Delhi. The research staff of Pathfinder presented 16 lesson plans on four broad areas of population education for discussion.
- Another workshop was organized by the Regional College of Education, Bhopal in 1970. The workshop was mainly concerned with a preparation of instructional materials and development of a methodology for the teaching of population in teachers' colleges.

The Bhopal workshop decided to divide population education for teacher education in six broad areas:

1. Characteristic features of Indian population in a world perspective.
2. Population growth and food supply.
3. Population and health.
4. Population and standard of living.
5. Small family and better living.
6. Population growth and education.

In March 1976, another workshop was orgamised at Regional College of Education, Ajmer by the NCERT. Teachers, Educators were made aware of population education. Research projects in population education were also finalised.

Strategies in Existence

The National Conference on Population Education 1971 states that in the light of the foregoing analysis of developing population education in the teachers' curriculum, the following strategies appear to be most appropriate:

Pilot Projects. More pilot projects in the light of what has been described above should be initiated.

Demonstration Project. There is need to demonstrate the effective results of some of the earlier projects.

Seminars. We had very many seminars on population education. The impact of these seminars is quite visible and many activities are followed as a result of these seminars/recommendations. Therefore more seminars must be organised at regional and state levels.

Workshops. Inviting a group of teachers to participate in a workshop to share their experiences and explore ways to meet their needs has been a good strategy in other areas of study. A large number of workshops be organised for secondary school teachers. The duration of the workshop can be for 2-3 weeks. This is the ideal time period. If it is of short duration, we may not be able to prepare much. The implication of such a programme of living together, working together, and solving actual curricular problems together are important for teacher education, especially for teachers in service. Working on a problem will give a new view point to a teacher.

Research and Study Groups. The emphasis on introducing population education in schools will be more effective if we have systematic research on this subject. Study groups can be formed to develop suitable materials on population education. More research will certainly help to formulate effective training programme for teachers in this subject.

Information Centres. There are hardly any information centres all over the country which provide information about Population Education. In many libraries, useful journals on population are equally missing. This is a very serious hindrance for any programme of training of education. Therefore, if support is available, every state can establish a library on population education and attach with it an information service.

Curriculum Development Experiment. Finally, we need to have several experimental projects on curriculum development in population education. There are several approaches being advocated such as family life education, health education, sex education and environmental education. All of them should be allowed and encouraged to examine these issues in the contest of school curriculum and conduct experiments in the class rooms.

The kind of preparation received by the teacher practically pre-determines whether the teacher will take an active and intelligent part in curriculum improvement.

Missionary Zeal

By puting a tremendous faith and responsibility on them, the National Policy on Education (1986) expects a lot from the teachers. It boldly opined. "No people can rise above the level of its teachers." It states that the 'Status of the teacher reflects the socio-cultural ethos of a society'. It has been recommended that : 'The Government and the community should endeavour to create conditions which will help to motivate and inspire teachers on constructive and creative lines. Teachers should have the freedom to innovate, to devise, appropriate methods of communication and activities relevant to the needs and capabilities of and the concerns of the community.'

Need for an Image

Well determined by the process of teacher education the ripe of the teacher, the society aspires to have. The desired image of the teacher has to be built up, keeping in view its the intellectual, the professional, the social and the personal aspects. As the Indian situation has certain peculiar characteristics, which are distinct from many other nations, we should keep in view the following specific characteristics while carving a composite image of the teacher :

(1) We are committed to political democracy as the way of life.

(2) We stand for peace and co-existence.

(3) We are a multi-religious and multi-religious nation.

(4) Our society is changing at a rapid pace.

(5) We have a cultural heritage which values the worth and the dignity of man.

(6) Explosion of population is giving rise to explosion of student numbers.

(7) Explosion of knowledge necessitates proper selection of teachers as well as the provisions of continuing education for the teachers.

(8) As there is explosion of needs and aspirations, there is need for spreading literacy and universalising education.

(9) The society judges educational standards and teacher's effectiveness from the pass percentage in public examinations.

(10) The certificates, and degrees, value continue to be the passports for getting jobs and entering lucrative careers.

Functions of a Teacher

Academic Functions

(i) Hard competence in his subjects of teaching and their contribution to the over-all education of the child.

(ii) Appreciating and understanding the changing needs of the society in a scientific age.

(iii) Understanding the psychological bases of education and the factors which influence education.

Professional Functions

(i) Acquiring ability to evolve and adapt methods and techniques suited to different situations and to evaluate their effectiveness.

(ii) Acquiring ability to improve and use audio-visual aids suited to different classroom situations.

(iii) Developing positive attitude towards teaching as a profession and create self-confidence as a teacher.

(iv) Understanding the development needs of children at various stages of their growth.

(v) Acquiring appropriate professional behaviour.

(vi) Acquiring knowledge about the existing education system and the latest Education Policy of the country.

Social Functions

(i) Acquiring desirable social attitudes.

(ii) Becoming an agent for social change.

(iii) Developing qualities of patience, impartiality and fairness.

(iv) Developing interest in modernity.

Competencies of a Teacher

A competent teacher is expected to possess following qualities

(1) He should be educated in the literal spirit of learning so that he my make his contribution as an individual and a citizen.

(2) He should be competent to represent the education profession and his subject-matter field in the school aid in the community.

(3) He should be thoroughly grounded in the theory and practice of his subject-matter and have knowledge and skills necessary for teaching theory and practice in an integrated manner.

(4) He should be able to contrive a variety of effective teaching-leaning procedures.

(5) He should be able to develop and use instructional materials including audio-visual aids.

(6) He should be able to select and organise subject-matter for instructional purposes.

(7) He should be able to use a variety of methods to evaluate pupil progress and the effectiveness of his own teaching.

(8) He should be capable of organising, supervising and participating in co-curricular activities.

(9) He should be able to select and use appropriate equipment and determine supply needs.

(10) He should be able to function effectively in the guidance programme of the school.

(11) He should be capable of functioning effectively as a teacher as evidenced by actual classroom performance.

(12) He should be interested in continued growth through participation in professional associations, community activities, in-service education, research and experiment.

Population Teachers being Trained

All the teachers should be trained but they should not be and also cannot be a specific training of teachers. Even the born teachers have to study the techniques of teaching craft. There are teachers who have acquired enormous success in teaching through training and experiences. Much wastage in teaching effort can be saved if the prospective teacher as subjected to teacher-education situations conductive for actualization of potential in him. A good deal of waste in teachers, efforts might be avoided by training. But a teacher is not a teaching craftman. He has to help his students to develop certain personality traits and also to realise desirable values. In past the training of teachers was born out of the necessity to bring up a 'literate' generation and to accomplish this task. The teachers were helped to develop a narrow technique and a highly, specialised professional approach. They, the need is to bring out a 'sophisticated and 'cultured' generation.

The schools of today lay emphasis on an integrated and balanced personality of the teacher as a whole man. The teacher of today must be the teacher of a whole man. He can never be this unless he is himself a complete man. We teach more by our actions than by our preaching. Training cannot be a matter of teaching professional tricks. A narrow vocationalism is wholly out of tune with modern educational thought. It is antipathetic to those generous sympathies and that consciousness of being one member in a self-education community, generally demanded from teachers. The new teacher will have to integrate the skills of teaching with his life style and also to help the students to develop not only intellectually but also emotionally.

Teachers are a section of community sharply segregated from the rest preparing themselves for their life's work in institutions for developing human attributes. The teacher education system set it exists today fails to educate the barium beings. The trained teacher is too often an untrained human being. Our aim must be the education of the right human beings for work in our schools. The era of the training of teachers is past; we are concerned with the education of the educators. With proper type of education to the prospective teacher, he will be in a more favourable position to correlate his knowledge with his experience, to see life steadily and to see it as a whole. The only means of strengthening one's intellect is to let the mind be a thoroughfare for all thoughts, not a selected party. From this open-mindednes, sympathy, tolerance, intellectual adaptability and width of interest will develop the attributes essential for successful riving and dealing with children. But all this requires a comprehensive philosophy of life and education, a map by which the future teacher may observe himself in relation to other teachers as well as other human beings activities. During his training course he must be given time and opportunity to think about education because he will have little time for it after completing his training as he will be engaged in the absorbing tasks of the classroom and the common life.

Therefore, the prospective teacher must be offered opportunities to associate with the best mind and to develop a disciplined intellect as well as the quality of appreciation of culture in its various forms. He will have an emotional life developed to a fine sensitivity but held in a strict control.

Today's teacher needs a philosophy primarily concerned with human beings to interact with each other. Humanistic programme for teacher education, seeks to develop a human teacher possessing such qualities as spontaneity, acceptance, creativity and self-realization. It would give an opportunity to the prospective teacher to relate theory to practice, to search for greater personal understanding of himself and for the learning processes of children. It would help him to develop compassion for weakness in individuals and sensitivity for the needs of human beings. It will make a teacher who knows how to help children to realize their potential. This humanistic approach to teacher-education will produce teachers able to exalt the continued process of education of human potential in our schools.

Competence and professional skills are the very heart of the programme of teacher education. The knowledge of the methods adopted by other teachers combined with other considerations will make the student try out various approaches to his work and during the practical work of the course. Thus a practicing teacher generally evolves and polishes his own method. He acquires technical skills in practice and not in the lecture room. He should possess such skills and competencies which make his task easy, useful and effective. He should know the techniques and procedures to be adopted in his profession. He should be able to effectively perform his duties. The most important task of education for the future is to improve the intellectual and technical competence in the teachers. It seeks to provide professional educated entrants to the profession in adequate numbers. It aims at maintaining or increasing the quality of entrants for the profession to satisfy society's needs. While the first aim is quantitative, the second one is qualitative.

Professional education should focus on the person as an individual who is in practice and seeks to broaden his mental, moral and emotional capacities. He should have a sound philosophy of education, knowledge of an adequate functioning of psychology along with a dynamic sociological perspective. Only such teachers will be to relate theoretical insight to practice and to improve preparation programme. They will be effective practitioners in their profession. Teacher education seeks to develop such competencies in the prospective teachers which will make him a successful teacher. It tends to increase the ability of the teacher to deal with a range of individual differences.

The teacher of tomorrow would design a teaching situation conducive to the growth of pupils, mental health. It would develop in them a commitment to a set of values. It would develop certain skills and competencies. The teacher requires a new type of knowledge and attitude, atmosphere and facility to make his task easy, fruitful and confirming for the demands of the students. His education, therefore, should be according to the necessities of the time and needs of the society. It should develop following :

(1) To relate learning with the individual diagnosis instruction.

(2) To analyse group development interaction and to perform a leadership role in a group.

(3) To communicate with the individual as well as the group.

(4) To acquire knowledge and skill in a disciplined manner.

(5) To structure the acquired knowledge, to choose from his specialisation, the need of knowledge that is important for a particular individual or group.

QUESTIONS

1. Explain the image and trends of its population teacher.
2. Describe some of the competencies which we needed to develop among teachers of population.
3. Describe the need of teacher-education for population of teacher.

14

Methods in Vogue

Effective learning takes place through the application of good methods of teaching. Ideal and lofty aims of education, functional and practical curriculum, are of no avail if correct methods for teaching are to be adopted. Following are the most important methods of teaching Population Education.

(1) Textbook Method.

(2) Lecture Method.

(3) Discussion Method.

(4) Project Method.

(5) Problem Method.

(6) Unit Method.

(7) Source Method.

(8) Socialised Recitation Method.

Textbook Method

According to Wesley, the text-book method my be defined as "that teaching procedure in which an understanding of the main body of information in the textbook is the immediate objective." According to this method mastery of the textbook is the immediate objective of teaching. The procedure of teaching revolves around the textbook. Almost all methods can be wed with the textbook as a basis of study. Textbook is a very useful means of getting concise and up-to-date information. However, the textbook procedure may become very "desirable if the teacher bases all of his teaching upon a single textbook.

Of course, only a judicious method of Population Education textbook should be made both by the teacher and the students. Textbook is not an end in itself. It is only one of the means. It is only an effective aid and must be taken as such one textbook should never be completely depended upon. Other textbooks, reference books and other resources should be consulted to supplement the subject-matter given in one particular textbook.

Merits

Meeting the needs of students: As the textbook is written from the student's points of view, it meets the needs of the average student.

Helping in the formation of the good reading habits: By reading the textbook intensively, and trying to grasp the maximum, the students develop good reading habits.

Furnishing an accurate amount of the subject: Students can very well depend upon textbook as it furnishes an accurate account of the subject.

Indicating the standard of achievement: The textbook reflects and indicates the standard of achievement expected of the students. It indicates what the pupils are supposed to learn.

Suggesting application of the material: Through assignments, questions, etc. a text book suggest application of the subject-matter.

Serving as basis of almost all other methods: Using any method of teaching, the teacher may always make the textbook as the basis. It is always profitable to base the study on the textbook and supplement the knowledge with reference and other books and materials.

The Limitations

Encouraging Cramming: Textbook emphasises cramming and memorisation rather than interpretation and understanding of the facts. This is against the principles of true learning.

Lack of Comprehensive Treatment: Due to the limitation of the space detailed and comprehensive knowledge cannot be given in my one textbook. Good students may not be satisfied with this insufficient knowledge.

Incomplete Method: Teaching-learning process should not be confined to a single textbook, as textbook is only one source of information and knowledge. Teaching must be supplemented by knowledged from our sources as well.

Thus, the textbook method may be used in combination with other methods. It may serve as a base for other methods. A judicious base of the textbook is recommended. In the secondary classes knowledge from the text-book should be supplemented by knowledge from other sources as well.

For example, take the topic, 'checking India's increasing population,' Knowledge about this topic can be supplemented from newspapers, magazines, government publications, etc. The textbook is only to be taken as a base.

Discussion Method

Teaching-learning process should be a co-operative process between the teacher and the pupils. In the discussion method the students participate actively in the learning process. Since Population Education deals with the population problem of mankind, discussion my be said to be an important means of discovering the problem and to suggest suitable steps for proper solutions. Discussion involve study and preparation, selection and organisation of subject-matter, exchanging ideas and learning procedures. It is a systematic procedure of collective decision-making . It seeks agreement but it is not reached. It has the value of clarifying the nature of disagreement. It my be informal or it may assume some such from as a debate, a symposium, a panel or a round-table conference. Any one of these forms may be adopted.

Constituents of a Discussion

According to Johnson, the constituents of a discussion are

1. The leader
2. The group
3. The problem
4. The content

The Leader: In discussion method, the teacher is the leader. He does the planning of the discussion, selection and organisation of the subject-matter etc. As a leader teacher's function is to lead and guide the discussion as well as to see that all the members of the group participate in the discussion.

The Group: The students of the Population Education class form the group. The students or the members of the group differ in their level of intelligence temperaments, interests, etc. Each and every member of the group may be encouraged by the leader to participate actively in the discussion.

The Problem: The problem or the topic for discussion should be selected co-operatively by the teacher as well as by the students. The problem selected must be real and touching the lives of the pupils and full of educative possibilities. It must challenge the minds of the pupils. It must be stated in definite and precise terms.

The Content: According to Johnson the content of the discussion is, "the body of knowledge, facts and generalisations which must be drawn upon if my problem is to be discussed and resolved." In discussion, we have constantly to resort to facts and generalisations. The different points of view are to be discussed and the differences are to be resolved, so that an agreement is reached.

Discussion is different from debate. While the debater always tries to win an argument and knows no compromise, discussion is a "sharing and weighing of all sides, which may be as many as there are conflicting interests or values". The participants in a discussion are inter-related in "a process of competitive co-operation." Agreement is the declared purpose of a discussion.

Merits

Helping self-expression: Discussion helps to improve verbal self-expression. It provides equal opportunities to everybody to express his views on the topic or discussion.

Collective decision-making: Discussion method is a process of collective decision-making.

Developing logical and critical thinking: The participants in discussion have arguments and develop their points of view logically, viewing the argument of others critically. This develops their critical faculty and logical way of thinking.

Providing right way of acquiring knowledge: Knowledge is not acquired through memorisation and cramming. It requires listening to various points of view. It also leads to better understanding are the facts me to be twisted according to the needs of the discussion.

Development of right attitude: Discussion develops the habits of patient hearing, trying to understand other person's point of view, tolerating the opinions of others, however contrary and different they may be, and putting forward one's own point of view calmly but convincingly. These are valuable qualities for a student of population.

Demerits

Absence of direct experiences: It does not provide first-hand information and direct experiences to the educands who keep themselves busy merely with the academic type of discussion.

Neglect of reading and writing: There is very little scope for reading and writing which are wry essential for learning.

Time-consuming: As much time is consumed in discussion, it is doubtful that much learning takes place by this method.

All students do not participate equally: Certain students feel shy or do not have the confidence to participate in the discussion. The bright students may dominate and do not allow others to speak.

In spite of these limitations, the Discussion Method can, most profitably, be used in Population Education particularly in teaching sex and family planning to the mature students. Supplemented by other methods, discussion method can prove to be very useful for the teaching of Population Education.

Lecture Method

Also called the Telling Method. Lecture method implies teaching by news of the spoken word. In the lower classes, this method may take the form of Telling, Story or Conversation method'. For higher classes, it may take the form of a 'Lecture' which means a formal talk by the teacher.

The students should be encouraged to ask questions to clarify their doubts if any. The lecture should be well illustrated with the help of models, charts, pictures, etc. The teacher should go on preparing blackboard summary so that the pupil may note it down from consultation in the future. Well-prepared and well-presented the lecture should stimulate interest and mental activity on the part of the pupils.

Lecture Method in the lower classes: In the lower classes, this method assumes the form of stories or conversation. Children are interested in stories, and therefore, whatever knowledge is to be given to the pupils, it is woven in the form of stories and narrated to the children in an interesting answer. A liberal and informal atmosphere is created in the class, so that the pupils may freely talk and put questions to the teacher to clarify their doubts and increase their knowledge.

Lecture in the higher class: In the higher classes, this method assumes the form of a formal talk or lecture. The teacher should prepare the lecture on the topic selected by consulting various sources of information so that each and every aspect of the topic is fully dealt with. The lecture must be delivered with full confidence. The teacher should encourage the students to ask questions to clarify their doubts, etc. The teacher should write the main points of the lesson on the blackboard. He should see that the students are noting down the main points and the summary of the lecture on their note-books.

Merits

More effective than simply reading: Wesley says, "spoken word is frequently far from effective than the printed one. The teacher can indicate by tomes, gestures and facial expressions the exact shade of meaning that he wishes to convey".

Adopted and modified: The teacher can adopt the lecture or a part of it to the requirements of the students. He can explain, clarify, remove doubts and illustrate the lecture for pupil's easy comprehension.

Economy in time and effort: As the lecturer generally prepares the lecture after consulting a number of books, this knowledge is communicated to the pupils within a very short time, saving a lot of time and energy of the pupils.

Multipurpose use: Lecture method can be used for various purposes. The curiosity of the students may be aroused in the beginning they may be motivated so that their interest in learning is aroused. In the middle of the lesson, difficult ideas and concepts my be clarified by the spoken word. The lecture also helps to supplement the knowledge of the pupils. The main points of the lesson are summarised. A brief lecture is helpful before any activity or project is undertaken by the pupils.

Demerits

Students are passive listeners: In the teaching-learning process, the students should actively participate. But, in lecture method, the students mainly remain passive listeners which does not helps to cultivate their minds.

Faulty and Inadequate method of training: Learning should be based upon the principle of learning by doing which is not the case in the lecture method. Lecture method provides only factual knowledge not based on the personal experiences or direct observation of the pupils. This is against the modern concept of learning.

Heavy teaching load on the teachers: It is rather too much to expect from a teacher to prepare five to seven lectures a day and to deliver them efficiently.

Not Possible by Every teacher: Everybody cannot deliver a lecture effectively.

Dull and monotonous: It makes teaching dull and monotonous. It is too much to expect from the children to listen actively and with interest a number of lectures delivered to them during the day.

The lecture method will prove useful if the lectures are well prepared, systematically delivered and well illustrated with the help of charts, pictures, diagram, etc. The interest of the students should be maintained throughout. The personality of the teacher plays a vital role in the success of this method.

Project Method

Project method evolved as a reaction against the theoretical, bookish and away from life type of education. It emphasises activity, direct participation and shouldering responsibility by the students.

The Definition

Dr. Kilpatrick, "A whole, hearted purposeful activity, proceeding in a social environment."

Stevenson, "A project is a problematic act carried to completion in its natural setting."

Prof. Ballard, "A project is a bit of rest life that has been imported into the school; learning by living is a better description of the project method than is learning by doing."

Basic Principles

1. The Principle of Purpose.
2. The Principle of Activity.
3. The Principle of Experience.
4. The Principle of Reality.
5. The Principle of Freedom.
6. The Principle of Utility.

The pupils take interest only when there is a purpose or aim before them, which involves activity, which provides educative experiences, which are realy related to their practical lives; which are pursued in a free atmosphere, and which have ability or usefulness for the pupils. All these principles are fully satisfied in the Project Method.

Steps in Conducting Projects

Providing a Situation: The project is not to be imposed upon the pupils. The teachers, provides a situation, initiating a discussion, etc, which may help the pupils to think of various projects touching their every-day life.

Selecting a Project: The Project is selected by the pupils with the help of the teacher. The project selected must be full of educative possibilities. It should serve some real need of the pupils.

Planning: The next step is to prepare a plan for the execution of the project. The responsibilities are divided according to interest and capacity so that the project my be executed co-operatively.

Executing the Project: The project is completed or executed co-operatively by the students under the guidance of the teacher. The students have to do various types of activities and perform multifarious responsibilities. The students learn by doing, while trying to accomplish the project learning takes place in real life situations; hence, it is practical and useful.

Judging and Evaluating: After the project has been completed, the students sit together for evaluating the project. It is an exercise in self-criticism which is a very useful type of training.

Recording: All the pupils should maintain a project book in which they should write down a complete record of all the activities connected with the project from the first to the last step. This serves as a reference for future guidance.

The Advantages

Eased on the Laws of Learning: The Project Method is based on the three laws of learning, i.e. the law of readiness, the law of exercise, and the law of effect.

Inculcating self-reliance in the pupil: As everything from the first to the last step, is done by the pupils, this method helps to make them self-reliant.

Teaching the value of co-operations: Co-operation is the underlying principle of the project method. It is accomplished through co-operation which helps the students to learn this quality.

Teaching the dignity of labour: Practical work rather than theoretical knowledge is required in the project method. The students have to do everything themselves which naturally teaches the dignity of labour.

A good preparation for life: The Project method is the best method for the accomplishment of the aims of education, that is, the preparation for life.

Correlated approach: Correlated and integrated knowledge is required to meet situations in practical life. This is provided by the Project Method.

Economy in learning: The students work in a free atmosphere, without any kind of strain on their minds. They use their brain as the entire responsibility is upon them. Instead of cramming and unnecessary memorisation, the emphasis on doing ensures maximum learning in the shortest possible time.

Disadvantages

No systematic knowledge is provided: Though knowledge is provided in four correlated manners, yet no single subject is taught systematically and there is no logical arrangement of the subject-matter. As certain portions of a subject cannot be touched through the project, hence no systematic syllabus can be covered by this method.

Expensive method: For its successful completion, the project method requires a lot of material. This makes it too expensive to be adopted by all the schools. It is expensive not only in money and material, but also in time.

Balanced learning for all pupils is not possible: Dominating students may be inclined to do the whole of the work themselves. This will make the work shirkers merely passive spectators.

Death of specially-trained teachers: For its successful implementation the project method requires specially-trained teachers without whom this method will be a complete failure.

Too much work load on the teacher: The teacher is required to guide the students individually, and though, he is to remain in the background, yet its ultimate responsibility rests upon him. This means too much of work load on the teacher.

No systematic time-table: It is nor possible to follow any fixed time table if the school is to ran on Project Method lines. No prescribed syllabus can be covered by this method.

Lack of suitable books: Lack of textbooks written on project uses is one of the greatest hindrances in the successful implementation of this method.

The project method is not the only method of teaching Population Education. Though complete in itself this method should not be depended upon because of its inherent limitations and problems of suitable textbooks and teachers trained on these lines. This method should be used as a supplement to class-room teaching. Projects may be carried on for all the day and classes may be held for the remaining half of the day.

Project in Working

The steps of the project will be as follows :

Providing a Situation: The teacher will initiate the discussion in such a manner that the students may become very keen and interested for the staging of a drama. The step implies motivation of the students.

Selecting a Project: The discussion will be guided by the teacher in such a manner that the students are led to the selection of a play.

Planning the Project: The staging of a play involve a variety of activities, e.g. writing of invitations, sending or posting of the invitations, distribution of the part to be played, rehearsal of the drama, setting of the stage, fight and wood arrangements, seating arrangements, etc. And these activities should be well planned and the duties are to be properely distributed and alloted to the various students. Good planning economises time and energy and provides a useful training to the students.

Executing the project: After the fun preparations, the drama is staged in front of the spectators.

Judging and evaluating the project: After staging the drama, the students sit together and try to assess their achievement as well as their limitations. This self-evaluation affords a very good training in self-criticism and helps to improve the performance in future.

Recording the Project: Everything done by the students is written by them in the project note-books for future reference.

This project will not only add to the knowledge of the students, it will also help to develop many desirable attitudes, e.g. co-operation, organisation, shouldering responsibility, etc, as well as many useful skills like, way of speaking, correct accent and pronunciation, eradication of the feeling of self-consciousness or shyness, etc. As development of all of these is the aim of the teaching of Population Education, this project will prove to be very useful.

15

Other Methods

Problem Method

Problem Method is of comparatively recent origin. It has emerged as a reaction against theoretical and away-from-life type of education. The aim of Population education is to prepare the individuals for life or to equip them in such a way that they can deal with the life situations effectively, competently and successfully. Life is full of problem with which we have to deal in our day-to-day life. Problem Method prepares the individuals for this purpose.

Definition

The syllabus consists of a series of graded problems which are taken up by the pupils who try to find solutions by reflective thinking. No ready-made solutions are obtained from the books. The method trains the individuals to solve their day-to-day problems. It also provides them training in original and creative thinking.

Problem Method differs from the Project Method. Whereas Project Method leads to physical accomplishment of a task, in the Problem Method only a mental solution is to be found. In the words of Bining and Bining "In the Project the activity both mental and physical, leads to the accomplishment of a task in the problem, the activity involved leads to a mental solution."

Problem-solving procedure

There are two procedures of problem-solving.

Deductive Procedure: In this very little effort and reasoning is required on the part of the students. The students mostly depend on their teachers, textbooks, etc., which provide ready-made solutions of the problem.

Inductive Procedure: Inductive procedure is the problem-solving procedure in the true sense: of the term. It requires reflective thinking on the part of the students as a result of which they reach a mental solution.

Steps in the Problem-Solving Procedure

As recommended by John Dewey in his book 'How We Think' the steps we as follows :

1. Selecting and defining the problem in definite terms.
2. Formulating various hypotheses or tentative solutions of the problem.
3. Gathering all relevant facts in connection with all the tentative solutions.
4. Judging and evaluating the tentative solution one by one in the light of the material collected.
5. Rejecting wrong and impracticable solutions and finally arriving at the best possible solution.

Characteristics of Good Problems

1. It must be the product of the student's environment and it must challenge the minds of the students.
2. It must be according to the mental level of the students so that they may be able to take interest in them.
3. It must have educational value and must provide the maximum of activity and practical knowledge to the pupils.
4. It must be accepted and undertaken by the pupils on co-operative basis.

Principles of problem-solving

1. The pupils must feel the problem a their own.

2. The problem must be stated definitely.
3. The means of solving the problem must not be vague to the pupas.
4. Solution must be definite and clear.

The Advantages

Fulfilling the objective of Population Education: The aim of population education is to prepare the individuals for life, so that they may be able to solve their problem. 1% method provides them a good training towards that.

Developing the power of reasoning and Judgement: The student's power of reasoning and judgement is developed because they discuss, investigate and evaluate themselves in order to reach a definite conclusion.

Correct way of acquiring knowledge: As knowledge means to the pupils as a bye-product while trying to solve a problem, knowledge is required with the express purpose of finding a solution to a problem.

Ensuring active pupil participation: As the students actively participate in the problem-solving procedure, the emphasis is on pupil activity rather than on teacher-activity.

Developing initiative and responsibility: Taking the initiative by selecting a problem for solution, the students bear the entire responsibility of solving the problem. This develops initiative and same of responsibility in them.

Disadvantages

Difficult to follow in actual practice: Though in theory this method seems to be very easy to follow, yet in practice, both the teachers and students, habituated to the traditional methods of teaching will find it difficult to follow.

No practical activity involved: Children are interested in practical activities and not in reflective thinking. This method cannot be used with small children due to lack of practical activity.

Time consuming: A lot of time will be consumed even in solving our problem. Much of the time will simply be wasted.

Difficulty in selecting right type of problems: The success of the problem-method depends upon the selection of right type of problem. It is not always possible to select problem to fun of educational possibilities.

Cannot be the only method: This method cannot be depended upon to achieve all the aim and objectives of teaching Population Education. It must be used along with other methods of teaching.

Actual Working

1. Selecting and defining the problem in definite terms.
2. Forming various tentative solutions of the problem.
3. Gathering all the relevant facts in connection with all the tentative solutions.
4. Judging and evaluating the tentative solutions one by one in the light of the material collected.
5. Rejecting the wrong and impracticable solution and finally arriving at the best possible solution.

Source Method

The Source Method implies the consultation of original sources of information and knowledge. Generally the books the students have access to, are compiled from the original books or the original sources of information. But, when a writer after reading the source material, expresses the same ideas in his own language, the ideas get distorted and therefore, the reader gets quite a different idea from what was expressed by the original author. Sometimes biased opinions are expressed, or the ideas are coloured by the personality of the writer. Times and ideas expressed by the original author get distorted to a very great extent. To know the original idea, the reader must consult the source book. This is known as the Source Method.

Source Method can be used by students of high class only. It cannot be recommended for the students of the iower classes.

The use of original material and original sources will give a better understanding of a subject like Population Education. Hence, this method is specially recommended for the teaching of Population Education, especially to the high class.

Various Types of Original Source

1. Material Sources, like ancient coins, monuments and buildings, old weapons and tools, etc.
2. Oral Account for example, folk songs, ancient stories, etc.
3. Hand Written or Printed Material such " old manuscripts, religious books, biographies and autobiographies and other books and printed material. All authoritative writings, whether ancient or modern, are included in this type. Methods of utilising sources not meant for general reading; source material are not to be studied from the first page to the last. It is used and coached when a particular topic is under study. It aims at some type of research work. The sources are consulted according to requirements. As the sources provide authentic proof, a particular thesis is maintained or rejected .

This method is generally used at the advanced stage but the students must be taught and made familiar with the use of this method. This can be done in the following ways :—

Settling Controversial Issues: Controversial issues and problem may be given to the students to be studied by them with the help of source material. The teacher can, thus, guide the pupils to discover errors in the textbooks, etc. This type of exercise is specially useful for high school students.

Demonstration by the Teacher: The teacher can demonstrate the way of making use of the source material after taking a particular passage from the original source, supporting or throwing additional light on his opinion. This will motivate the pupils to consult such sources for clarifying certain controversial issues or for are living at truth about a certain point.

Assigning Passages for Reading: The teacher introduces the sources by assigning selected passages to be read by trained students. These Passages should be in connection with the topic under study.

By using these methods, the teacher can motivate as well as teach the way in which the pupils can make a profitable use of the source material according to their needs and requirements.

Merits

Developing scholarly attitude of mind: By making use of the source material detailed study of selected topics, develops a scholarly bent of mind which is very useful for the advancement of learning.

Lending to met and authentic knowledge: By making use of the 'source', the pupils come to acquire exact an authentic knowledge.

Leading to the development of critical faculty: As various types of sources may be available giving contradictory views on the same topic the student will have to think, reason out and judge before arriving at the final truth. This develops the critical faculty of it, student.

Arousing interest and curiosity for learning: Use of original sources increases the curiosity of the students. Because of the conflicting views contained in these, they arouse their interest to go into the depth and find the truth.

Great educational value: The habit of using the source material provides training which leads to the discipline of mind. Hence, it has a great educational value.

Demerits

Difficulty to be used by school students: Source Method is generally used for advanced studies. It may be used for the high and higher secondary classes, but cannot be recommended for the lower classes.

Difficulty of language: Source material is generally available in the classical languages like Sanskrit, Persian, Arabic, Greek, etc. with which the school students are hardly familiar.

Paucity of source material: Source material of real worth is not available in abundant quantity. Even whatever source material is available, cannot be made use of by the school students.

Conflicting views of writers: As conflicting and contradictory views are expressed by different writers of source books, this creates confusion in the minds of the students.

All teachers cannot use this method: To use this method, the teacher must have a good knowledge about all the source material available. This is possible only if the teacher knows many languages especially the classical languages, in which most of the source material is available. This is too much to expect from every teacher.

In spite of these limitations and difficulties, the Source Method can be usefully employed in the higher classes. With a little bit of effort, the teacher will be able to make use of this method to the great advantage of the pupils.

Unit Method

Unit Method is a modern innovation, the outcome of the growing tendency towards correlated and integrated approach in the teaching of various subjects. As knowledge given in the form of isolated facts is of no practical consequence, unit method tends to be only theoretical. Even within a subject, the division of the instructional material or the content into a number of chapters is criticised on the ground that knowledge given in this form is not functional and practical. Population Education requires to be taught in an integrated form. Therefore, its subject-matter may be divided into larger divisions, called units.

What is a Unit ?

In Population Education we have to present an integrated picture of population and its impact. Hence, the facts of knowledge are not to be taught in isolation. The vast subject-matter of Population Education has to be organised in larger divisions. Each such division is called a unit. A unit is, thus, "The orgamisation of material in related groups, each large enough to be significant, but small enough to be seen as a whole by the pupils."

Definition of Unit

Dictionary of Education: A unit is a major sub-division of a use of study, a textbook or a subject-field.

Preston: "A unit is as large a block of related subject-matter as can be overviewed by the learner."

Hanna Hageman and Potter: A unit can be defined as a "purposeful learning experience focussed upon some socially significant understanding which will modify the behaviour of the learner and enable him to adjust to a life situation more effectively." This is exactly what the Population Education aim at.

The unit my be subject-matter unit or an experience unit. It is an instructional device to give knowledge or experience or both. It is an organised body of information and experiences, designated to effect significant outcomes for the learner." The unit should be comprehensive enough to have utility and contribute directly to the pupils, adjustment in society.

Criteria of Units

1. They should be according to the class or the mental level of the pupils.
2. They must be comprehensive, yet small enough to be seen as a whole by the pupils.
3. They should centre round the pupils' interests.
4. They should involve pupils in learning activities through their active participation.
5. The specific objectives to be achieved in a given unit should be clearly stated.
6. They should provide opportunities for creative experiences and in various form of creative expression.
7. They should provide scope for the use of a variety of materials like books and other reading material pictures, charts and graphs, etc. drawing of maps, discussions, etc.
8. They should be well-integrated. The Unit Method Procedure.

Dr. H. C. Morrison, the chief exponent of the Unit Method has suggested a procedure, which, like Herbartian Steps, consists of five formal steps, and which, according to him, will enable the pupils to accomplish and master the unit. The steps are as given below :

Exploration: It consists of motivating the pupils as well as testing their purview knowledge about the proposed unit.

Presentation: The teacher presents a complete outline of the unit, which serves as a guide for the detailed study of the unit.

Assimilation: During this step, pupils are busy in reading discussing, writing and taking notes, and in this way, gathering information and material for the completion of the unit.

Organisation: The material collected is organised and written logically and systematically.

Recitation: It implies giving a systematic oral account of the whole or of significant portions of the unit. This will promote clarity of expression on the part of the pupils.

The Advantages

Integrated knowledge: Integrated knowledge is more functional and practical. This method provides knowledge in an integrated manner.

Variety of activities: This method emotes a lot of activity like reading, writing, discussing, etc. in which the pupils participate actively for the completion of the unit.

Traits of citizenship: Many traits of citizenship like cooperation, sympathy, respect for the opinions of others, etc. are acquired by the pupils through this method.

Instruction according to individual differences: This method does not aim at fixed and uniform standard of achievement for all pupils. Teaching is adapted to the requirements of individual differences

Disadvantages

Difficult to prepare good units: This difficulty arises because the teachers are not trained on unit method.

Lack of equipment and reading material: When the needed equipment and other reading material is lacking, the units cannot be completed properly by the students. The lack of textbooks written on unit lines is a genuine difficulty.

No Systematic knowledge: Knowledge provided in an integrated manner rather confuses the pupils, as no systematic knowledge is provided.

Copying: Instead of doing genuine work, certain pupils may copy the prepared units from the notebooks of more intelligent students. This defeats the very purpose of the unit method.

Socialised Recitation Method

Meaning: An outcome of the modern concept of teaching-learning process, the socialised recitation method is the result of the philosophy that instead of being only a passive recipient of knowledge the learner should actively participate in the learning process. This method is the product of a reaction against the dictatorial role of the teacher. It emphasises co-operative learning under the guidance of the teacher. It is a type of class-room instruction with emphasis on group consciousness and the sense of individual responsibility towards the group. The word 'recitation' implies 'discussion'; and socialised' implies the social atmosphere.' Hence, socialised recitation means 'discussion in a social atmosphere' that is created in the class-room.

In the past, the emphasis was on teaching rather than on learning. The teacher was all important. He did most of the work himself and there was little activity on the part of the pupils. The modern concept of teaching-learning process emphasises active participation on the part of the learners. In specialised recitation, the emphasis has been shifted from the teacher and the subject-matter to the pupils. Learning process is meant for the child and not child for the learning process.

Moreover, in Population Education the emphasis is laid more on ideals, attitudes, habits and skills, rather than on aquisition of only the facts of knowledge. The socialised recitation affords maximum training in formulating ideals, attitudes, etc. This more important part of education takes place in the socialised atmosphere and active participation by the pupils in the learning process.

Role of the Teacher. The teacher does not play a dictatorial role in the socialised recitation. His role is to guide the pupils and pose himself as a member of the class or the group. He sits with the pupils and does not sit or stand at a higher level. The problem or the topic selected is discussed co-operatively by the pupils as well as by the teacher. The teacher provides necessary guidance if and when required by the pupils. Socialised recitation makes group discussions of paramount importance. The pupils get training in independent and group thinking. The pupils are socialised because of their active participation in the discussions under an expert guidance of the teacher

Recitation Procedure

As a classroom procedure socialised recitation takes the form of group-discussion. Hence, it is also known socialised discussion, which may carried on informally or in some formal manner. It should involve maximum pupil participation.

Varying from a simple informal organisation to a complex parliamentary one sacialised recitation may assume any form. It may be only a form of socialised group discussion in which members decide on an agenda, express their ideas freely, share their information willingly and draw some definite conclusions about a certain topic, issue or problem.

Taking his seat among other members of the group and thinks himself one of them, the teacher acts as a friend, philosopher and guide in the true sense of the terms.

The Advantages

Active participation: In socialised recitation, each and every student takes active part in the discussion.

Firm expression: As compared to the traditional class-room teaching, where the emphasis is on rote memory, the students are required to think and express their ideas logically, clearly and impressively.

Socialisation: Socialised recitation affords ample opportunities to the individuals for their socialisation.

Development of right attitudes: As compared to mere factual knowledge development of right attitudes and ideals is very much emphasised in Population Education, socialised recitation is one of the most important class-room procedures for the development of desirable attitudes, skills and ideals.

Respect for democratic lines of life: As a class-room procedure, socialised recitation is organised on democratic lines. The president and the secretary are elected according to parliamentary procedure. The students learn to cooperate with others and hence, they begin to respect the democratic way of life.

Disadvantages

Neglect of Reading and writing: As this method mainly revolves round discussion there is very little scope for reading and writing by the students, which are of worse essential for the acquisition of knowledge

Damination by a few pupils: As a few intelligent students endowed with the quality of impressive speech, they dominate and the discussion and other students may not actively participate. Thus equal opportunities are not provided to the students for learning.

Wastage of time: As discussion often tends to wander away firm the topic, and certain students are in the habit of arguing things for the sake of argument alone, much of the time is wasted.

Slow Learning: Through this method, facts which can be told by the teacher in a very short time, take very long time to be learnt by the pupils. Learning becomes a very slow process and make it difficult to cover the courses in time.

Thus, howsoever good this method may be, its exclusive use cannot be recommended. This method should also be supplemented by other methods of teaching Population Education.

Effects of Methods

Education is an organised and systematic activity. In this methods of teaching have a unique and important place. We have to think of suitable methods of teaching whenever we want to convey an idea or a topic. Same is true with population education.

In fact, one big problem of population education has been that we were not able to think of the methods with which to convey this to students. Now this problem appears to have been solved. Many writers and thinkers have given thought to this and they have listed the following methods of population education.

(1) Value Clarification; (2) Play and Drama; (3) Help of Audio-Visual Aids; (4) Inquiry Method; and (5) Programmed Learning.

In this scheme, prominent role is played by Audio-Visual Aids, such as:

(a) Charts

(b) Suitably-Illustrated Books

(c) Slides

(d) Posters (Printed Chart)

(e) Radio-Talks on it
(f) Tape Recorder
(g) Gramophone
(h) T.V. & Cinema/Film
(i) Drama

The audio-visual aids listed above will project education as population oriented. All aids must project this and highlight this.

We describe in brief some of the methods. The author do not claim any originality.

Value Clarification. Population education is a sensitive issue. People have wrong notions about it. Some consider it bad/obscene. This misconception had to be erased/removed. A clear viewpoint about small population, rising population and related problems has to be developed. People are to be exhorted to develop right social and cultural values. The teachers should collect facts and weigh these on proper scales. You can give a lecture, talk to people, discuss and clarify their feelings and traditions. Ultimately you are to tell them that population education is not bad. It is moral, just and good to have small family. Liberty and social justice depend upon these. Let there be thorough discussion so that people do not show unnecessary guilt or shame.

Drama and Play. Drama and play have great use in teaching population education. Play and drama depict reality of life. Economic problems can be brought home with the help of play and drama. Many situations can be depicted through play and drama. Many plays and dramas can be staged on various themes. Here the main theme will be population education. These can be on the education of the child. It can be on earning one's livelihood.

We need not go into the difference between play and drama. Entertainment rules in play. In drama, there is some dryness. People can play role. Role-playing is educative in itself. Various problems related to population can be highlighted. This is an effective method but the teacher will have to be very innovative in this. He has to find time also for these to be staged. Money, time and power are required but when there is a will there is a way.

Teaching Population Education on Inquiry. This method is also known as problem method. We try to reach the roots of the problem. There is no cramming. There is free discussion. The steps as under.

1. Defining the problem in clear, meaningful terms.
2. Critically evaluating the facts to see the differences and relations among them and to draw meaningful conclusions.
3. Inquiring about the presented conclusions.
4. To draw conclusions.
5. To put into effect those conclusions.

There are various uses in teaching through this technique:

1. There is an active participation of the learners. Thus teaching is based on the activity and not on the subject-matter.
2. As the students remain active. Thus this is child-centred technique.
3. Here the ultimate end is not subject-mater but this subject-matter becomes means for finding the important conclusions.
4. This method is as useful as traditional lecture method because through this method also knowledge is appropriately given to the students.
5. There is much scope for creative thinking and critical examination.
6. This method is very useful in teaching population education because by using this method necessary information is given regarding various problems related to population education and thus it broadens the individual's knowledge.

But one has to face many problems while using this method:

1. The success of this method depends on able teachers, students and administrators, in the absence of whom it loses all its utility.
2. This method is time-consuming. If there is less time for teaching, then this method should not be used.

3. All the topics of population education cannot be taught through inquiry method. Thus it should be used only after selecting appropriate topics.

Programmed Learning. Skinner gave us this method of teaching. It states that reinforced behaviour is repeated again.

Programmed learning is learning with the help at machines. It is also known as self-learning. Entire knowledge is broken into units and the units are fed into machines. You learn at your speed. You are given feedback on your answer. If the answer is correct, you learn more and more. The machine can be cheap. The machine can be costly like a computer. It can be a specially-designed textbook.

In most of the developing countries, this method of programmed learning is being applied to population education, because students are mature and educated. They enjoy learning by this method.

Best Method. Is there a best method of population education or which is the best method of population education ? The answer is combination of all these—Lecture can use of aids Conversation and Question-answer method without guilt or shame.

The Assessment

The concept of Evaluation is clear to all. By evaluation in population education, we want to know as to how much does a student know about it.

Under the overall guidance of Professor B.S. Parakh, the NCERT in July 1985 published a series a Population Awareness Tests. The Tests are for three levels:

Level A: For Students of Schools and for Teachers of Elementary Schools.

Level B: For Teachers of Secondary Schools.

Level C: For Professionals.

There are three tests for each level:

(a) True-False Items
(b) Opinion Statements
(c) Multiple Choice Items

A sample is given here:

TEST NO. 1

Given below are certain statements on different aspects of population education. They are either TRUE or FALSE.

Against each statement, two alphabets namely, T and F have been mentioned. T stands for True and F stands for False.

Please read each statement carefully and indicate whether it is TRUE or FALSE by encircling either T or F, as the case may be.

1. Population education is another name of sex education. T/F
2. Population education is yet another separate subject to be taught at the school level. T/F
3. Every year India adds over 13 million people which is the population of Australian Continent T/F
4. If we draw a map according to population, Delhi would appear bigger than Himachal Pradesh, Arunachal Pradesh, Nagaland and Sikkim put together. T/F
5. Population growth rates have considerably declined in those countries where most women are in jobs. T/F
6. Research has not confirmed that reduction in birth rates must precede reduction in death rates. T/F
7. Demographic factors and socio-economic development are independent of each other. T/F
8. Population education stands for better fulfilment of our basic needs than mere survival. T / FF
9. Population education does not confine/itself to the well-being of the present generation alone and also that of the generations to come. T/F
10. For a population educator, girls' education is less important than boys' education. T/F

QUESTIONS

1. Briefly explain the various methods of teaching Population Education.

2. What is the Textbook Method of teaching Population Education ? Give its merits as well demérits.
3. How would you use the Population Education textbook in the secondary sense ? Elucidate with the help of an example, choosing any topic from the syllabus.
4. What is the Discussion Method of teaching Population Education ? State and explain the various constituents of a discussion and give its merits as well as drawbacks.
5. What is Lecture Method ? Explain its merits and limitations.
6. What is Project Method ? Enumerate its principles, steps, advantages and limitations.
7. What is Problem Method ? Explain the procedure and steps for Problem-solving. Give its advantages and limitations.
8. What is Source Method ? What are the various types of original sources? Give the advantages and limitations of the Source Method.
9. What is the Unit Method of teaching Population Education. Explain the procedure of the unit method. Explain its advantages and limitations.
10. What is Socialised Recitation Method ? What are its advantages and disadvantages?

16

Audio-Visual Aids

Acquisition of knowledge, learning or experiencing is one of the important aims of Population Education. Now, they are two fundamental means of acquiring knowledge :

Through Direct Experiences: Direct experience implies personal observation, which provide immediate sensory contacts with the actual objects. According to an old Chinese proverb, "One seeing is worth a hundred tellings." Also, nothing teaches like an experience. Excursions and field-trips provide first-hand experience. Thus, direct experiences are the best teacher.

Through Indirect Experiences: As first-hand experiences or direct experiences may not be always available, and may sometimes be too costly dependent upon indirect experiences is essential. Indirect experiences are vicarious or representative experiences as these are obtained 'through something.'

Definition and Meaning

Audio-visual aids imply a variety of materials which help to provide exepriences indirectly or through something. Films, radio, pictures, charts, maps, models, etc. are some of the audio-visual aids widely used in Population Education.

Meaning: Audio-visual aids, as the name implies, means certain types of 'aids' to teaching, which we can 'hear' as well as see'. For example a motion picture. Sometimes, however, we have either audio aids; i.e.. which we can 'listen to or we have 'visual aids, which we can see but, in fact, all of these are called by the technical line, 'audio-visual aids. These aids make teaching effective and help in the easy comprehension on the part of the students.

The Advantages. Audio-visual aids are so important and useful in Population Education that these have become an inseparable part of teaching. Their use is based upon sound principles of psychology and they help to make teaching effective and learning easy and lasting. Following are the advantages of audio-visual aids :

Sensory aids to burning: Our five sense are the gateways of knowledge. It is a psychological fact that if more than one of our senses are being used simultaneously for learning a particular at the impression created on the mind will be deeper and vivid which will make learning tiny, clear and lasting. If, for example, a teacher shows a picture or a chart also along with his verbal explanations, the students will be making use of two of their senses, hearing and as well as seeing. The impression on the mind will naturally be deep, clear and lasting. This shows the importance of audio-visual aids in teaching.

Create interest in the lesson: The use of audio-visual aids make the lesson interesting because they bring variety in the lesson. Variety is the spice of life. Audio-visual aids help to arouse curiosity and thus create interest in the lesson.

Substitutes for direct experiences: Direct experiences cannot be had always. Everybody cannot go round the world to see the impact of over-population on developing societies. The audio-visual aids can serve the purpose of direct experiences. For example, in the above instance a film on the world population may serve the purpose well.

Useful for the slow learners: Students with below normal intelligence cannot follow the verbal teaching entirely. The use of audio-visual aids makes teaching mom concrete. It enables the slow-learners learn easily and quickly.

Making teaching effective: The audio-visual aids help to make process of teaching more effective, because, audio-visual aids make the students learn quickly, easily, clearly and permanently.

Aids in Use

Population Education is a subject whose scope is very vast. It is an integrated subject and its boundaries touch the various social sciences such as History, Geography, Political Science and Economics, etc., In fact it is a subject which derives its content or the subject-matter from these subjects. Therefore, all those audio-visual aids which can be used for the teaching of all these subjects, can also be profitably used in Population Education.

Personal observations and first hand experiences which can be provided through excursions and field-trips we greatly stressed for the young children.

In the class-room the teacher can make use of a large variety of audio-visual aids for the teaching of different types of lessons in Population Education. Such audio-visual aids as the maps, various types of models, charts, pictures, black-board sketches, diagrams graphs, etc. are specially useful for the teaching of Population studies.

Kinds of Audio-Visual Aids in Population Education

Field Trip: Organise a field trip to slum to see the population problem among the poor. A field trip must be property planned. Some contacts and prearrangements between the leader of the party and these incharge of the places to be visited is most essential. The most important part of field-trip is the planned procedure during the trip. The leader must look to the minutest details so that the trip is successful from every point of view and the students benefit the most, After the trip is ever, the students must review it. Specially to note thew limitations; for their future guidance. Describing the details of the trip in writing by the students will also prove useful. Including it in the form of an article in the school magazine along with the photographs taken during the trip will arouse interest of other students for such trips. Thus excursions and field-trips will prove to be very useful for understanding population problem.

Models: Direct experience or observation of the actual objects is not always possible, either because the students cannot be taken to those places or because those things cannot be brought into the class-room or it is too expensive to do it. Under these conditions, a 'model' of that object will very well serve the purpose. The example of technique of family planning may be cited in this connection. Sometimes, the models my prove to be better than even the actual objects for illustrative purposes. This happens when the actual object is difficult to secure for observation under these conditions a model of the convenient size will serve the purpose better. In Population Education, we can use the models of small family, family planning tools, etc.

Pictures: Pictures are the most important form of audio-visual material which can be profitably used in Population Education. Pictures of over-crowded cities, slum, poverty, insanitation, insufficient countries, child marriage to many children life in over-crowded places, etc. serve a very useful purpose in illustrative media. All these types of pictures are easily available. Some of these may be drawn by the teacher himself.

Charts: Charts are specially prepared or got prepared by the teacher for the express purpose of using these in a particular lesson for illustrative purpose. An advantage of the chart is that it contains only those things which the teacher wants to show to the pupils. Charts of various characteristics of population may be useful in population education.

The pictures and charts should be simple and not very colourful or highly finished, as these will arouse too much curiosity on the part of the students which will distract their attention from the actual lesson.

Maps: Maps are specially useful for teaching population statistics and world demography. The maps can be printed ones in drawn in a big piece of thick paper by the teacher himself. The teacher can also draw the maps on the blackboard, which, of course requires a little practice on the part of the teacher.

Diagrams: A special advantage of diagrams and graphs can be drawn on the blackboard by the teacher, and he is not required to take the trouble of preparing charts, etc. Population data are generally shown through diagrams.

Graphs: Graphs are specially useful for the teaching of the economic aspect of population diagrams and graphs are indispensable for illustrating the various laws and principles of population dynamics.

The teacher can encourage the students also to draw the diagrams or graphs on the blackboards. This will have an added advantage of creating a sort of activity in the class.

Films: Films are the full-fledged audio-visual aid. These are the best audio-visual aids for family planning and family welfare used by the government. Film depict the reality in a most life-like matter. If rightly used it can prove to be a wonderful medium for population education. To a very great extent, it cain serve as a good substitute for field-trips. It can be more useful because, even the far-off places and their interiors can be exhibited through the films. Film specially prepared to disseminate the knowledge pertaining to population problem are greatly to be recommended. Films depicting population events, morality, fertility, migration unemployment over-crowding, etc. in their multifarious complexity and variety, are very useful as a supplement to the class-room teaching in the subject of Population Education. Developed countries are specially making use of this medium for sex and Aids education as well as for the family planning and family welfare. In India also, film should be got prepared specifically for the teaching of various aspects and problem of population as well as for providing general population education. The use of films is very much recommended for the teaching of Population Education.

Film Strips. Film strip is a short spool of cinematograph film, having photographed on it a number of illustrations for projection. Its length varies according to the number of photographs, which of course, depend upon the nature of the lesson; and which are to be decided by the teacher. The filmstrip does not run like a film; rather only one photograph is projected at a time on the screen, and it can be held them for any length of time, during which the teacher will explain things from the projected image to the class. The film-strip is made where the growth or the developmental features of a particular object, human anatomy are to be shown. Various photographs will show the various parts of human anatomy and the teacher will explain these properly it elaborately while providing sex and Aids education. The subject of Population Education affords numerous opportunities where the teacher can make use of the film-strip. Various stages of the development of human being, homes for living, various stages of the economy, stages of development of the means of transportation and communication, and a variety of other developmental phenomenon can be illustrated with the help of film-strips.

Radio. Radio is a wonderful educational medium which combines learning with entertainment. It is specially useful in Population Education because, in addition to entertainment and recreation radio covers a variety of fields like social, political, economic, historical, geographical and educational fields. In all the fields, radio helps us in keeping our knowledge up-to-date. The persons who deal with different topics from the broadcasting stations, are specialists in their fields of activity. So, they are in a much better position to make their subject-matter real and full of life. Radio helps to widen the outlook of the students about the world and its population problems. In India some of the programmes braodcast from the radio about India government, concern over family planning. Radio-listening is an art. It requires proper training and guidance. Keeping in view the age-group of the students the teacher must make a selection of the broadcasts. Before the broadcast, the nature and substance of the broadcast must be explained to the students. After the broadcast is over, the students should have a discussion on it under the guidance of the teacher. This will very much enhance the educational value of such programmes. It must be remembered, however, that radio is an aid to teaching and not a substitute for it. Radio should be used occasionally to supplement the knowledge of the students about population problems.

Histrionics: Histrionics include discuss, plays, pageants, etc. Histrionics or drama can prove to be a wonderful and very useful aid to the teaching population problem, family planning, etc. Drama is a most life-like and realistic representation of life. The knowledge and insight gained through drama is deep, vivid and lasting. Hence it may be utilised to educate rural people about family welfare and family planning, etc.

Population education, as we know does not aim simply at the of knowledge and information, it also aims at the development of socially desirable and useful attitudes and skills towards population issues. Drama, when planed organised and staged by the students themselves, helps to develop numerous desirable attitudes towards population issues.

The Blackboard. Blackboard is one of the most utilised aids of teaching. Its greatest advantage is that it is most handy and available. It is used for various purposes; such as for writing the topic of the lesson, for developing the summary of the lesson, for illustrating the lesson with the help of diagrams, sketches, graphs, etc. The use of coloured chalk proves to be very useful for creating interest for emphasising certain points and for clarity and vividness.

Blackboards writing is an art and must be practised by an aspiring teacher. Some suggestions for blackboard writing are given below :

(i) The letters written on the blackboards should be of moderate size; neither too big, nor too mall.

(ii) The teacher should stand at an angle while writing on the blackboards. If he writes with his back towards the students, they may take it as an opportunity to talk or do some sort of mischief.

(iii) The writing should be in straight lines.

(iv) The teacher should see to it that whatever he is writing on the blackboard, is visible to all the students.

(v) The teacher should make use of coloured chalks to emphasise something.

(vi) The teacher should cleanse the whole of the blackboard in the beginning of the period and keep it ready for use.

(vii) The teacher should always make a good use of the blackboard while teaching. The use of this aid will make teaching effective and easily comprehensible to the students.

(viii) The teacher should occasionally call the students and ask them to write the answer, etc. on the blackboard. This will create activity in the class.

Bulletin Board: Bulletin board is a sort of board fixed on the wall inside or outside the class-room. On this board are displayed various types of articles, pictures, cartoons, posters, maps graph, news item etc. We may display such material on the bulletin board which is related to and is useful for the students of population. It is, therefore, an effective aid to the population teacher. The articles etc., should be contributed by the students and these should be changed quite frequently to maintain the interest of the students. If properly used, the bulletin board call prove to be a very useful and effective aid as a supplement to the teaching of Population Education.

Globe: Globe is a very useful aid for the teaching of population in various countries. It is an inexhaustible source of help to the pupils. Population education being a vast subject, which takes under its purview the whole of the world, many things related to geographical, historical and economic aspects can very well be taught with the help of the globe. A frequent study of globe aids the mental horizon of the students. They begin to consider themselves the citizens of the world. This international outlook is the need of the how to which contribute frequent references to globe. To inculcate the feeling of international understanding, the students must be given an idea that the whole of the world belongs to us. Frequent presentation of the globe to the students will put this idea into the minds of the students. For this and for many other purposes, specially related to the teaching of population issues, globe could be of great help and utility

The School Museum: The school museum is developed by the efforts of the students and the teacher. Children are eager collectors, and they can help a lot in reflecting various articles of use which can be kept and exhibited in the school musuem. In the museum, we can have various types of models, charts, pictures, maps, specimens, etc. which can be brought and used by the population education teacher while teaching in the class-roam. The school museum will be a store-house of audio-visual material, on which the population education teacher can frequently draw for illustrations.

The Gramophone. Gramophone can mostly be used for letting the students have records concerning population issues.

The Tape Recorder. For teaching Population issues tape-recorder is even more useful. Good speeches of prominent personalities can be recorded on the tape. The students can listen to those again and derive benefit from the same. Similiarly, many other types of programmes or item can be recorded on the tape and the students can derive benefit from the same.

The slide Projector. The slide projector is an instrument by which slides specially prepared for illustrative purposes are projected on the screen in wall. Various types of slid" rout be used for illustrations in the teaching of population education, for example life in a village life in a town or life in foreign countries Over-crowding slums, etc. Thus, while providing entertainment for the children, the slide projector also prove to be very useful for instructional purposes.

Epidiascope: Epidiascope is also a similar instrument having an added advantage that there is no need of preparing slides for this. Any object placed in the front of it will be projected on the screen or the wall. A picture, a photograph, a mosquito or a fly; anything can be projected with the help of epidiascope. Its uses are the same as those of the slide projector.

Celebration of Festivals, Fairs and National Days: Fairs, festivals and the celebration of national days can serve a very useful purpose for imparing knowledge of Population Education. A number of fairs and festivals are celebrated in India. The students take a keen interest in them; and therefore opportunities should be provided to them to witness these. The students will naturally put a number of questions in this connection; the teacher should consider it as an opportunity to impart knowledge about those and in this way try to quench their thirst for knowledge. The students will come to imbibe the national heritage and develop a feeling of pride for their country in addition to acquiring a lot of knowledge. Similarly, observing national and international population days will prove to be of immense value specially for the students of Population Education.

Thus, audio-visual aids are of great importance and value in Population Education. Their right use will make teaching effective and full of interest. The teacher of Population Education can equally benefit from their use and make his teaching effective and useful for the students.

QUESTIONS

1. What are audio-visual aids ? Discuss their Population Education.
2. Enumerate it explain some of the important audio-visual aids that can be used profitably in population Education.

17

The Curriculum

Education has to integrate two processes- the individual process and the social process. In the former sense, it is identical with individual growth and the development of latent power in the child. From the latter point of view it is identical with socialisation, adjustment to environment and imbibing of culture. Both the processes are integrated.

While education is a process, curriculum is a means to the process. While education is learning, curriculum signifies situations for learning. While education deals with 'how' and 'when' curriculum deals with 'what' While education is the product curriculum of the plan.

The Definition

Etymologically the term "Curriculum" is derived from the Latin word 'Currere' which means 'run'. Thus curriculum means 'a worse to be run for reaching a certain goal'. In recent years the term curriculum has come to me" all the planned activities and experiences which are available to students under the direction of the school. In the words of Kerney and Cook, "It is a complex of more or less planned or controlled conditions under which students learn to behave and to behave in their various ways. In it, new behaviour may be acquired, present behaviour may be modified, maintained or eliminated; and desirable behaviour may become both persistent and viable." Curriculum includes both the curricular and co-curricular activities. It is the sum total of good learning experiences that the students have in order to achieve the goals of education which determine the direction of these experiences.

The Aims

(1) To draw out, cultivate, excite and inspire the full development of each student.

(2) To create an atmosphere in which students will learn to think critically and constructively and seek truth and solve problems.

(3) To help students in establishing values through intimate acquaintance with the humanities, the arts, the natural sciences, the social sciences and religion.

(4) To develop the character of students-integrity, honesty, judgement co-operation, friendliness, and goodwill.

(5) To prepare men and women for citizenship in a democratic society where freedom and liberty go hand in hand with law and justice and where responsibility, national and international, is a characteristics of the individual.

(6) To meet the needs not only of mine students, but of students with a wide range of ability, aptitudes and interests.

The Significance

According to Cunningham,: "Curriculum is a tool in the hand of the artist (teacher) to mould his material (pupils) according to his ideals aim in his studio school."

The curriculum of population education includes the learner's experience in or outside the school that are included in a programme which has been divided to help him develop mentally, physically, emotionally and morally. Thus, curriculum and population education were inseparable. The unprecedented growth of number is one of the powerful challenges of the second half of the present century. Children and youths of today should understand the impact of population on the life of mankind should be able to act wisely and rationally by deciding about their reproductive behaviour. Educationists all over the world and economic reformers of all the countries agree on the issue of including population education in the curriculum of educational institutions at all levels. While divergence of opinions is found on the possible content of a population education programme. This is because of social and economic growth of the country and its cultural and traditional background, However, there is an area of agreement about the core concepts in the content of population education programme all over.

Practical Aspects

There are three main factors of population education programme:

1. The aims and objectives of population education.
2. Curriculum in population education.
3. Instructional methods.

The teacher of the population education programme has to achieve the prefixed aim and objectives. He has to employ suitable instructional methods and procedures. He can do it only when he knows what effect he has to make and in what order. He should know the content of population education curriculum its subjects, activities and experiences in a property graded form. Curriculum is the "warp and woof' of the whole educational process. Followings are the needs and importance of curriculum in population education :

Achievement of Aims: It is futile to define the aims of population education, without well-planned efforts and organisations to achieve the aims. The teacher must know the knowledge, activities, experiences and other influences which help in the achievement of aims of population education.

Criteria for Suitable Rockers: The curriculum can show what type of teachers are required for new types of educational systems, what type of work they are required to do according to the requirements of the curriculum.

Selection of Suitable Methods of Teaching: The curriculum, of population education enables the teacher to select suitable methods of teaching. "How to teach" is determined by 'what to reach'.

Trends in Education: The aims of population education are dynamic. They go changing with the changing social requirements. The curriculum of population education reflects the trends and growth of population in education. For example, modern population education places the following demands on the curriculum :

Providing Suitable Knowledge : The curriculum should include suitable knowledge helping in the achievement of aims of the population education.

Providing Suitable Activities and Experience : The curriculum includes well selected activities and experiences needed for the development of pupils according to population requirements.

Providing Wholesome Influences : The curriculum should provide wholesome school programme to develop the desirable behaviour patterns in the pupils to check population growth.

Problems

According to Prof. Jayasurya thinks that the curriculum development in Population Education has to confront the following difficulties :

(1) The relative newness of the concept of population education.

(2) The traditional, conservation of the educational professional.

(3) The necessity to draw the content of population education from a number of disciplines.

(4) The lack of personnel specially trained in the field of population.

Relative Newness of the Concept of Population Education: Population education is relatively a new area of study. It has not yet reached a stage of sufficient clarification of related concepts and ideas. This is not a special feature of population education alone. All educational innovations have to overcome these difficulties. After generalising the difficulties of population education one will have to find remedies in the light of experience.

Traditional Conservatism of the Educational Professional: Conservative and orthodox teachers and administrators block the progress and development of the population education programme though all the teachers and administrators are not conservative by nature. If they are convinced of the horrible consequences especially socio-cultural and economic consequences of population growth as they affect their life, they will favour the inclusion of population education in the programme. Therefore, administrators and teachers should be involved and oriented to the concept and need for population education for the coming generation.

The Necessity to Draw the Content from a Number of Disciplines: Another difficulty faced in curriculum development of population education is its multidisciplinary nature. Its concept draws its content from a number of disciplines like economics, demography, sociology, health sciences, social studies, medical science etc. This makes curriculum development a joint effort on the part of the educational administrators, teachers, parents and experts in the field or education. All the persons should work together to construct and arrange an effective curriculum.

Lack of Personnel Specially Trained in the Field of Population: Lack of trained persons is another hurdle in curriculum construction of population education. Population education is a relatively new field of education. For the last 60 years much progress has been made in this field in the Western countries. In the United States of America systematic population education programme has been organised. Our problem about the lack of trained personnel is temporary problem which shall disappear gradually.

Various Levels

Educational matter presented to the child should be at his level of understanding. The makers of curriculum should always bear this inspiration fact in their minds while planning the curriculum. Having fixed the content of population education, the next step is to find out the type of content at different stages, so that the objectives of population education can be achieved. At the Asian Regional Workshop, it was the unanimous consensus that elements of population should eventually be incorporated into all levels of the school system. However, it was also recognised that limitations of human and financial resources demanded that initial programmes be somewhat narrower at these stages :

1. Primary Level (Class I-V)
2. Middle Level (Class VI-VIII)
3. Secondary Level (Class IX-X)

Primary Level (Class I-V): "Well begun is half done" is a well known maxim. The superstructure of the population education programme of a country rests on primary education. If the child is well looked after at the primary stage, the stage of secondary education automatically takes care of it. Thus, a rightly organised primary education is the first and the most important platform from where educationists should launch the attack to obviate the alarming problem of the country.

Begining from the Primary Stage

Large number of students : By a primary level programme a large number of students can be influenced. At the primary level, i.e, up to class V, children are below 10 or 11 years of age. A large number of pupils can be met at this level. Important attitudes towards life and social values are formed at this age. Most of the pupils who complete their primary education and go for secondary school are compelled to leave the village because of lack of educational facilities.

Minimum benefit to the dropouts : Those who complete primary education and do not go for secondary schools remain in villages. The population education programme at the primary stage shall help them in playing the role of an adult and married person. This minimum population education shall help them to understand the dreadful effect of population growth on the quality of life.

Easier to include : It would be easier to include population content to a primary school syllabus. In most of the developing nations a single teacher system prevails in primary schools. There is also a common curriculum for all pupils in the same class. As there are no provisions to option the subject it is comparatively easy to include population topics in the existing textual materials.

Ground for attaining large objectives : In including population education in the primary school syllabus the intention is to make children aware of simple population data and facts about population growth. According to Prof. Jaya Surya the most important objectives to prepare the ground for the attainment of larger objectives may be achieved at the elementary or the primary level. The population knowledge to be imparted to the children of primary level should be limited to own important facts related to population. This knowledge and education must be according to their age. According to Dr. Adlefarit students on the elementary level, starting from 7 or 8 years of age, can be made to understand the pattern of population growth in their rare country with particular attention to the birth and death rates and the rates of population growth.

Children are the future citizens : Today's children in the school would be the responsible adults of tomorrow. The new information should be introduced little by little so as to keep their appetite keen for more knowledge regarding population. What we teach to them today is reflected tomorrow.

Sowing the seeds of disaffection : The population education at the primary classes may create in the children a sense of disaffection for their parents and hatred for their brothers and sisters in case they constitute a large family. In this stage it is likely to be presented in an over-simplified manner that could sow the seeds of disaffection.

Right time for right ideas : Very simple ideas regarding family size and happy family life may be given at the primary level. One can took them that "a small family is a happy family". One can make them alert towards the war of basic needs of large family in comparison to those of a small family.

Basic of the educational ladder : Educationists throughout the world agree to introduce population education at all levels of schools and colleges. As the primary stage is the base of the educational ladder, where a maximum number of students are taught, so, it is the best stage where the population education programme ran be started with greater hope and aspiration.

Less burden on examinations : A single teacher system prevails in the country at the primary classes. There is less burden of the examination. So, it will be very easy to infuse small topics of information about population education through different subjects like languages and social studies. This requires an imagination and understanding on the part of the primary teacher. No opportunity should be lost to touch on the population concepts while teaching science, mathematics and social studies. The primary stage is the foundation on which further programmes of population education may take place.

Begining at the Secondary Stage

Curricula have more freshness : Secondary school students are very near to their reproductive ages. They are older than the primary school students and are around 16-17 years of age when they leave the secondary school. They are, therefore, on the threshold of their reproductive field which they will enter within 3 to 4 years. The impact of the population education programme on their minds shall have the freshness in comparison to the primary school pupils.

Passing through a transitional period : In this period sex development is a very significant, remarkable, problematic development. In this phase primary and secondary sex developments are noticed. Various types of sexual abnormalities are found among students. Therefore, sex guidance, sex counselling and sex education should be given through the population education programme.

The future leaders : The Asian Regional Seminar held at Bangkok remarked that secondary pupils constitute the society's future leaders. Most students who have received secondary education go to cities and towns for different jobs and occupations. They are likely to occupy a middle level leadership. As such they may influence the masses to a considerable extent. Their comprehensive knowledge of population education can make them capable of transmiting it to others.

Easy to prepare : At the secondary level the curricular materials are easier to prepare than the primary level, because the students are more advanced in age and have a broader experience. They are in a position to understand the fundamental relationship between population growth and other variables. Therefore, population education materials developed in several countries are largely for the secondary level.

Better equipped teacher : The teacher at secondary stage is both professionally and academically better equipped, in comparison to the primary level teachers. They are also smaller in number and more efficient. This makes the introduction of population programme easier at this stage.

Easy to teach and explain : Considering the comprehension level and the physical growth of the pupils at the secondary level it is very easier to talk to them about population problems. Physiology of human reproduction, structure and function of the sex glands, cannot be taught at the primary level. Controversial topics of population education can be included in the programme at secondary stage. Because of their maturity and development difficult topics may be better learnt by the students at this stage.

Quick and accurate education possible : The population education programme at the secondary level can be imparted more quickly and accurately, because of smaller number of pupils and better trained teachers. The students at the secondary and higher secondary stage should not develop critical thinking on population issues and problems. They should be encouraged to synthesise what they have learnt and to apply knowledge in day-to-day life. According to Dr. Bloom these are definitely higher levels of achievement in the cognitive domain. The above aim should be taken into consideration while framing the curriculum of population education at the school stage.

Curriculum in Details

Primary Step

Primary education is the foundation on which the superstructure of higher education stands. The pupils at this stage are small and growing. The curriculum is to be arranged in accordance with their age, need, growth, development and interest. It cannot be equivalent to that of the secondary stage. The population education curriculum at the primary stage can be categorised under important headings:

Social Life

i) Population growth and its social causes.

ii) Population growth and superstitions.

iii) Population growth and standard of life.

iv) Population growth and social disharmony.
v) Population growth and beggar problem in India.
vi) Population growth and lack of discipline.
vii) Disadvantages of early marriage.
viii) Rapid growth in population and its impact on the socio-economic life.

Economic Life

i) Population growth and food problem.
ii) Population growth and less per capita income.
iii) Population growth and unemployment.
iv) Population growth and less availability of consumer goods.
v) Education and employment of women.
vi) Scarcity of means and vastness of demand.

Environment

i) Population growth and air pollution.
ii) Population growth and water pollution.
iii) Population growth and soil pollution.
iv) population growth and noise pollution;
v) Population growth and its pressure on soil, water, air, and sound pollution, deforestation, soil erosion and threat to wildlife.
vi) Population growth and natural calamities.

Family Life

i) Parents and their role as family.
ii) Population growth and marriage.
iii) Population growth and remarriage.
iv) population growth and universality of marriage.
v) Population growth and belief in such norms as "Child is the gift of God."
vi) Population growth and family tension.

vii) Population growth and lack of care, love and affection.

viii) population growth and low standard of living .

ix) A daughter is as important as the son.

x) Small size family for a better quality of life.

Health

i) Population growth and diseases.

ii) Population growth and poor quality medical facilities.

iii) Population growth and shortage of medicines.

iv) Population growth and shortage of doctors.

v) Cleanliness, safe drinking water, balanced diet and health facilities.

vi) Healthy mother, healthy child, need to have fewer children.

Nutrition

i) Population growth and low quality food.

ii) Population growth and adulteration.

iii) Population growth and lack of nutritious food.

iv) Population growth and hunger.

Educational Life

i) Population growth and poor quality of education.

ii) Population growth and overcrowded classes.

iii) Population growth and shortage of schools and colleges.

iv) Population growth and shortage of efficient teachers.

v) illiteracy.

Demographic Implication

i) Population dynamics.

ii) Size, structure and composition of population at local and national level.

iii) Causes and consequences of population growth.

iv) Impact of migration to rural and urban areas.

Secondary Stage

In the comparison to the primary school children, children at the secondary stage are more mature and grown-up. The curriculum at the secondary step should be arranged and constructed according to the growth and development, age, maturation, and interest of the children. While framing the curriculum a number of points will have to be taken into consideration as the period of adolescence starts at this stage. During this time children pass through a critical and transitional period. Thus, guidance and counselling from the teachers and parents are always needed. The curriculum at the secondary stage can be divided into the following headings:

Social Life

i) Marriage-types and necessity.

ii) Effect of divorce.

iii) Unscientific explanation of prejudices and social tradition.

iv) Population growth and social disharmony.

v) Role of women in social and national development.

vi) Population growth and quality of life.

vii) Interrelationship between various aspects of marriage and quality of life.

Economic Life

i) Population growth and per capita income.

ii) Population growth and economic life.

iii) Demand and production.

iv) Population growth and price rise.

v) Population growth and national income.

vi) Population growth and unemployment.

vii) Population growth and lack of industrialisation.

viii) Population growth and labour supply.

Demographic Implication

i) Mortality, fertility and migration.

ii) Population policy.
iii) Birth rate and death rate.
iv) Methods of family planning.
v) Estimation of world population in general and population of India in specific.
vi) Population growth in developed and developing regions of the world.
vii) Occupational structure of India.

Sex life

i) Sex education.
ii) Concept of sex deviations.
iii) AIDS-causes, symptom and prevention.
iv) Sex mechanism.
v) Physiology hygiene of human reproduction.
vi) Structure, type and function of different glands.
vii) Basic knowledge about different sexual diseases like VD, STD, etc.

Environmental Life

i) Environmental pollutions like water, air, noise, soil, etc.
ii) Adulteration of food materials.
iii) Control of environmental pollution.
iv) Environmental pollution and its effects on human life.
v) Better environment for better living.

Family Life

i) Concept and type of family.
ii) Merits and demerits of joint family system.
iii) Origin of the family.
iv) Small size family and large size family, a comparative picture.
v) Government benefits for green-card holders.

Transaction Approaches

The Asian Regional Workshop on population and family education has suggested different approaches of including population education programme in the school curriculum. Following are the important approaches and their advantages and disadvantages :

Single Subject Approach : It consists in developing a year course based on population education. In it population education becomes an independent subject taught like other subjects at one or more grade levels.

The Advantages

i) It enables one to study the subject in proper depth.

ii) It requires a fewer number of teachers to be trained.

iii) As the imparting of population education is so crucial to the welfare of people, it should be given a separate status. Heaviness of curriculum should not stand on its way.

Disadvantages

i) It will be another addition to the already over burdened school curriculum.

ii) It is difficult to find and train teachers in sufficient number to teach such a course adequately.

iii) There is practical difficulty of the situation on primary as well as on the lower secondary level which compells us to think of alternatives.

iv) If the course is introduced at the primary level there would be many concepts which could not be adequately covered because of very low intellectual level of children at this stage.

v) Introduction of a single course will defeat the very purpose of population education. To quote Prof. Jayasurya, "in the case of children at the elementary or the primary level it is perhaps out of question trying to introduce population as a distinct subject."

vi) The addition of an extra subject may make the condition of lowering of standards at all levels still worse.

vii) The single subject approach is against the inter-disciplinary nature of population education.

viii) It is psychologically unsuitable and economically non-viable.

Unit in a Subject Area : Under this approach a number of units can be checked out in different school subjects and at different grade levels. In spite of introducing a single course on population education, some units can be selected and included inside the curriculum. The UNESCO's regional office for education in Asia states: 'A series of related concepts may be women into an introductional scheme which takes roughly from 1 to 4 weeks of classroom time."

Disadvantages

1. This system is a slight alteration in the school curriculum which is a difficult task.
2. To give training to the teachers in many subjects and grades is not an easy job.
3. It suffers from all the drawbacks of single course approach.

The subject areas identified for this purpose are: science, maths, social studies, language, geography, economics, etc.

Penetration Approach: It is generally known as the infusion method in which the concept and data of population education can be introduced in the normal instructional materials without developing separate courses or introducing units in a subject area. When they consider it logical, appropriate and necessary the teacher can introduce the concept of population education in the curriculum. The success and failure of this approach depends on the efficiency and training of the teachers on population education. Permeation is the most widely adopted approach for the infusion of population concepts and contents in the existing curriculum. It is the systematic incorporation of population concepts into the existing textual material as different school subjects, more or less which are amenable to such infusion.

The National Seminar on Population Education held at Mumbai in 1969 emphasised that "Population education should be introduced into the curriculum of schools and colleges by including it in so far as it may be possible, in the areas of study new common in the educational curriculum such as social studies, health education, mathematics, languages, etc. The Seminar was of the opinion that it might be possible to achieve all the objectives by including population education suitably in the curricula of appropriate subjects already comprised in the curriculum. As population problem permeate in many curricular areas, this fact assumes that curriculum framework in these area has a certain flexibility. This approach is based on the interdisciplinary nature of population education.

Unsuitable for Overcrowded Curriculum: The present curriculum in the school stage is already over-crowded. Abha Bai Wadia remarks: "Overcrowded syllabi are becoming the base of modern education, partly due to clinging to old and out moded facts of knowledge and ways of teaching and, to a considerable extent, due to the 'explosion of knowledge taking place when new discoveries are emerging at breathtaking speed."

Undesirability of Single Course : In overcrowded syllabus it is not all desirable to introduce population education as a single course. Because of its multi-disciplinary nature and difficulty in its introduction as a special subject, population education should be taught necessarily to small childrens incorporating with other academic materials.

Usefull for Continued Learning : In order to provoke better understanding population education curriculum should be presented before the students throughout their entire period of schooling. This objective can be achieved if population education programme is started from the primary classes. As a special subject system cannot work effectively in lower classes permeation is highly needed. Therefore, the need of integration of population materials with other content is realised.

Integration Levels

Status Study- It refers to a systematic study of the existing curriculum to find out in it the relevant curricular areas. Its purpose is to locate a 'plug point' for injecting population education materials. The curriculum areas where the "plug points" can be found easily are: Social Studies, Mathematics, Economics, Geography, Home Science, Geometry, Art and Painting, Biology, Languages, etc.

Selection of Concept and Ideas : In order to integrate population education with normal school curriculum one should select the concepts and ideas of population education, which are to be infused. These concepts can be like environment education, family life education, pollution, economic development, health education, demographics, sex education, family, the marriage, etc. Following questions are to be answered while selecting the concept and ideas :

(i) What is the age of children ?

(ii) Whether they are grown up and matured to receive such concepts and ideas ?

(iii) How easy are they to implement ?

(iv) How does the concept impact the thinking of the children?

(v) How can the objectives of population education be achieved?

(vi) What motivational technique can be utilised ?

Dissemination Phase: In order to disseminate concept and ideas of population education, guide materials, leaflets, newsletters, bulletins are published. The teachers are the potential factor of the new curriculum. The new curriculum is to be communicated properly by the curriculum constructor and agents. This phase is undertaken by panel discussions, seminars, orientation programme, in-service training programmes.

Execution Phase: This phase is the practical aspect of implementation of integrated curriculum in the schools. After the arrangement of all curricular materials, curriculum are introduced in the school from class I to class X. At this stage the involvement of the school personnels, cooperation of the parents and different social organisations and social members is solicited. The schools are to organise various outdoor programmes in order to implement the permeation approach effectively.

Evaluation Phase: This phase is undertaken in terms of cognitive as well as behavioural and attitudinal outcome in every programme necessitates evaluation, so also the integration of population concepts and ideas in normal school curriculum.

Population Concept Integrated

Mathematics: Mathematics is a form of abstract thinking. It has a utilitarian value in modern life. It forms a suitable background for advanced study and research in all sciences. Demographics of population can be suitably integrated through different parts of it. Mathematics is a prerequisite of all technical or sociological advancement in the space age.

Geometry

Problem 1 : The percentage of population in Asia is 58.2 per cent of the world population. Draw a circle and shade of the population of Asia as a black.

Arithmetic

Problem 1 : In a family there are 10 members and among them, 8 members depend only 2 earning members. Find out the ratio between the earning members and unemployed members.

Problem 2 : According to the 1991 census the male and female population (in millions) are 437 and 406 respectively. Find out how much less is the female population in comparison to the male population of India.

Problem 3 : Read the following population numbers of 1981 Census in the International System and write them in words

(i) Karnataka : 37,041,451,

(ii) Punjab : 16,669,755,

(iii) Kerala : 25,403,217,

(iv) Tamil Nadu : 48,297,456,

(v) Orissa : 26,272,504,

(vi) West Bengal : 54,580,647,

(vii) Which state is the most populated and which the least ?

Language: Language is the best media through which the concepts and ideas of the population phenomenon can be effectively integrated and infused in normal school curriculum. It is the best media of communication.

(i) Press

(a) Population growth and problem:

(b) Population growth and quality of life.

(c) Population growth and environment pollution.

(ii) Composition

Write the essays and state your opinion and suggestions.

(a) Population growth and social indiscipline.

(b) Population growth and unemployment problem.

(c) Population growth and environment.

(d) Food problem and population growth.

(e) Our superstitions and high birth rate.

(iii) Letter Writing

(a) Write a letter to your friend describing how you participated and organised the NSS programme to staging a one-act play on family planning in village areas-

(b) Write a letter to CDMO to make necessary arrangements for delivering a speech on physiology on human reproduction.

iv) poetry

Compose a poem on small family, environment, pollution, "We two, our two".

Social Studies : Social studies is the field of knowledge drawn from various social disciplines concerned with man in relation to his physical and social environments. Social studies is the appropriate subject through which demographics of population growth of the world in general and India in specific can be imparted.

(a) History

(i) Population growth and industrial revolution.

(ii) Growth of population and urbanisation in the pre-independence period.

(iii) Growth of population and its impact on occupation in the British period and in post-independence period.

(iv) Expansion of agriculture in historical periods.

(v) Socio-economic condition of modern India.

(b) Geography

(i) The climatic condition and density of population.

(ii) Population and agriculture.

(iii) Area of the different nations in square kilometers.

(iv) Population growth and city life.

(v) Interpretation of world map.

(vi) Survey of world maps and India maps.

(vii) Land forms and density of population.

(viii) Energy resources and minerals.

(ix) Factors of density.

(c) Civics

(i) Population growth and civic amenities.

(ii) Population growth and its impact on education.

(iii) Civic bodies.

(iv) Role of voluntary organisations in social service programmes.

(v) Computing population of different states.

(d) Economics

(i) Population growth and poverty.

(ii) Migration.

(iii) Economic development.

(iv) Causes and consequences of population growth.

(v) National income.

Physiology/Hygiene

(i) Physiology of human reproduction.

(ii) Structure and functions of glands.

(iii) Pollution and its impact on life.

(iv) Physiology base of sex.

(v) Keeping the body clean.

(vi) Hygienic and unhygienic environment.

Home Science : Home science is the combination of both home and science. The nature of home is changing very rapidly in modern times. The concept of population growth and consciousness can be imparted through home science.

(i) Role of mother in child development.

(ii) Family life education.

(iii) Food and nutrition.

(iv) Keeping home, and environment healthy.

(v) Home furnishing and household equipments.

Art and Painting :

(i) Save the environment.

(ii) Symbol of family planning.

(iii) Symbol of literacy.

(iv) A sketch on "Small family, happy family."

(v) Ecological balancing circle.

(vi) Ecological balancing rests on population.

(vii) Industrialisation and environmental pollution.

(viii) Teach your parents well.

Evolution and Development

Several definitions of curriculum are available. The curriculum is commonly defined as all the experiences that a learner has under the guidance of school. It is a complex of more or less planned and controlled conditions under which students learn to behave in various ways. Curriculum is both written and unwritten activities in a school. Curriculum is a wider term than syllabus. Curriculum includes syllabus.

We continue to update our school curriculum. It is a period of knowledge explosion and this warrants that some new topics are included in the course—old topics are deleted from the course. The school curriculum thus remains in a state of flux. The contents of courses undergo a change. India is no exception. Our Commissions on education have devoted considerable number of pages to this aspect of Indian education. It is safe to conclude that curriculum improvement is a process which is continuous. And in all, three characteristics of time directly affect curriculum reform:

(i) Knowledge explosion (already referred to).

(ii) Cataclysmic social and technological changes (like computer education these days).

(iii) Population explosion.

We are concerned with Population Education curriculum or the place of population education in school curriculum.

Population explosion is a problem. We have already summed up the ill effects of large population earlier. This should be enough to convince us that Population Education forms an integral part of general education. We are thus clear that it has a place in school curriculum.

Bruner has suggested the criterion for any subject to be included in the curriculum. A subject when taught in the primary grades and fully developed at the end of the school period is worth knowing as an adult, and if studying as a child makes for a better adult. He stated further, "if the answer to both questions is negative or ambiguous, then the material is crowding the curriculum." Population education satisfies the above criteria. Therefore it must find a place in school curriculum.

There are two ways to teach population education in our schools:

(i) To integrate it with the relevant topics in all the action subjects, i.e., social studies, general science, mathematics, physiology, social studies form the most suitable subject for integrating most of the population concepts.

(ii) To teach it as a separate subject. And for this NCERT organised a workshop on population education at New Delhi in July 1970.

It suggested that the following five areas should form a part of curriculum of population education

1. The population growth.
2. Economic development and population.
3. Social development and population.
4. Health, nutrition and population.
5. Biological factors, family life and population.

Faneff C.T. (Ph. D. thesis 1971) suggested the following curriculum :

1. Birth rate, mortality rate and population.
2. Health and population.
3. Food production and population.
4. Family size and population.
5. Standard of living and population.

D. Gopal Rao suggests the following topics forming contents of Population Education :

1. The history of population growth—World in general, India in particular—Causes, trends and implications.
2. An introduction to demography with particular reference to India—Components of population growth, population distribution and its composition.
3. Effects of rapid population growth on economic, social, cultural and political aspects of national development.
4. Effects of rapid population growth on individual and family life-standards of living.
5. Effects of rapid population growth on the physical environment, food, natural resources and quality of life.
6. An elementary knowledge of the physiology of reproduction wherever feasible.
7. The population policies and programmes of the world in general. Before you finally think of curriculum in population education, in "Task and Challenges" publication of NCERT, a few questions posed for "change of ideas and clarification of views in this regard could be as follows:

What are the general and specific goals of population education as an area of study at different school stages? What values, perspectives and knowledge should be expected at the end of each possible terminal point of formal education for a large number of students such as primary, middle and secondary?

What are the existing subjects that lend themselves admirably to integrate population education ideas and values?

What are the different ways or patterns that we can follow in development of curriculum, for organizing knowledge and development of values? How can we ensure active participation of students in discussing population problem and its implications for individuals, families and communities? How best can we identify children's experiences and relate new contents to the same?

How do we spot potential talent and nurture it in the State for the development of curriculum? What are the systematic procedures of curriculum development? What range of specific expertise shall we need in developing balanced curriculum? Would it be ensured by participation of different subject specialists, subject teachers, masters of methods, curriculum specialists, text-book writers and the like?

What needs to be done or emphasised for inculcation of proper attitudes and values related to population education suited to different school stages?

Are there any patterns and models of curriculum and curriculum development in population education? If so, where are they?

Would population education curriculum vary from State to State in view of their varying situations, socio-economic conditions and cultural backgrounds? If so, to what extent and in what manner?

Co-curricular Activities

Even more significant would be the role of co-cioricular activities in conveying the message of population education not only to the students but also to the community at large. We have to think of appropriate co-curricular activities for imparting population education. One such activity can be preparing charts, another can be writing slogans.

Thus, population education offers a big challenge for curriculum workers. We have to identify population education ideas, values and contents and then grade them, articulate them vertically, i.e., from class to class and horizontally in different subjects in a given grade or a class.

Remember, that curriculum development is an on-going process. It calls for continuous review and refinement in the light of evaluation and feedback. This is true not only of curriculum as a product but also of curriculum development as a process. The states should always scrutinize the soundness and effectiveness of procedures and strategies adopted in curriculum development and its evaluation from time to time. It may be worthwhile to have in-built evaluation of curriculum development procedures and their end products.

Concepts Developed

Dr. Rao says that modern research in the field of curriculum has indicated that concepts can be the basis for developing curriculum and conceptualization facilitates learning.

Concepts are a tool of thinking. A concept is a generalised ideas of an object or a thing. It is a subjective interpretation of the perceived objects or events. There are definite steps of concept formation—actual experience or perception, abstraction and then generalisation. Concepts have several advantages in thinking:

(i) It reduces the complexity of environment.

(ii) It reduces the need to relearn every situation.

(iii) It helps provide for direction, prediction and planning.

(iv) It is an essential tool for thought.

D. Gopal Rao says that for developing curriculum in population education, we should develop key concepts in it and he lists the following key concepts;

1. The causes of population growth.
2. Consequences of population growth.
3. The need for population control.

These three concepts broadly covering the contents, form the basis for organising the elements of curriculum. They also indicate the scope of population education in the curriculum.

QUESTIONS

1. Describe the importance and difficulties of Population Education.
2. Give population education curriculum at different stages.
3. Explain and evaluate various approaches to curriculum contraction in population education.
4. How shall you integrate population concept through different subjects ?

18

International Trends

Till twentieth century, no complete and reliable estimates of world population were available. After carefully reviewing all the information available, the United Nations prepared estimates for the population of major regions of the world since 1920. The estimates given by Walter E Wilcox and A.M. Carr Saunders for the period 1650-1900 are considered as the most authoritative region-wise estimates of world population. The history of population growth has been traced since 10,000 BC to 1975 AD as given in the table on next page. The table shows that the growth has been zig-zag and very gradual. Before 10,000 BC, at the end of the Ice Age, men were sparsely scattered over the earth. The size of boom population was between 1,00,000 and 10,00,000. In 5,000 BC this population grew upto between 5 and 20 million. It is estimated that from 8,000 BC upto the beginning of Christian era, the population of the world increased at the rate of 0.06% per annum. By 1300 AD, it increased to 400 million. From 1300 AD to 1650 AD, there was an addition of only I million in the world population. In the next 50 years, however, one million was added. Yet other million grew during the period 1700 AD to 1750 AD. From 1750 AD however, population increased by 2 millions in the first 50 years and by 3 and 4 millions respectively during the next 50 year periods. Thus, prior to 1650 AD the growth of world population was slow, while after 1650 AD it increased rapidly.

While it took 123 years for the world population to grow billion from to two billions, it grew six billions from five billions in just 12 years.

In 20th century the world population increased rapidly except for the period 1940-1950. The average annual growth rate during the period 1900-1950 was 0.8%. This rate low to 1.9% during 1950-1970. During the next 20 years however, the population has increased very fast, registering on an average an annual growth rate of 2.22%.

Trends and Directions

According to the Washington Post of November 1978, the world population trends were as follows : For the first time the world has reversed itself and has stopped growing so fast, the US Census Bureau has reported. Since 1970 the world's population has gone up 1.9 per cent annually, while in the previous 18 years it had been rising 2 per cent each year. According to the Bureau's study, funded by the Agency for International Development.

According to the Washington Post of November 1978 the world population trends are as follows : For the first time the world has reversed itself and has stopped growing so fast, the U.S. Census Bureau has reported. Since 1970 the world's population has gone up 1.9 per cent annually, while in the previous 15 years it had been rising 2 per cent each year. According to the Bureau's study, funded by the Agency for International Development.

"We didn't expect a downturn in the rate of increase until the early 1980s, but is happening a decade earlier and is very significant" said Samuel Baum, the Bureau's Chief of International Demographic Statistics. The difference of a tenth of a percentage point "is not a tremendous decline. But it is important because the numbers were so high and it represents a change in direction, which is more important", Baum added, "The encouraging thing is that the direction has shifted in all regions of the world except Africa and now there a number of countries-Tunisia, South Africa, Mauritius and Reunion-have had substantial declines," he said (The latter two are islands in the Indian Ocean). Baum noted that more people are being added to the world and predicted that a growth rate of zero will not be reached, at the earliest, until the years 2020 to 2025." The world's population increased from 3.5 billion in mid 1967 to an estimated 4.3 billion in mid-1977 the report said. At current (1976) vital rate, the world registers a net gain of over 2,00,000 persons each day.

Baum said two trends account for the reduced rate of growth: a rapid decline in fertility and not-so-rapid decline in mortality. "People are being born at a slower rate and deaths are not going down as rapidly," he explained. The census report does not project future world population, but the World Bank has predicted it will reach six billion by 2000. The United Nations has predicted 63 billion by that year.

A study released recently by University of Chicago demographer Amy Ong Tsui and Donald J. Bogue projected a 5.8 billion total and said the world's population time bomb may have been defused by birth-control programmes in some of the most populous countries.

"Only 10 years ago doomsday prophesizing called for mass starvation, world chaos and possible world war by the year 2000," their study said. "If recent trends continue, the world population crisis appears resolvable."

The new census report seems to support that optimism. The report noted growth rate declines in less developed as well as developed nations. It cited Sri Lanka, where the 1966 growth rate was 2.3 per cent and the 1976 rate was 1.5 per cent. The Phillippines, Thailand and the Republic of Korea each had a decline of 0.7 per cent; Colombia had a decline of 0.6; South Africa, 0.4 and Turkey and China, 03. The estimate for China was made by John Aird, Chief of the Bureau's foreign demographic analysis division and was based primarily on provincial population figures that have been released since the death of Chairman Mao.

China's population was estimated to be 982.5 million, 23 per cent of the world figures. India's growth rate will 2.2 per cent in 1976 and 1977, about the same as it was in the mid-1960s.

Asia, with 2.5 billion people had 58 per cent of the world's total in 1977, the report said. Because of the sheer size of its base population, its population growth accounted for two-thirds; of the world's increase. The United States had a growth rate of 0.8 per cent between 1976 and 1977 compared with 1.1 per cent between 1966 and 1967. The United States had 5 per cent of the world's population last year. North America, Europe and the Soviet Union, combined had 23 per cent, the report showed. Africa's annual growth rate between 1975 and 1977 was 2.8 per cent. It has been rising steadily since 1950, when it was 2.1 per cent.

According to Michael Palmer's estimate, between now and the end of the century the actual number of people in the world will still increase from just over 4 billion to just over 6 billion, 90% of the extra 2 billion people will be born in the economically poor countries of the World. The World population will grow to 6196 million in the year 2000. This is an increase of 40% on the earlier estimate of 4413 million population in 1980. Of this total world population the break up between the poor and the rich world will be 4848 million and 1348 million respectively. The poor World will increase 50% of the earlier estimate of 2332 million in 1980. On the other hand the rich World will only increase 14% of the 1980 estimate of 1181 million. Similar projections have been made by other demographers all over the World. According to S. N. Agarwal, "It took nearly two million years for the human population to reach one billion. The second billion came in a hundred years, the third in thirty and the fourth in fifteen years. At the present rate of growth, the fifth billion will be reached in eleven years and the sixth billion in only nine years." According to a United Nations estimate the world population will be 6.25 billions in 2000 AD. Of this while only 1.36 will be of the more developed regions, as much as 4.89 will be of the less developed regions.' China and India are now contributing around 37% of increase in World population. Brazil adds more people per year than the Soviet Union. Therefore it has been concluded, "thus, the more developed regions during the period 1965-1985, would add to their population at an average rate of 5 per cent per quinquennium, while the less developed regions would gain at an average rate of 13 per cent per quinquennium. Because of the higher rate of population growth in the less developed regions, their population in 1985 would be nearly three times that of the more developed regions (the ratio being 2.9 to 1) whereas in 1965 the ratio was only 2.2 to 1.

Development Hampered

This change in World population will considerably decrease the quality of population. It will increase the burden upon the non-developed regions. Thus it will create problem of health, food supply, employment and education, and housing. The demographes have started thinking how to maintain the pace of development with the increasing population. A recent survey of population and development in the eighties by Michael Palmer presents some interesting ideas in this connection.

In some population circles, the 1980s have been hailed as the Decade of New Integrations. Even if you are distrustful of these seemingly all-embracing labels, it remains a certainty that in the next few years more and more research and ideas will be devoted to the link between population and the whole process of development.

Scene in UN

Each year the world's population grows by almost 90 million, an increase of 2.8 people each second. The world's population will continue to grew at least until 2050. The world's largest countries, which play a critical role in determining future population growth, are a diverse group. They range from Iran, were the average woman has 6.6 children, Germany, where the average is 1.3.

It is no more than a logical outcome of the changing perception of population from the initial focus on morbidity and mortality through the height of the so-called 'population crisis' and its emphasis on the fertility factor in population growth to the present decade when population is universally recognised as an integral factor in development Now that recognition is due to be turned into reality and population to take its full place in development programmes and policy-making.

Education : Easier and Wider

Already a number of areas have been identified which illustrate the strong interplay between population and development. In the field of increased education for women, for example, there are potentially significant implications for the lowering of the fertility rate as is known by what has happened in Sri Lanka and Kerala in India. In Kerala, where the birth rate has fallen from 39 in 1961 to 28 in 1976, the female literacy rate is twice as high as any other state. The same story of high literacy and falling fertility can be told in Sri Lanka. Moreover, in both instances, the decline in fertility has been achieved without the classic precondition of an economic boom.

Trade and Commerce

Major investments and new transportation and trade policies can also have a marked effect on population factors, particularly those relating to the location of people and the growth of cities both problems which are becoming increasingly acute in many countries".

Growing Cities

All over the world the move to the cities is gaining pace. In developed countries, half the population lived in urban men in 1950; by the end of the century three-quarters are expected to do so. Similarly, in less developed regions in Africa, the urban population tripled during 1950-1975 and will triple again by the year 2000. Individual examples are equally horrendous Mexico City will be increased its population from 2.9 to 31.6 million in the period 1950-2000 and Greater Mumbai will have jumped during the same period by over 650 per cent to 19.1 million people. It almost goes without saying that these population figures are of vital importance to those with the responsibility for planning and providing for the services needed to keep these 'exploding cities alive.

Migration at World Level

International migration is equally important to the planning of manpower needs in the economy. The phenomenon of workers from South-East Europe and Asia flocking to the factories of West Germany and Northern Europe is well-established, equally significant are the figures for migrant workers in some of the states of the Middle East where economics are booming but which lack their own manpower resources. In Qatar and Kuwait 77 and 71 per cent respectively of total employment is taken up by immigrant labour. The economic consequences of these population shifts are vital also. In 1977 the total remittances to Egypt Jordan, Morocco, Tunisia and the Yemens met close to 30 per cent of the total value of foreign exchange carried through exports.

Workers' Force

It is only through the careful analysis and marriage of population statistics and manpower needs that the necessary cooperation among developing countries in the flow of Labour can be achieved. This complex relationship between population growth and manpower needs will certainly continue in the future. When the present numbers of children in the developing world start entering the labour form, the future growth of that force may well exceed the growth rate in the population as a whole. This phenomenon has, indesed, already occurred in certain countries leading to increasing numbers of unemployed and under-employed.

Smooth Relationship

The relationship between population and development, than, is a two-way one to take simplified examples, rapidly rising population have been seen in imposing enormous strains on the environment and contributing to the depletion of the earth's natural resources. Conversely, we can see that effect of greater educational opportunities can have in reducing fertility and stabilizing are reducing the birth rate.

Sheer numbers may be the raw material of demographic statistics but increasingly sophisticated analysis of those numbers have shown further examples of the tie-up between figures and social and economic concerns. Take the growing problem of an aging population. The consequences that arise when the relative size of a population's younger members rapidly declines, as is happening particularly in the developed world are manifold : the need to shift resources from assistance for child health and education to welfare systems for the aged; major impacts on residential and labour form mobility and the probable need for changes in political attitudes towards immigration to bolster a declining labour form.

Mortality on Decline

Then there is the effect of declining mortality rates both in advancing life expectancy and combating previously high infant death rates. Not only has this had probably profound effects on family formation attitudes and behaviour and, beyond that, for overall fertility figures but it poses a challenge to policy in public health and medical and health education. Since the potential for increasing control over death and diseases is more and divorced from the constraint of social and economic underdevelopment, there are now new opportunities to be in making further gain in Africa, Asia and Latin America. It is perfectly feasible to expect five-year gained or more in the life expectancy over the next decade in sub-Saharan Africa, South Asia and the Middle East.

The examples of the connection are legion and, once set out almost so self-evident as to be in danger of being dismissed as understood and, therefore, relegated to the background : hence the need for the Decade of New Integration.

As the recently published State of the World Population 1979 pointed out, "Population policy is fast transcending the point where it can be regarded as a fiscal sideshow. Rather, much enhanced sophistication will be necessary in future in selecting among policy alternatives, in assessing their benefits and cost effectiveness, and in allowing for demographic development reciprocities. Not the least among the mining decide's major mods for improved demographic policy-making will be the rapid evolution of evaluative tools for analysing all these question. Such tools might well, in time, come to constitute entire new areas of research in the social sciences and in the literature on administration."

The various members of the United Nation system are already giving attention to those aspects of the inter-relationship between population and development which fail within their respective mandates. For example, the International Labour Office is executing UNFPA-funded country projects which deal with population and employment planning as well as carrying out global and national research activities which examine the various aspects of migration and the numerous inter-reactions between production, female employment opportunities and fertility change.

Transition Theory in Demography

The demographic transition has been defined by Ansley J. Coale and Edgar M. Hoover, when countries of Europe, North America, Australia, New Zealand and Japan evolved, "From a predominantly agrarian peasant economy to an economy with a greater division of labour, using more elaborated tons and equipments, more urbanised, more oriented to the market sale of its products and characterised by rapid and pervasive changes in technique." These countries have shown a demographic stability or the low population growth, not through high fertility and high mortality but through low fertility and low mortality. The theory of demographic transition has been also supported by Warren Thompson, C.P. Blacker and Frank Notestein. Various stages have been maintained as essential in the progress towards the demographic transition. These stages exist before, during and after the transition. These have been explained as follows :

Pre-Transitional Stage. In this stage population growth is almost static. Both birth and death rates are very high. The society has an agrarian peasant economy with a traditional organizational system. High death rates are achieved due to wars, famines, epidemics chronic malnutritions, etc. High birth rates are supported by social norms and customs regarding marriage and reproduction with emphasis upon prolific child bearing. This stage shows high potential growth and lack of man's control over fertility and mortality. This stage may be pointed out in India particularly in the nineteenth century and early 20th century.

Transitional Stage. This stage has been further classified into three types : Early, Mid and Late.

(i) *Early Transitional Stage.* In this stage death rates start decreasing but birth rates continue to remain high with the result that the population grows rapidly.

(ii) *Mid-Transitional Stage.* During this stage death rates continue to decline, but a decline in the birth rates also begins. However, since the birth rates are higher than the death rate the rate of population growth is fairly high.

(iii) *Late Transitional Stage.* In this stage death rates continue to be low while birth rates remain moderate. Therefore the population growth is again low. In India the early transitional stage could be observed under British Rule. With the independence of the country and the effort to control diseases, etc. the country has now come to mid-transitional stage. The aim of late transitional stage is near though not yet achieved. In so many other countries however, one may see late transitional stage. This is in developed countries. The developing countries however, such as India, China, Thailand, Korea, the Philippines, Indonesia, Sri Lanka and some Latin American countries, are still in mid-transition or late transition stage.

Post Transitional Stage. In this stage both birth and death rates are low. The country reaches a stage where population is almost stationary and can't be changed by change in fertility. The theory of demographic transition describes in a simple manner the historical trends of population growth. However, most of the demographers have challenged its value as a demographic theory.

Reasons for Fast Development

All the surveys of world population growth show that the rate of growth is very fast. Therefore, United Nations are trying everywhere to check the growth rate. The problem, however, is different in different countries, since as has been already pointed out, different countries are passing through different stages of the demographic transition. The following may be listed as the main causes of rapid population growth.

Fall in Mortality Level. A review of almost any country in the world shows a fall in mortality levels in 19th and 20th century. It is most explicit in the countries of Europe and North America. The fall in mortality level is firstly due to agricultural revolution, secondly, due to industrial revolution, and thirdly, due to progress in medical sciences, public health and environmental sanitation.

Accelerated Growth Rates. After 1950 the world population increased rapidly due to the accelerated growth, particularly in the developing countries in Asia, Latin America and Africa. This firstly, due to decline in the death rates, secondly, due to the prevention and control of diseases, and thirdly, due to expansion in medical public health services. Of the above mentioned causes the extension of technology and expansion of medical and public health services together with industrial revolution are those which cannot be checked out their control is desirable. Therefore, the only hope lies in family planning and control of birth rates. This again will be planned according to the ratio of growth of population and the increase of means of subsistence in a particular country. Population control is particularly required in the developing and not in developed countries.

QUESTIONS

1. Write an essay on World Population Trends.
2. Show the inter-relation of Population and Development.
3. What are the causes of rapid population growth. Explain with reference to India.